MEN AND DIVORCE

Men and Divorce

MICHAEL F. MYERS, M.D.

The Guilford Press
New York   London

© 1989 The Guilford Press
A Division of Guilford Publications, Inc.
72 Spring Street, New York, NY 10012

All rights reserved

No part of this book may be reproduced, stored in a retrieval system,
or transmitted, in any form or by any means, electronic, mechanical,
photocopying, microfilming, recording, or otherwise, without written
permission from the Publisher.

Printed in the United States of America

This book is printed on acid-free paper.

Last digit is print number: 9 8 7 6 5 4 3

Library of Congress Cataloging-in-Publication Data

Myers, Michael F.
    Men and divorce / by Michael F. Myers.
      p.   cm.
    Bibliography: p.
    Includes index.
    ISBN 0-89862-386-3
    1. Divorced men—Psychology. 2. Divorced men—Counseling of.
3. Divorce therapy. I. Title.
HQ814.M94   1989
   306.8'9—dc19   88-35101
                                                        CIP

To Joice—for her love, steadfastness, and much more.

ACKNOWLEDGMENTS

There are many individuals whom I want to thank for contributing directly and indirectly to this book. My interest in the male patient, and in men's issues in general, is in large measure attributable to Dr. Joseph Pleck. Since we first met at the Wellesley College Center for Research on Women, Wellesley, Massachusetts, in 1983, Joe has been both an inspiration and an invaluable resource person for me. Through him I became involved in the National Organization for Changing Men, and I have been enriched by the scholarly work of many of its members and its various task forces. Dr. Harry Brod, founder of the Program for the Study of Women and Men in Society at the University of Southern California, Los Angeles, met with me in April 1987 and was helpful in alerting me to the work of other individuals whose work dovetails with mine.

My ideas about men and divorce have been supported and refined by my having taken part in two important symposia presented at annual meetings of the American Psychiatric Association. The first, Divorce and Individual Development, took place in 1986 in Washington, D.C., and included Dr. Judith Gold, Dr. Martha Kirkpatrick, Dr. Elissa Benedek, Dr. Leah Dickstein, Ms. Elyce Zenoff, and Dr. Fred Gottlieb. The second, Male Gender Issues in Psychiatry, took place in 1987 in Chicago, Illinois and included Dr. Peter Jensen, Dr. Leah Dickstein, Dr. Theodore Nadelson, and Dr. Henry Grunebaum. Dr. Jean Baker Miller had submitted an abstract on men's psychological development as seen by women, but unfortunately she was not able to participate. I want to thank all of them for their knowledge and expertise in this area of psychiatry.

Dr. Robert Lewis, Professor in the Department of Child Development and Family Studies of Purdue University in Indiana, has assisted me with my writings on abandoned husbands and aging men who are divorcing. Dr. Carolyn Robinowitz, Dr. Alexandra Symonds, Dr. Leah Dickstein, Dr. Kristin Sivertz, Dr. Terry Stein, and the late Dr. Nancy Roeske have all contributed to my work on men's issues in psychiatry when we have given presentations together or taught together. Dr. Frances Forrest-Richards, with her rich clinical insights, has helped me enormously with the chapter on older men with younger women. And Dr. Carol Nadelson, well known for her work in marital and divorce therapy, has been, as usual, a catalyst and tremendous friend to me.

The other psychiatrists and the support staff who work with me at the University Hospital, Shaughnessy site, of the University of British Columbia have been essential throughout the writing of this book. Not only have they stimulated my thinking with their ideas and clinical observations about men who are divorcing, but they have been very kind and encouraging about my writing. Unbeknownst to them, they have helped me through the slumps. My secretary, Mrs. Gisela Murray, has been untiring and ever patient through many drafts and revisions. I am tremendously grateful to her.

This book would not be were it not for Seymour Weingarten, Editor-in-Chief of The Guilford Press. The idea of the book is his. I thank him for believing in my ability to develop and to expand on my earlier writings on men who are struggling with divorce. His support and suggestions have been extremely helpful. Dr. Ellen Berman of the Marriage Council of Philadelphia and the University of Pennsylvania Medical School read the text in its entirety and gave me invaluable help with several parts of the book. I am particularly grateful for her suggestion to consolidate and enlarge upon the theoretical substrate to the book, and her insightful queries about some of my clinical findings and therapeutic strategies.

This book also would not be were it not for all the men, women, and children whom I have seen as patients over the years. Although this book is about men and divorce, I could never fully understand men without the assistance of their wives and children, and the assistance of the many significant other people in their lives. Many of them are a bit jarred when, at the end of an interview, I say: "Thanks for coming in. Talking with you has helped me to understand your husband's [or father's] situation a lot better." I don't think that many "helpees" realize how much they help the "helpers."

Finally, I want to thank my family for all their love and support throughout the writing of this book, a book that has come on top of all of my daily responsibilities to my patients and students. Fortunately, my wife, Joice, my daughter, Briana, and my son, Zachary, have an exquisite ability to let me know when enough is enough. I hope that I have respected that.

PREFACE

My interest in divorce began when I was a teen-ager, long before I became a psychiatrist. My father was a lawyer, and I recall an incident that occurred when I was about 13 or 14 years old. We were driving home from his office, and he pulled the car off to the side and proceeded to tell me about one of his clients. I knew that this must be serious because he never discussed his work with me.

He told me that one of his clients was a man who had come to see him about a divorce. I don't remember the details, but I do know that divorce wasn't very common in those days (mid-1950s), so I certainly was interested in hearing about this man's situation. My father went on about how hard it was for the man living on his own and how upset the man would be when he would come to my father's office for legal counsel. Then my dad told me that that very afternoon, he had received a call from the police that the man had just murdered his wife and his four children and then shot himself to death. I was stunned. So was my father. We sat there in the car, silently in the dark, for a few minutes before driving home for dinner.

I have thought a lot about this incident throughout the writing of this book. I know that I did feel troubled for my father, although I don't recall ever bringing it up again or trying to comfort him in any way. I didn't realize until I was much older that he must have felt very guilty about this horrible tragedy, that maybe he could have prevented it in some way. Just his taking me into his confidence about it must have been one measure of his tremendous sense of personal upset. I remember thinking about the man's wife and children. What did they do to deserve this terrible fate? I remember also thinking about the man himself. I certainly couldn't understand why being divorced made someone act like that, but I do recall thinking that the man was better off dead; it would be impossible to live with yourself after doing something so ghastly.

Years later, another incident took place that has remained vividly in my memory. It was 1966, and I was an intern at the Los Angeles County General Hospital. I was rotating through the Jail Service, and one evening when I was on call, the police brought in a man in his 60s who needed medical attention. This man was covered from head to toe with blood—he had cut himself all over his body with a butcher knife. He was extremely agitated and very suicidal; despite being in restraints, he continued to try to do anything to hurt himself further. I remember his pleading with me for mercy killing—he wanted me to give him an injection of some sort to put him out of his misery. The man had been admitted to the Jail Service because he had just been arrested. Earlier in the evening, he had bludgeoned his estranged wife to death with a baseball bat after seeing her with another man. Despite typical intern fatigue, I didn't sleep a wink that night. I found myself feeling very anguished, both for this aging man and for his wife of so many years.

Now it is the 1980s and the newspapers, from the headlines to the back pages, tell us all too frequently about those separated husbands who murder their wives, their children, themselves, and sometimes the wives' new lovers. Although these men are only a segment of men who are newly separated or divorced, and a small segment at that, they do exemplify the most extreme form of psychological trauma associated with the stress of divorce. There are many other manifestations of symptoms and behavioral change in men when a marriage ends.

My purpose in writing this book is based on two very simple premises: that men have a lot of difficulty coping with divorce and that many divorcing men fall between the cracks—that is, they either receive no treatment at all or they receive less than adequate treatment. Because men do not easily or directly ask for help, they tend to be an underserved population of people in distress. Some abuse alcohol, some overwork, some commit criminal acts, and some become depressed and kill themselves. Behind the social persona that all is well and the male ethos of self-reliance, there is often a powerhouse of pain.

A number of men develop physical symptoms at some point in the separation process. Again, many live with these ailments and don't go to their family physicians or internists. Those who do may not think to mention to their doctors that they are unhappily married and about to separate or are newly separated. They either don't think that it's relevant or downplay its relevance. Not all physicians ask about psychosocial stressors in their patients' lives when the patients come in with physical problems. And when they do, they too may underestimate how tremendously stressful separation and divorce can be for some of their patients. In short, divorce makes a lot of people feel sick.

As a physician and then a psychiatrist for over 20 years, I have treated scores of men whose lives have been affected by divorce. The plight of these men forms the substance of this book. Many have been patients that I have seen in my private practice; others have been assessed and treated at the Shaughnessy site of the University Hospital (a teaching hospital of the University of British Columbia), where I supervise medical students and residents in psychiatry. They are a diverse mix of men from many different racial and ethnic groups, from all socioeconomic groups, from many different occupational groups, and from a range of ages. Some initially have come for treatment with their wives, both before and after separating. Most have been referred as outpatients, but many I first met in the emergency room or on the medical wards or on the inpatient psychiatric unit of the hospital.

The book begins with a brief history of divorce from early times until present day, followed by a chapter on the theoretical underpinnings of marriage and divorce. I then describe the prodromal stages of separation, psychological separation if you like, that precede the actual or physical separation. I try to differentiate those separations that are husband-initiated, wife-initiated, and mutually initiated, because the dynamics and the symptomatology are very different. How people divorce also varies with their ages, the length of time married, and whether there are children or not. This is discussed at length. I have included a chapter on divorcing men who are coming out as gay men, not because these men are so common but because these separations are so complicated and the men and their families do not always receive thoughtful care. Another chapter is about fathers and their relationships with their children after divorce and after remarriage. The book concludes with three chapters on therapy in which I emphasize the importance of a biopsychosocial perspective when treating divorcing men and the importance of paying close attention to transference and countertransference issues at all times.

Although this book is about men and divorce, I have not attempted to exclude the other members of the family whose lives are affected by divorce. I do attempt to place the men in the context of family dissolution and family redefinition throughout the body of this work. However, this is no easy task. There are times when I fear that my analysis has suffered from being overinclusive, and other times from being underinclusive. Also, my preoccupation with divorcing men is purely thematic. I am trying to further our understanding of men who are facing and living through divorce. I do not have a professional bias for or against divorce, nor do I have a bias for or against the rights of men in divorce. I hope that my efforts are not misconstrued as a political statement.

I am very aware of the fact that I am a man writing about men. I cannot avoid bringing a male perspective and a male consciousness to this work. I am deeply affected by those men who feel abandoned by their wives, by those men who batter their wives, by those men who are separated from their children after divorce, by those men who rape their wives, by those divorced men who are with women 20 years their junior, and by those fathers who neglect their children. I make no apology for the range of emotions that is a part of my prose.

Finally, I have used many case examples in this book to illustrate a finding or a clinical observation. These have been disguised and edited, and many are composites of many cases, in order to protect the confidentiality of all of my patients.

Michael F. Myers
Vancouver, B.C.

CONTENTS

MEN AND DIVORCE

I

History and Theory

CHAPTER 1

Historical Perspective on Marriage and Divorce

To have a better understanding of contemporary men and their attitudes and reactions to divorce, it is helpful to glance briefly at the history of marriage and divorce throughout the ages. Because of the proliferation of divorces over the last 20 years and of studies of individuals coping with divorce in this same space of time, there is a tendency to deny the fact that divorce is as old as the institution of marriage. What have changed are the religious and legal ramifications of divorce, the social and personal meanings to those people who are divorcing, and the sheer numbers of divorces in Western society.

Marriage was considered a religious duty for the ancient Hebrews (Bohannan, 1980), and it was particularly incumbent on men to fulfill this moral and social responsibility (Mayer, 1985). Single life was frowned on, as it was through marriage that the family name, the family heritage, and property were passed on to posterity. Husbands' rights to divorce were far greater than those of their wives, and it was the men who wrote the bill of divorcement, the "*get*." For the ancient Greeks, marriage was both a civic and religious duty; divorce was possible for both spouses but easier for husbands to obtain (Bohannan, 1980). The Romans had many marriage and divorce forms depending on one's tribe; divorce was by mutual consent or the wishes of one party.

From the beginning of Christianity until the Reformation of the 16th century, marriage became a sacred ritual that could not be reversed (Bohannan, 1980). Dissolution was by canon law through ecclesiastical rather than civil courts. Divorce was granted by Roman Catholic courts for adultery, cruelty, and heresy (Scanzoni, 1979). After the Reformation and the beginnings of the Calvinist and Lutheran churches on the Continent, marriage became secular with the option of sanctification. Divorce cases went to civil courts. In England, the Anglican church retained control of marriage and divorce until 1669; after that, the House of Lords could grant divorce by legislative decree (Bohannan, 1980).

In Colonial America, laws of marriage and divorce were left in the hands of the individual states. With modernization of attitudes and citizens beginning to assert control over their lives, the rate of divorce began to increase during the 18th century (Scanzoni, 1979). The difference in status between husbands and wives at that time meant that the majority of the petitioners were men. They were less shy of the authorities, less affected by the stigma of divorce, and more independent financially. They could pay the legal fees and could more easily initiate acquiring a second spouse. More males than females advertised for "runaway spouses." However, by the end of the 18th century, records show that increasing numbers of wives successfully petitioned for divorce on the grounds of adultery. This trend has continued until the present day.

In the middle of the 19th century, the women's movement concerned itself with marriage and divorce with some gain in divorce rights for women (Bohannan, 1980). During the late 19th and early 20th centuries, American marriages began to collapse at an unprecedented rate (May, 1980). Between 1867 and 1929, the population of the United States increased by 300%, the number of marriages increased by 400%, and the divorce rate rose by 2,000% to become the highest in the world. By the end of the 1920s, more than one in six marriages ended in court. "Divorce conservatives" blamed feminists who were vigorously advocating the right of divorce (Scanzoni, 1979). Scholars also linked women's emancipation to the climbing divorce rate, but they were divided in their reaction; some were negative and judgmental, whereas others applauded the liberalization as long overdue (May, 1980). The panic and public outcry were so fierce that between 1889 and 1906, as the divorce rate began to accelerate rapidly, state legislatures across the country enacted more than 100 pieces of restrictive marriage and divorce legislation in an effort to stem the tide. What people failed to realize was that marital stability had hardly been universal prior to the liberalization of divorce laws because wives and husbands simply deserted each other (Scanzoni, 1979). Divorce itself does not undermine the family—it is a safety valve, a symptom, not the fundamental issue.

During the Victorian era, sex-role expectations were clearly defined, that is, how a good husband and a good wife were to behave (May, 1980). However, as time passed, many Victorians found it increasingly difficult to abide by their own code of conduct. Women who were not paragons of virtue were deemed "whores." Gambling, drinking, and the visiting of prostitutes were condoned for men with the idea that they would then be more sexually restrained at home. When this wasn't successful, marriages broke down. Wives petitioned that their husbands' lust for them impaired their health, and many women were forced into the workplace by economic necessity. With increasing urbanization and the advent of factories and businesses in the late 19th century, more jobs became available to women.

What has happened during the 20th century? By the 1930s and the 1940s, liberalism had grown tremendously in the United States, and this trend has continued (Bohannan, 1980). The women's movement reemerged in the 1960s. California made irretrievable breakdown of the marriage the basis for marital dissolution in 1970. Many states have followed suit, and public attitudes toward divorce have softened immensely. The divorce rate itself increased after World War I, decreased during the Depression, increased after World War II, stabilized during the 1950s, and then began to increase again in the early 1960s. It rose sharply (it actually doubled between 1966 and 1976)(Cherlin, 1981) and steadily until 1979 and 1981, when it peaked at 5.3/1,000 population (Hiebert, 1987). Since then, the divorce rate has been leveling off and falling to a rate of 4.8 in 1986.

Cherlin (1981) advises caution on how we interpret divorce rates. If we compare the annual rates from the 1950s with those of the 1970s, we are comparing a period of relatively low rates with a time of very high rates. But this recent upturn in divorce rates looms larger this way than if we compare it with the overall trend since 1860, the earliest year for which data are available from the U. S. Census Bureau. The lifetime proportion of "ever divorced" people among those marrying in a given year has risen steadily over the past century.

Most people who divorce do so early in their marriages—50% of the divorces occur by the seventh year of marriage (Cherlin, 1981). Although half of divorcing couples are childless, the other half average two children per family. In each of several recent years, some one million divorces involved two million adults and one million children (American Psychiatric Association, 1986). Most people who get divorced remarry: five out of six men and three out of four women, and half of all remarriages occur within 3 years of divorce

(Cherlin, 1981). A number of studies have demonstrated a modestly greater risk of marital disruption for remarriage after divorce than for first marriages, but the reasons are far from clear. Most remarried adults are satisfied with their current marriages and believe them to be far superior to their failed first marriages. And although several statistical studies suggest that people whose parents divorced are somewhat more likely to end their own marriages in divorce ("intergenerational transmission of marital instability"), this is controversial and may reflect lack of sophistication in research design (Cherlin, 1981).

A few final notes from the sociology of divorce. Poverty and lower socioeconomic status contribute to higher divorce rates. This in part accounts for higher divorce rates in black Americans. There is a greater risk of divorce for those who marry young, especially teenagers, and for those whose marriages are forced by pregnancy (American Psychiatric Association, 1986). The number of Catholics in a state sometimes affects the rate of divorce (that is, the rate is lower). Interracial and interfaith marriages have a slightly higher divorce rate than homogeneous ones.

Clinical Research in Divorce: An Overview

What is the relevance of divorce to our work as clinicians? Its increased prevalence since the 1960s has generated study of the separation and divorce process by many different disciplines: sociology, psychology, social work, psychiatry, law, and theology. Research on divorce had really just begun in the 1950s, with a focus particularly on its impact on children. This research has become more refined, especially its longitudinal aspects, and children at various ages when the divorce occurred have now been studied. In the literature of the 1960s and 1970s we also begin to see the study of gender and its relevance to divorcing women and divorcing men, especially women as divorced mothers and men as divorced fathers. Research on remarriage and stepfamilies began in the 1970s. The study of individuals in nontraditional families—single-parent families, dual-career marriages, cohabiting couples, and gay male/lesbian families—is being carried out in the 1980s.

Although my focus in this book is on men and divorce, I cannot proceed without discussing the context in which divorce occurs. Divorce begins as a psychological process (and I emphasize process; it is not an event) that affects two individuals, that is, the couple who is separating. When there are children, and, as mentioned above, there are in 50% of divorces, they also become involved in this process. But the impact does not stop here. Parents and grandparents, friends and acquaintances, classmates and workmates, even neighbors feel its effects. On the Social Readjustment Rating Scale (Holmes & Rahe, 1967), marital separation earns 65 points and divorce 73, surpassed only by the death of a spouse at 100 points.

In order to appreciate our patients' experience of separation and divorce, it is best to think of them as people in mourning. Indeed, divorce is a type of mourning in which the individuals are coming to terms with *loss*—a loss of what once was, loss of a happier and more harmonious time, loss of a strong and protective family unit. As one woman patient said to me, "I have lost my refuge against the storms of the world." Some people divorcing are also losing contact time with their children, their homes, their neighbors, friends, and in-laws. And less tangibly, some are losing status, privilege, social conformity, predictability, and stability.

Our patients will be at various stages of this mourning process when they consult us—some will deny what is happening, some will be raging, some will be despairing and suicidal, some will be numb and detached. All will have feelings of failure and variable amounts of self-blame. As with widows and widowers, many will pine for the spouse. This results from the sense of bonding and attachment that occurs in marriage, especially enduring marriage, and it will be present in those individuals who no longer like, admire, or respect their spouses. One woman said of her ex-husband: "I can't stand him any more. I could kill him; his alcoholism has ruined my life. But after 27 years of marriage I can't help but be drawn to him. I'd take him back in a minute if that were possible."

The research of Bowlby (1980), especially his attachment theory, is helpful in understanding this sense of bonding that is seen so commonly in people who are separating and divorcing. Affectional bonds or attachments between child and parent (and later between adult and adult) evolve during the course of normal development. They are not confined to childhood but continue actively throughout the life cycle. Intense emotions arise during the formation, the maintenance, the disruption, and the renewal of attachment relationships. Threat of loss precipitates anxiety, and actual loss arouses sorrow; each situation is likely to give rise to anger. In adult life, the characteristic ways in which an individual's attachments are organized will be determined by the experiences he or she had with attachment figures during infancy, childhood, and adolescence.

Separation distress as a response to intolerable inaccessibility of the attachment figure has been described by Weiss (1975, p. 42).

It includes anger, pining for the lost person, loneliness, apprehen-
siveness, anxiety, and panic. Feelings of sadness and regret are common and, when they are severe, persistent, and accompanied by
other symptoms such as loss of appetite, sleep disturbances, impaired concentration, or severe guilt, suggest clinical depression.

Also helpful in appreciating the dynamics of people who are
separating is the work of Kressel (1980). Expanding on the work of
others who have studied people's reactions to traumatic life events,
he has described four stages in the coping response to separation
and divorce—denial, mourning, anger, and readjustment. Spouses
whose separations are unexpected or who clearly do not want to be
separated or divorced are most vulnerable to separation distress. In
fact, nonmutuality of the decision to divorce is quite common
(Kressel, 1985). One should also remember that the initiator of the
separation may also be struggling, but differently. He or she may
feel guilty, ambivalent, and self-doubting.

What about the biomedical aspects of separation and divorce?
How do people react physically to divorce? The biological links between emotional stress such as divorce and the development of
physical illness are still being uncovered. It has long been known
that individuals who are separating and divorcing have poorer mental and physical health than the married, widowed, or single
(Bloom, Asher, & White, 1978). In fact, separated individuals have
about 30% more stress-related acute and chronic illnesses and visits
to their doctors than married adults (Somers, 1979; Verbrugge,
1979). Recent research on a sample of separated and divorced
women has found poorer qualitative and quantitative immune function in those women who were separated less than 1 year compared
to their married counterparts (Kiecolt-Glaser et al., 1987). A paral-
lel study of men who were separated and divorced has yielded similar findings (Kiecolt-Glaser et al., 1988).

In a sociological survey of data on morbidity, mortality, and
mental health, Riessman and Gerstel (1985) confirmed that the
married, whether male or female, are less depressed than either the
separated or the divorced. Women who are separating and divorcing are more likely than their male counterparts to have acute illnesses, to visit physicians, to restrict activity because of illness, and
to report feelings of depression. However, separated and divorced
men are at greater relative risk than their female counterparts for
the more extreme physical and mental health problems, including
mortality and hospitalization of all types. And where milder physical and mental health problems are concerned, separation tends to
be worse for women, whereas divorce tends to be worse for men.

What this means in everyday terms is that family doctors are more apt to see their women patients before and during separation, but later on down the road, if and when divorce becomes inevitable, they may be more likely to have estranged husbands coming in with symptoms.

Women and Divorce

The most recent data on marriage and divorce in the United States are from 1985 surveys of women conducted by the Bureau of the Census and sponsored by the National Institute of Child Health and Human Development (Norton & Moorman, 1987). Results are the following: first marriages are occurring at an older age; more adult women are not marrying at all; divorce has likely peaked; the majority of women who divorce eventually remarry, but the proportion who remarry is becoming smaller; redivorce for women married twice is declining; and among current adult cohorts of women, those representing the first 10 years of the baby boom are expected to have the highest frequency of divorce. Women who first married in their teens are more likely to divorce, as are women who marry after a premarital birth or give birth within 7 months of marriage; first marriages of women over age 30 are the most stable; the presence or absence of children does not affect either divorce or remarriage figures to an appreciable degree; women with incomplete units of education are most likely to divorce; and educational attainment is inversely related to remarriage.

Historically, the rules governing marriage have favored husbands and penalized wives (Bernard, 1979). Despite the fact that the material costs of divorce are considerable for both parties, women remain economically worse off after the divorce. Weitzman's (1986) 10-year study of no-fault divorce in California has shown that a woman's standard of living decreases by an average of 73% 1 year after the divorce, whereas that of her former husband increases by 42%. Even though the psychological costs of divorce are higher for men (men have higher morbidity and mortality rates), the psychological costs of marriage are higher for women (for example, many women in marriage are physically and psychologically battered) (Bernard, 1979). This fact accounts in part for the higher percentage of women wanting to leave their marriages (in 9 of 11 separating couples in one study, the wife desired termination) (Spanier & Casto, 1979) and initiating the divorce action. The only thing that seems to have decreased over time is the social cost of divorce; that is, there is now far less stigma attached to being divorced. However, this may be only partly true for those women whose socioeconomic status has dropped considerably after divorce; they may not be stigmatized for being divorced, but they are certainly stigmatized for being poor.

Kressel (1985, p. 51) has argued that women may be at a disadvantage in the male–female context of divorce negotiations. Husbands have a high degree of power *vis-à-vis* wives over the bargaining table, but they tend to have a relative insensitivity to the interpersonal and emotional dynamics that operate during negotiations. Wives may be attuned to these dynamics, but they have only a low degree of power. This imbalance of power exists because of the general economic dependence and disadvantages of wives relative to their husbands. The stronger party is likely to be less motivated to compromise and more likely to use coercion and intransigence. The less powerful party may react with passive concession-making or reactive defiance. Kressel reviews and summarizes the recent literature on sex-linked differences in personality and the negotiating process and concludes that in a competitive social encounter with a partner of the opposite sex, the man will be more "powerful" than the woman. Women react to divorce in a highly interpersonal manner; men are more apt to react in a nonpersonal manner and use instrumental and nonemotional ways of coping.

What else is different for divorced women? Their rates of depression are higher than those of men and married or widowed women. They also seek psychotherapy more often than men. They have a completed suicide rate that is 3½ times higher than that of married women. Wallerstein's (1986) longitudinal study of 60 middle-class divorcing California families has noted several distinguishing trends for women. At the 10-year follow-up, two-thirds of them had improved in their psychological functioning and had enhanced the quality of their lives; for women who were 34 years or older at the time of marital separation, anger, bitterness, and loneliness remained persistent emotions; women were less likely than men to accept their share of responsibility for the break-up; and most importantly, age appears to be a significant factor in a woman's capacity to rebuild intimate adult relationships and to re-establish social and economic stability. Women over age 40 at the time of the separation were living in economic, social, and psychological conditions well below those they had achieved during their marriages. None had remarried. Women in their 20s and 30s, by contrast, were more resilient and showed economic and emotional progress.

Men and Divorce

Bloom, White, and Asher (1979) have noted that divorced and separated men have higher admission rates to psychiatric hospitals than do divorced and separated women. The admission ratio of divorced men to married men is also higher than the admission ratio of divorced women to married women. Although divorced and separated women attempt suicide more often than their male counterparts, the deaths from suicide are higher among men. Indeed, separated and divorced men have higher mortality rates from nearly all causes including homicide, motor vehicle accidents, and cirrhosis of the liver than do separated and divorced women (Bloom et al., 1979; Verbrugge, 1979). Other deaths may result from lethal combinations of drugs and alcohol, lung cancer, diabetes, and arteriosclerotic heart disease.

Kressel (1985) and other investigators have concluded that compared to women, divorced men seem less able to articulate plausible psychological explanations for the marriage breakdown and generally seem more bewildered by the entire separation experience. This seems to hold whether they had actually initiated the divorce or not. Kitson and Sussman (1982) have found that men more often than women respond with "I'm not sure what happened" to inquiries about the cause of divorce.

Men become stressed because of the many disruptive changes that occur in their lives once they separate. Most have one or more changes of residence within the first couple of years of separating. They must adjust to cooking, cleaning, and shopping for themselves, and the ease or difficulty with this will depend on how much independent responsibility they assumed before and during their marriage. In an articulate and moving first-person account of his divorce after 22 years of marriage, newspaper columnist Darrell Sifford (1982, p. 147) gives a vivid description of his difficulty with marketing: "Grocery shopping was for me the worst of the strange and unfamiliar domestic ordeals, not because I didn't know what to buy but because, to my amazement, I was uncomfortable in the supermarket aisles . . . with my cart and shopping list." He wonders if the other shoppers who scrutinize him think his wife is out of town, or that he's unmarried, or that he's homosexual. He begins to keep his left hand in his jacket pocket; later he begins to put his wedding ring back on before going food shopping. "In a bizarre way I had become paranoid in the supermarkets, convinced at times that others were concerned more about me than about their shopping."

Hetherington, Cox, and Cox's (1976) study of divorced fathers has noted these types of adjustment difficulties and several other findings: divorced men spend more time at work, possibly out of loneliness, possibly because of enhanced financial pressures; 75% of divorced fathers felt they were functioning less well socially, especially with women, and 19% reported sexual difficulties; noncustodial fathers reported extremely painful and persistent emotional distress associated with seeing their children less frequently and with having little to say in the decision making regarding visitation.

Divorcing (Jacobs, 1983) and divorced (Hetherington et al., 1976; Greif, 1979; Wallerstein & Kelly, 1980) fathers have been studied more extensively than divorced men who are childless. This research has focused specifically on the father's post-divorce adjustment, the father–child relationship in pre- and post-divorce situations, noncustodial fathers, and single fathers. Most data suggest that those fathers who have continued contact and involvement with their children after separation are less depressed. Furthermore, one cannot predict the nature and quality of the post-separation fathering from the relationship during the marriage: some "closely involved" fathers before separation do not maintain this behavior after separation because of inability to adapt to visitation status; other men become more active and interested fathers only after separation.

Tepp's (1983) study of noncustodial but involved fathers 3 years after divorce is noteworthy. These men reported feelings of loss, dysphoria, sadness, and struggle regarding their not having custody of their children. They described feeling shut out of parenting functions, decreased feelings of being special, a sense of displacement, and a sense of confusion and difficulty about their status as parents. Anger is not mentioned as a specific emotion in these men who were examined 3 years after divorce, but Wallerstein's (1986) research is illuminating in this regard: almost 30% of the men in her study continued to feel angry and bitter 10 years after the separation.

Wallerstein's (1986) 10-year follow-up study of divorced families has yielded several other important findings. Two-thirds of the 52 men had remarried, a figure that is somewhat less than the highly reported remarriage rate of 80% for men (Cherlin, 1981). Half of these remarried men had redivorced or separated. One-third of the unmarried men were in a stable relationship, including three men in homosexual relationships. Wallerstein noted defensive posturing in several of the fathers who had largely phantom relationships with their children. These men, who had rarely paid child support over the years and who referred to their children not by name but by size or birth order, spoke proudly about their close, sustained relationships with their children as well as their regular support payments.

One of Wallerstein's most startling findings is that in most of the families the divorce had resulted in an enhanced quality of life for only one of the partners, more often the wife. Despite the passage of a decade, only 16% of the men had improved psychologically, 12% had deteriorated, and 72% remained unchanged. This may be explained in part, but certainly not completely, by the fact that only 35% of the men had actively sought to dissolve their marriages—the remaining 65% of the men had opposed their wives' initiation of the divorce. Those men and women who had initially sought the divorce were more likely to have enhanced the quality of their lives than were those who had opposed it.

In my own clinical research on divorcing men, both in our teaching programs for medical students and psychiatry residents at the University of British Columbia and in my private practice, I have found the following behavior to be characteristic: violent behavior directed against their wives (especially battering and sexual assault); violence toward their children and strangers; decreased work efficiency and productivity including absenteeism from work; compulsive and frenetic dating; indiscriminate sexual behavior including first-time involvement with prostitutes and first-time engagement in homosexual behavior; isolation from family and friends; limited and superficial relationships with other men; and early entry into new relationships with women (M. Myers, unpublished research). These findings are not unique and are familiar to any clincian who assesses and treats a large number of separating and divorcing men.

CHAPTER 2

Theoretical Background: Developmental Aspects of Marriage and Divorce

Before discussing the clinical aspects of men who are divorcing, it is necessary to look at contemporary marriage patterns from both a developmental and a sociocultural perspective. The past few decades have witnessed several changes that have affected family forms and the length of many marriages. An increased life span and the widespread use of contraception mean that many couples have the potential for a longer marriage with fewer children to raise to adulthood. This also means that never before in history have so many couples had so many years together after the last child leaves home before one of them dies. "Till death do us part" may seem like a very long time for many couples, and many argue that a marital expectation of remaining with the same partner for a lifetime is becoming an anachronism.

The resurgence of the women's movement of the past 25 years has had a profound impact on the norms, values, roles, and expectations of marriage. Since the pioneering work of Betty Friedan and the publication of her classic work *The Feminine Mystique* in 1963, women have come to realize, and to accept, that doing something for themselves is a legitimate act even if this does mean upsetting the status quo. Consequently, many married women are now more highly educated and are assured a higher degree of financial independence from their husbands. Many married women, with or without children, work outside the home for pay and, in some marriages, earn more money than their husbands. Unlike gender-defined marriages of the past, where women gave up jobs and careers to run their homes and to be wives and mothers, current types of marriages are fashioned along much more egalitarian and partnership lines. Nowadays, unhappily married younger women can and do feel with more certainty that if their marriage ends they can survive financially. Few women could say that before the 1960s.

In order to understand divorce, one must understand marriage. Although I treated many divorced and divorcing men as a resident in psychiatry and in my early years of private practice, I do not think I fully understood or appreciated the complexity of their conflicts until I began doing, and became more knowledgeable about, marital therapy. Treating men in their marriages, both individually and conjointly with their wives, has given me a richer and more dynamic perspective on men. Before that time, my tendency was to see the divorce as the precipitant (and a major precipitant at that) of the man's illness, the trigger for his symptom complex and disability. However, one must guard against seeing the divorce as an event rather than a process and refrain from viewing the patient's distress cross-sectionally rather than longitudinally. Conceptualizing divorce as both a form of marital activity and a process of grieving assists the clinician who treats men who are divorcing.

Why do people marry? From an Eriksonian (Erikson, 1963) perspective on psychosocial development, individuals who have achieved a stable identity approach marriage out of a need and capacity for intimacy with another person. Marriage represents a commitment that they are prepared to make to each other and a sharing of parts of each other. Gilligan's work (1982) on morality and how women and men differ in terms of moral expectations and intimacy in marriage is applicable to why people marry. Women define morality in terms of responsibility in relationships and responsibility to others. Men define morality in terms of ethical behavior and in terms of right or wrong. Women's sensitivity to the needs of others is different from that of men: women define themselves in terms of relationships with others and often in relationship to a particular person, in this case a husband. I find Gilligan's observations helpful in understanding the high level of thoughtfulness, caretaking, and nurturance that many divorcing women feel toward the husbands whom they are leaving. Gilligan's notions on responsive engagement and connectedness with others also help to explain the common clinical finding that women who are divorcing classically have a supportive network of family and women friends, whereas quite frequently divorcing men have no one.

People also marry for security. This may be psychological; that is, they do not feel complete or independent without someone. Often, they have problems with dependency and marry so that the can be looked after and protected. Some are late adolescents or young adults running away from unhappy home situations where they have felt unloved or controlled, or where they have been physically or sexually abused. Their need for security may also be financial, and by marrying, their basic needs for shelter, food, clothing, and so forth are met. In many marriages, especially when the partners are quite young, time has a way of "maturing" one or both of the individuals, the dependency on the other passes, and the marriage ends. One partner outgrows the other, or both outgrow each other.

Most people marry with the desire to have children, sooner or later. Developmentally, this is Erikson's stage of generativity. This powerful and fundamental need to procreate, present in most adults, accounts for the anguish in many couples who divorce before having children together. It also accounts for their heightened interest and drive in meeting someone else and remarrying while they are still biologically capable of having children.

Individuals also marry for social reasons—they have felt parental pressure to marry, or they feel they have reached an age when they should be married in order to feel socially accepted and not ostracized. It is intriguing that so many divorcing individuals, when asked to explain why they are separating, mention social expectancies and pressures as the reason they married in the first place. Perhaps individuals are more subject to social norms than one would think, or perhaps "blaming" social factors is a way of avoiding a more individualistic or introspective analysis of their divorce dynamics.

The unconscious factors in why people marry and whom they marry are extremely important in understanding the uniqueness of the couples whom clinicians assess and treat. In all couples that I treat in marital therapy, I insist on one, sometimes more, individual visit(s) with each partner to enable me to obtain a complete personal and family history. Only in this way can I achieve a psychodynamic sense of how the two individuals have become a couple and remained a couple. By examining their parents' marriages (and any earlier significant relationships or previous marriages that the distressed couple may have had), I can then begin to decipher the interpersonal forces that work well for them and those that don't. For those couples who are divorcing, a psychodynamic and interpersonal approach is necessary, perhaps more necessary, to comprehend what is happening to each individual and to gauge and predict what might happen down the road.

Divorce can also be examined as a part of the psychological and social development of a person (Gold, 1988). Indeed, it is often the catalyst of the personal development of an individual, which might not have happened had the relationship remained intact. There is a tendency for individuals who are in the midst of the most painful aspects of the divorcing process to be unable to see this at all because of the confusion, panic, and hopelessness that they feel. In this way, the clinician not only assists the patient through those dark days but also acts as a beacon toward positive growth for the individual down the road. As I will explain in a later chapter, it is usually those persons who initiate their separation (not those who feel left) who view divorce as a necessary and positive developmental stage in their life course. They, rather than their partners, have felt unhappy, stifled, or stagnant in their marriages.

If one were to ask the question "Why do people divorce?" responses range from the most microscopic and idiosyncratic of reason, such as intrapsychic and interpersonal reasons, to the more macroscopic and global reasons, the sociological and cultural ones. Yet, one of the most common responses would be that one or the other of the individuals was not happy. Happiness is indeed a major expectation of most people who marry in North American society. Whether this is realistic or not is not the point—individuals expect to be happy, for the most part, with their marital partners. Divorce, then, is viewed not merely as an escape from unhappiness but as an opportunity for renewed happiness, either as a single person or with remarriage to someone else (Gruncbaum & Christ, 1976).

Therapists who do marital and divorce work need to come to their own insights about divorce and what divorce means to the individuals whom they treat. Therapists need to be conscious of their own biases and conflicts about divorce, which may be a by-product of their own personal backgrounds, their own experiences with divorce, or their own views on marriage and commitment. Therapists who hold extreme or rigid positions—that divorce always represents failure, divorce is always liberating, divorce is morally wrong, divorce is inevitable in these times, and so forth—should not be doing divorce work. Not only do the individuals and couples whom we treat need to come to their own decisions about separation and divorce, but they do not need their therapists' personal views, whether latent or expressed, heaped on top of the distress and challenge that they already feel. My position is that marital and divorce therapists must strive to attain as value-free a context as possible in doing their work, fully aware that we are never value-free but honest and self-knowing enough to recognize when we are not.

The therapist's mettle is often most put to the test when he/she has been treating a couple for several weeks or months, thinks the marriage is improving, and suddenly learns or realizes that husband and wife are going to separate. With particular couples, this news may be quite jarring for the therapist, who may be besieged by worries or self-doubts. Have I failed in some way? Is their separation a failure of marital therapy (a not uncommon myth about the purposes and goals of marital therapy)? How do I quickly change my mental set to assist them to proceed with separation? How do I hide my feelings (of surprise, of anger, of sadness) that they are going to separate? Should I hide my feelings?

Many individuals who divorce can be understood and conceptualized according to developmental psychoanalytic psychology (Singer, 1975). Divorce, like marriage, provides another opportunity for psychological separation from one's parents (or one's spouse as parent). Divorce, like marriage, provides an opportunity for working through early sexual inhibitions. Divorce, like marriage, can assist in the development of a new level of object relations, that is, the ability to relate to others with mutuality and recognition of the other's needs. And most important, divorce, like marriage, can provide an opportunity for autonomy, for the ability to be close and at the same time retain a sense of one's own personal identity.

Cantor (1982), drawing on the observation of Horney (1967) that divorce is often related to unresolved conflicts that are brought into marriage from childhood development, has hypothesized that many divorces result from working through the task of separation–individuation at an adult level. The marital couple is seen as an analogue of the mother–child dyad, wherein the nondifferentiating spouse assumes the role of the mother and the differentiating partner is the child/spouse. A child/spouse, sufficiently differentiated, can break up the marriage and seek to fill rapprochement needs with another partner or through other, emotionally supportive adult relationships. Most clinicians have seen many couples with this type of separation dynamic.

The presence of unresolved intrapsychic conflicts in the individual as a cause of divorce pertains to only a segment of couples who divorce. Individuals who divorce and remarry someone else who is similar to the original spouse fit into this category, but they are really a small minority. Most individuals in this group are ones with quite severe neurotic conflict or with serious character pathology antedating their marriages. Many of these individuals are treated by general psychiatrists before and during their marriages and often during and after a divorce. Although there is not a clear line of demarcation, these individuals and couples can be differentiated from those individuals and couples who enter treatment only at the time they are divorcing and end treatment once the crisis has passed and resolution is underway. These individuals do not seem beleaguered by intrapsychic conflict, and the individual treatment they require is supportive only. The reasons that they divorce are more often interpersonal or sociocultural in nature—they are unable to communicate with each other, one has outgrown the other, one wants to pursue a different lifestyle, there is role strain in one or both, there is conflict over sex-role change, and so forth.

In his book *Marriage and Mental Illness*, Hafner (1985) reviews and summarizes some of the recent research on sex-role stereotyping, marital intimacy, and psychological symptoms. Men who adhere to a male sex-role stereotype have difficulty talking about feelings of vulnerablility and dependency, thereby making honest, open communication within marriage very difficult. Since rigid adherence to a male sex-role stereotype also increases the likelihood of sex-role strain and conflict, men with these attitudes bring a double problem into their marriage: they maximize the likelihood of sex-role problems and minimize the likelihood of their resolution through mutual discussion between husband and wife. Hafner cites the well-known research of Brown and Harris (1978) that found that women who had an intimate, supportive relationship with their husbands or boyfriends were protected from depression even if they had been subjected to major stressors. If we accept that sex-role stereotyping is a powerful obstacle to emotional intimacy within marriage, then we can hypothesize (says Hafner) that the likelihood of psychological symptoms emerging in a married person is directly related to the extent and rigidity of sex-role stereotyping within the marriage.

Hafner's observations and theorizing do have clinical relevance. Many couples with distressed marriages describe conflict over their respective role behaviors and a complete inability to communicate and problem-solve in a constructive way about their differences. Likewise, as I discuss later in Chapter 7, male sex-role rigidity is a contributing factor to divorce and a complicating factor in divorce adjustment and divorce therapy.

Before leaving this subject, I want to highlight a segment of the population who consult mental health professionals and who are at especial risk for divorce: those individuals with psychiatric disorders. It has long been known that there is an association between psychiatric illness and marital turmoil and divorce (Blumenthal, 1967; Briscoe et al., 1973; Woodruff, Guze, & Clayton, 1972). Likewise, the prevalence of primary affective disorder is significantly higher among divorced individuals than among controls. In her study of assortative mating (the tendency for married couples to be more similar for a phenotypic trait than would be expected if they were chosen at random), Merikangas (1984) found that 30 of 56 married depressed patients had psychiatrically ill spouses. On follow-up, the entire group had a divorce rate nine times the expected rate for the population, and those couples in which both members were ill had a significantly higher divorce rate than those in which only one member was affected. The implications of this research are serious and underscore the need for clinicians to treat their depressed inpatients and outpatients with both an individual approach (supportive psychotherapy and/or medication) and an interpersonal approach (psychoeducation about depression and/or marital therapy).

Male Development

Earlier I mentioned two of Erikson's stages—intimacy and generativity—as essential to understanding marriage. In traditional terms, these are the tasks that the man and the woman must face and complete for a wholesome and functioning marriage and family. If we now consider the stereotype of the North American male role with its emphasis on autonomy and self-reliance, disavowal of feelings, pursuit of achievement outside the home, and denial of personal vulnerability as "weakness," we begin to see how much these tasks for men work against the completion of Erikson's developmental stages. These concepts help us clinically to understand men who recoil from marriage and marry later in life, men who have trouble communicating in marriage, and men who are facing and struggling with divorce.

Building on the work of Erikson are the longitudinal study of normal men by Vaillant (1977) and the retrospective study of normal men by Levinson (1978). Vaillant's work is grounded in ego psychology—intrapsychic development is based on a progressive negotiation of life-cycle stages. Adaptation to life is the goal, and this adaptation, superimposed on biological givens, encompasses absorption in relationships with other people, internalization of objects, and identification. Vaillant makes the following conclusions: early childhood events have a role to play; individuals' lives have many discontinuities; "adaptive mechanisms" correlate with health and maturity, and they are the key to understanding mental health and mental illness; psychological development is a lifelong process; and positive mental health can be described free from moral and cultural bias (Vaillant, 1977, p. 29).

Levinson also sees human development as a lifelong process or cycle, and he talks in terms of "seasons," those periods of development that are universal in adulthood, each with its own distinct form. Levinson's observations embrace the self of the man (his wishes, conflicts, ways of feeling and acting, and so forth), the sociocultural world about him, and his interactions with this world. His description of the masculine/feminine polarity in men is superb (Levinson, 1978, pp. 228–233) and has particular relevance to how men conduct themselves in marriage and in divorce. I will try to summarize: as a young man starts to make his way in the adult world, he tries to live in accord with the images and values that are most central to his sense of masculinity. Simultaneously, he must neglect and repress the feminine aspects of his self, which are perceived as dangerous. Hence, much of the self cannot be lived out or even experienced in early adulthood because the man would be frightened by feelings and interests that seem womanly.

Levinson defines five different qualities that are included in the masculine/feminine polarity and that define a man's sense of masculinity or femininity. First, one meaning of femininity in a man is homosexuality, although femininity and homosexuality are far from identical. Nevertheless, homosexual feelings or desires in many young men cause them severe anxiety (and moral outrage in those around them) and are experienced as unmasculine. Second, bodily prowess and toughness are associated with manliness. This includes the stamina to undertake long, grueling work (and sports) and to endure severe bodily stress without "quitting." Third, achievement and ambition are associated with masculinity, and this usually means paid work, preferably with status, outside the home sphere. Success at work and getting ahead are important, so that the man is defined as a "breadwinner." The more traditionally "male" the work is, the greater the sense of masculinity. Fourth, power and masculinity are closely associated. Exercising control over others and being (and being recognized as) a person of strong will or a leader who "gets things done" contribute to this sense of power. Its opposite, weakness, is so deplorable and frightening to some men that they have to fight it or deny it at all costs, and this accounts for the very authoritarian nature of some men. And fifth, the masculine/feminine polarity may be reflected in the distinction between thinking and feeling. Men by nature are assumed to be more logical and "reasonable" than women—more analytical and intellectual, "cooler" emotionally, and more interested in how things work. In its extreme form, this polarization requires a man to be some kind of thinking machine. He must be assertive, rivalrous, and task-oriented. He is not permitted feelings that involve dependency, intimacy, grief, sensuality, and vulnerability. They are associated with childishness and femininity.

Social psychologist Joseph Pleck has been a major contributor to our understanding of male psychology and masculine development (Pleck & Sawyer, 1974; Pleck, 1976, 1981). He has challenged the theory of male sex-role identity (MSRI), which has been the dominant paradigm in American psychology for understanding male experience (Pleck, 1987). This theory holds that for individuals to become psychologically mature as members of their sex, they must acquire male or female "sex-role identity" manifested by having the sex-appropriate traits, attitudes, and interests that psychologically "validate" or "affirm" their biological sex. For males especially, there are many factors that thwart the attainment of healthy sex-role identity, for example, the actual or relative absence of male role models and women's changing roles in our society. The resulting problems for males include effeminacy and homosexuality (too little masculinity) or hypermasculinity (too much masculinity).

Pleck argues that psychoanalysis is not the ultimate source of MSRI theory but that it merely provided an intellectual vehicle for the expression of cultural concerns about masculinity that were prevalent in American culture before psychoanalysis (Pleck, 1980). He notes that Freud had very little to say about the issues of central concern to male sex-role identity theory, and he also cites evidence of articles such as "The Effeminization of Man" appearing as early as 1894 in America, long before Freud's early writings. Further, states Pleck, male sex-role identity theorists borrowed three of Freud's earliest concepts (identification, psychosexual development, and homosexuality as a fixation in psychosexual development) and developed their own ideas with little further exchange or contact with psychoanalysis. Male sex-role identity theory and contemporary psychoanalytic theory now share hardly anything intellectually in common.

Pleck is a proponent of male sex-role strain theory. In other words, men are products of their culture. They attempt to take in societal dictates about what constitutes masculinity or maleness, and if they don't spontaneously fit in, they may force themselves to do so. This can mean adopting hypermasculine behaviors, not because they have some unconscious anxiety about femininity or lack of maleness but because they will be rejected or ostracized from society (or fear that they will be) if they don't conform to traditional male role norms or standards. Male sex-role strain theory does not fault the individual or the individual's mother or the individual's wife but, rather, attributes the responsibility to society's unrealistic expectations of what is considered "manly" in our culture.

I find that Pleck's ideas have a lot of relevance to our work as marital and divorce clinicians. Because the theory of sex-role strain is respectful of *both* women and men, especially their differences and similarities, and not attacking and blaming of women (as mothers or wives), we are able to work more honestly and with balance as both marital and divorce therapists. Further, specifically when working with divorcing men, it is easier to see them speaking or behaving in particular ways that are culturally determined and thereby typical, or appropriate, for either North American culture, their culture of origin, or some amalgam. This is especially so for divorcing men who are very young, divorcing men who are aging and involved with younger women, divorcing men who are coming out as gay men (or who have underlying sexual orientation conflicts), or divorcing men who feel abandoned by their departing wives. These are all subjects that I will elaborate on in later sections of this book.

Fathering

The study of men as fathers is quite new, about 15 years, and like the field of male psychology in general, it is largely a corollary of the women's movement with its emphasis on changing sex roles and changing family forms. Because half of the divorces in North America involve men who are fathers, it is fitting to have a deeper understanding of developmental theory about fathering. This helps us in our clinical understanding of the behavior and feelings of men as they approach (and resist) divorce and how they adjust to divorce.

Ross (1982), a psychoanalyst and major contributor to our knowledge about fathering, has called the father the "forgotten parent" in psychoanalytic literature. He observed 65 boys between the ages of 3½ and 10 years and noted a variety of intense wishes on their parts both to have babies and to care for babies (Ross, 1983). He believes that the paternal identity of an adult man does not just exist in a vacuum but begins much earlier in life and is merely activated or crystallized by the birth and presence of his children. Ross refers to the earlier work of Benedek (1970), who noted that fatherhood had instinctual derivatives that were not restricted to the father's role as provider but also included mutually reinforcing ties to his children. She used the term "genuine fatherliness," which refers to the father's ability to respond to his children in an immediate and empathic manner. Later, Greenberg and Morris (1974) used the term "engrossment" to describe the excitement, joy, and fascination that fathers manifest with their newborn infants. Diamond (1986) further documents that the father's attachment and relationship to the infant begins long before conception and birth in his paper "Becoming a Father." He reviews much of the literature of the past decade about expectant fatherhood and paternal identity formation and proposes a seven-stage sequence of prospective fatherhood: getting ready, conception, the first trimester, midpregnancy, the turn toward one's father and fathering, toward the end of the second trimester, and the last trimester.

Moving further along the life cycle, as both fathers and their children develop, we see what important contributions fathers make to healthy family functioning. Fathers are more than providers, authority figures, and protectors. Indeed, what have been most noteworthy over the past 15 to 20 years are the nurturant activities and abilities that fathers have demonstrated toward their children and toward the running of the family home. There is now more emphasis on each parent's unique role in the rearing of children and less focus on the specific mother–child dyad when there are psychiatric problems with children. We can hope that the skewed way of conceptualizing psychopathology and the era of "mother blaming" are over.

Cath's emphasis on the dynamic interplay between the man and the woman and how they view each other as parents of their children is significant (Cath, 1986). The father's role is implicated in his wife's nurturing capacities, just as her role is implicated in his fathering capacity. In other words, how the man nurtures his wife helps to assure the nurturance of their offspring. Cath calls this the "alliance of couplehood," that is, the father's positive and negative contributions to family mutuality that begin long before conception. Fatherhood itself thrives with the mother's permission and support. How she conceptualizes and understands her husband's role as father may be one of the most important determinants of how their child will relate to his/her father and to other men and women later in life. Divorce, with its severance of attachment bonds and its intense emotions, has a profound impact on this alliance of couplehood. How the man views his former wife as a mother and how the woman views her former husband as a father significantly reinforce or denigrate their ongoing capacities to parent their shared offspring.

There is other research that highlights the importance of fathers in child development that I will mention just briefly. Yogman (1982) has illustrated how much infants are able to elicit loving and competent caretaking not only from their mothers but also from their fathers (regardless of how reluctant or hesitant their fathers may be) and that this is done in a mutually reinforcing manner. Fathers parent differently: they tend to be more stimulating and physically arousing, whereas mothers tend to be more soothing and lulling. Parents always bring their own individual pasts into the rearing of children: most contemporary fathers long to be better fathers to their children than they felt their fathers were to them. Sometimes this quest plays a part in whether they decide to divorce or not. Divorce for some men means an opportunity to be a better father, even though in the short term the man may feel he is being a worse father "for breaking up the family." And finally, Cath (1982) has written about the importance of grandfathers in the development of their grandsons because they can more easily facilitate a boy's acceptance of the feminine side of himself. Grandfathers may act as neutralizers of excessive parental demands for action, toughness, and competitiveness. Cath's observations are particularly relevant to the tragic weakening (or severing) of the grandfather–grandson bond that occurs with those divorces where the father's contact time with his children is drastically curtailed. His statement, "We need a broader commitment not only to involve fathers but to make ourselves available to them in the implementation of all therapeutic family plans from the cradle to the grave" (Cath, 1986), echoes my feelings totally.

Before concluding this section on male development, I want to mention the academic discipline of men's studies and its impact on men and divorce. In tandem with the discipline of women's studies over the past 20 years, there has been a reworking and reassessment of our understanding of men, exemplified in the research of Pleck that I reviewed earlier. This field of study is quite new and is just beginning to earn some respectability in our universities. There are many assumptions and so-called "givens" about men that are being explored and questioned.

One of the leading scholars of this subject is Dr. Harry Brod, former Assistant Professor in the Program for the Study of Women and Men in Society in the Department of Philosophy at the University of Southern California in Los Angeles. In "The Case for Men's

Studies," Chapter 2 in his edited book *The Making of Masculinities* (Brod, 1987, p. 40), Dr. Brod has the following to say:

> While seemingly about men, traditional scholarship's treatment of generic man as the human norm in fact systematically excludes from consideration what is unique to men qua men. The overgeneralization from male to generic human experience not only distorts our understanding of what, if anything, is truly generic to humanity but also precludes the study of masculinity as a specific male experience, rather than a universal paradigm for human experience. The most general definition of men's studies is that it is the study of masculinities and male experiences as specific and varying social–historical–cultural formations. Such studies situate masculinities as objects of study on a par with femininities, instead of elevating them to universal norms.

There are many themes and issues about men, their relationship to women, and their relationship to each other that are being researched under the rubric of men's studies. Let me name a few: fathering, men and violence, gay rights, homophobia, men and aging, men and pornography, men and spirituality, sexual harassment, men and infertility, the male sex role, and male sexuality. Many of these subjects are germane to men and divorce, and I will refer to them both directly and indirectly in the chapters that lie ahead.

I want to turn now to the final section of this chapter on background and summarize briefly my philosophical beliefs about treatment of couples and treatment of men who are in the process of divorce. These are generic beliefs and ideas only; the specifics of treatment are mentioned sporadically throughout the book and in more detail in Section III.

The theoretical underpinnings of marital therapy stem from three broad schools of thought: behavioral, systems, and psychoanalytic–psychodynamic. My approach to couples is an integrated one that not only utilizes concepts from these three schools (in varying degrees, depending on the particular couple) but also borrows from others: communications theory, role theory, and feminist theory (Myers, 1986a). A feminist approach to marital therapy encompasses many principles of social-role and sex-role theory and argues that traditional marriage values, rules, and expectancies have been unhealthy for women (Laws, 1975). A feminist approach espouses egalitarian principles and is particularly apropos during this contemporary era of rapidly changing roles for men and women both within and outside the boundaries of marriage. Because so many distressed couples at the moment are struggling with issues related to sex-role change and are striving for equality in their relationships, I find it only natural and sensible that contemporary therapists be comfortable with feminist scholarship and its marked relevance to women and men in marriage. My approach to divorcing men is also eclectic because, whether I have treated the man originally with his wife or not, I find that certain men who are divorcing may respond to behavioral interventions, others to psychodynamic interpretations, and so forth.

Let me elaborate briefly on my feminist perspective in the treatment of men coming to terms with separation and divorce. Some might argue that feminism and divorcing men are incompatible, contradictory, perhaps mutually destructive. I would argue the opposite: that is, a feminist approach to a divorcing man is salutary, educative, and, most of all, empowering. Many people, not only laypersons but also professionals, have gross misunderstandings about feminist theory and feminist therapy. They see feminism as separatist and divisive, as anti-male and man-hating, as anti-family, anti-heterosexism, and pro-lesbianism. Mainstream feminism is nothing more than promotion and preservation of equality of women in a male supremacist society. As a male therapist in North American society, I am very aware of the injustices and inequities that plague women in the workplace and in the home. As a marital therapist, one cannot *not* be affected by the male-domination communication patterns in marriage. One cannot *not* be affected by the anguish and shame of the battered wife. One cannot *not* be affected by the terror and numbness of the women who are raped by their husbands. My feminism is rooted in and shaped by my clinical day-to-day work.

I have both an academic and a clinical interest in women's and men's studies. I teach a course, with a woman psychiatrist colleague, to residents in psychiatry at the University of British Columbia entitled "Women and Men: Issues in Training and in Practice." My clinical teaching of medical students about ambulatory psychiatry emphasizes the many gender-specific issues in clinical psychiatry and in the doctor–patient relationship. My work in marital and divorce therapy, and my one-to-one work with divorcing men, especially men who feel abandoned by their wives, is both woman-affirmative and man-affirmative. Many newly separated husbands at the moment have a lot of concerns about our changing societal sex roles. They are bewildered and angry. They blame "feminism" for their marriages ending, and they lash out at women in general. Especially hurt and angry are those men whose wives have "come out" as lesbian or who are exploring lesbianism. These and many other men seem to respond to a therapy that is respectful of the revolutionary upheaval of men's and women's relationships that we are immersed in at this moment in history.

It is time now to talk about the clinical aspects of divorce for men, beginning with men who have not yet separated from their wives, the subject of the next chapter.

II

Clinical Presentation
of Divorcing Men

CHAPTER 3

The Not-Yet-Separated Man

Mike and Monica were in crisis when they came to see me for marital therapy. One week earlier, Mike had admitted to being involved with another woman when confronted about this by Monica. To Monica's surprise, Mike was agreeable to coming with her for marital therapy. In that first visit, both expressed the desire to work on and improve their marriage if at all possible. The idea of separating and divorcing was disturbing to each of them.

Mike was a surgeon who taught part-time at the local medical school and maintained a busy private practice the rest of the week. He was 45 years old. Monica was 43 years old, a former flight attendant and model, who in addition to full-time mothering and homemaking was very involved in unpaid fundraising for several community agencies. They had been married for 20 years and had three children aged 17, 15, and 7. They had no previous marital therapy or individual therapy. Fay, the woman with whom Mike was involved, was 25 years old, and she was an intern at the same teaching hospital. They had been seeing each other for 6 months.

I learned in that first conjoint visit that things had not been going well at home for at least 2 years, maybe longer. Both Monica and Mike described "less communication" than previously: they were no longer able to discuss anything without bickering or making sarcastic quips. Mike was spending less time at home and taking on more work. Monica complained of trouble sleeping, premenstrual mood swings, and weight loss. She volunteered that she was drinking more than usual. The two of them could not remember when they had last made love. Both were alarmed about their 15-year-old daughter's obsession with thinness and feared she was developing anorexia nervosa. I arranged to have an individual visit with each of them.

Monica was the middle child in a family of three daughters, having grown up in a small logging town where her father was the only doctor. He had worked night and day, and she described her relationship with him as "respectful." Her mother, who had a degree in Fine Arts and who was from a large city, was described as "chronically unhappy." Monica described her parents' marriage as "barren"; she suspected that, had her mother been living in another era, and had she not given up her career to be a mother and homemaker, she would have left her father.

Monica was an attractive and popular teenager who was never without a boyfriend and who was involved with many school activities. Her grades were "so-so." After high school, she left home to begin nursing school but dropped out after several months. She took a course in modeling and enjoyed this for a couple of years before training as a flight attendant. About this time she met Mike at a dance; he was an intern. She was attracted to his "good looks, his energy, and his sense of humor." They were married a year later.

My visit with Monica was quite straightforward. She was very worried about her marriage and had been for some time. Attempts on her part to talk with Mike about her fears made him angry. She loved him as much as ever, she said, and clearly felt devastated and furious about his relationship with Fay. Her manner was one of sadness—and panic.

Mike's background was quite different from Monica's. He had grown up "on the other side of the tracks" in a large Eastern city. His father was a bricklayer, and his mother a cleaning woman. When asked to describe his parents' marriage, Mike said: "Well it seemed to work for them—I never saw them talking or doing anything together or ever showing any affection, but they never fought either." His mother worked full time during Mike's childhood years, which meant that Mike was largely responsible for looking after his younger brother after school and for preparing dinner during the week. Mike grew up resenting this amount of responsibility and the lack of time for sports and other school activities. He worked for 2 years after high school to earn college fees and to buy a car. He had wanted to be a surgeon since high school and somewhat humorously described "Ben Casey" as his idol. He did very well in medical school and had no difficulty being accepted into a "plum" surgical residency.

Mike's visit with me was another story. He described himself as "disengaged"—from Monica, from the home, from their possessions and furnishings, from their couple friends, and partly from the children.

This emotional estrangement had been increasing slowly for about 2 years. "There's a sheet of plexiglass between Monica and me," he stated. He recalled with vivid clarity the precise moment of something changing in his feelings for Monica. They had been at a party with friends, and a small group were gossiping about a senior colleague's recent separation from his wife: "I don't know what happened—something just went click—I looked across the table at Monica—I remember she was laughing at the time—and I said to myself 'I don't love you any more.' And that feeling—or lack of feeling—has persisted," he stated.

Mike spoke warmly and lovingly of Fay but described a terrible sense of guilt and responsibility for the family and everyone in it. He told me that he had had several "brief flings" over the years of his marriage but none that he felt was serious or threatening to his marriage. These were never discussed at home, and he doubted that Monica knew of them. He told me that he had had the reputation of having a "roving eye" since he was a medical student.

Mike promised Monica that he would stop the affair and work on the marriage. I began to see them weekly in conjoint therapy. One month later, when Monica called him at his hotel in another city where he was attending a conference, Fay answered the phone. Mike begged for forgiveness when he returned from the conference and vowed to try harder to stop seeing Fay. This time he did sever the relationship completely, but he remained distant and bitter at home. Three months later, the day before they were to leave on a "romantic 3-day weekend," Mike canceled, stating that he just couldn't afford the time away. Once again Monica was understanding. Three months later, when Monica developed genital herpes and communication was as difficult as ever, she decided to file for divorce.

What I have attempted to illustrate in this brief vignette, is the dilemma of many men who no longer love their wives but cannot face the possibility of separation. They are so overwhelmed with feelings of bewilderment and guilt and terror that they do nothing in a constructive or problem-solving way about their marriages. Some become stuck or paralyzed in a state of morose or hostile inertia, others throw themselves into their work (or hobbies or recreational pursuits), and still others become extramaritally involved. Most are mourning their marriages but are not in touch with feelings of sadness and sorrow; they are more apt to be irritable and angry, withdrawn, and hard to live with. Unfortunately, what begins as a very valid and legitimate constellation of feelings that are easy to empathize with (as in Mike's case when he realized he no longer loved Monica) becomes twisted and covered over with behaviors that are harder to remain empathic about, such as lying, continued withdrawal and hostility, and a return to deception and repeated sexual acting out.

The time before actual physical separation has long been known to be a stressful time in marriage. Despert (1953) called it "emotional divorce." Kressel and Deutsch (1977) describe two stages that antedate actual separation—"the pre-divorce decision period" and "the decision period proper." Federico (1979) has described the concept of a marital point of no-return (N/R) reached when a marital partner reaches a point at which he/she cannot return to a previous emotional investment in the marriage. As in Mike's case above, this feeling can be so threatening that the individual immediately suppresses or denies it, professing that he/she wants the marriage to continue with or without professional help. All marital therapists are familiar with this type of individual or couple, who, despite their best intentions at the beginning of therapy, are not able to truly work at their marriages as therapy proceeds. Further, as Federico goes on to elucidate, they may develop very convoluted marital termination strategies. One is by provocation, which is exactly what Mike did. Initially, Monica accommodated to Mike's behavior, but, eventually exasperated, she initiated the divorce proceedings. At separation, then, she looked like the rejecting one, but it was originally the other way around.

I might just add that at the time of assessment of Mike and Monica, especially after my individual visits with each of them, I was able to sense intuitively that Mike was not ready for conjoint work. I felt that he needed individual therapy to help him understand more clearly his feelings about Monica, Fay, and his notion about the preservation of family at all costs. I proposed this to him, but so alarming were his feelings about the reality of his failing marriage that he insisted on the two of them coming together. Much later, when Monica demanded that they separate, then and only then would Mike begin to do some individual therapy with me.

What follows is a second example of an unhappily married man, but one in whom there is less denial and more insight:

David, a building contractor, came to see me with a chief complaint of "I'm miserably unhappy in my marriage, but I don't know what to do." He went on to tell me that he had been married for 12 years and had two sons, aged 9 and 7. His wife, Tara, was a teacher but hadn't worked outside the home since their younger son was born. He de-

scribed her as being at loose ends—wanting some type of paid work but not wanting to return to teaching. He dismissed this as irrelevant to his lack of feelings for his wife and spent most of his time with me reciting a litany of unhappy anecdotes about their life together as a couple. He listed many areas in which he thought they were incompatible. He complained at length of Tara's shortcomings—and refreshingly, about a few of his own! He felt frustrated, demoralized, and trapped. They had been to a marital therapist a year earlier but dropped out after four sessions: "I didn't really like the guy—he picked on me a lot for not really trying—for not doing my 'homework'—he was right—I didn't work at it at all."

Toward the end of David's visit with me, he told me that he had considered separation and considered it seriously but that he had three reservations—his wife, Tara, his two children, and their respective families. He told me that he still loved Tara in many ways but not in a marital sense: "I love her as I would love a friend—she's like a sister to me; I care about her and her welfare." He told me that they had not been sexual with each other for about 5 years, that he no longer shared as much with her as he used to, and that he no longer felt like doing things alone with her just as a couple. He said that the idea of even discussing a separation with Tara made him shudder: "I just can't imagine it—it'll kill her."

David went on to talk about his children and his fears of putting them through a separation. He stated that he didn't feel it was fair for the kids to have divorced parents, especially children the ages of his two sons. He believed that all children need and deserve a solid and single family. He mentioned that he also feared losing his children if he and Tara separated. He feared losing his children both with respect to custodial time now (he would not get to see them as often as he wished), and he also feared losing his children permanently, that is, that Tara would obtain sole custody and move several thousand miles away to the city in which she had grown up.

Regarding their families, David dreaded the impact of their separation on his and Tara's parents. He described their marriage as the model marriage of all the siblings in each family. Neither set of parents would have any reason to suspect anything amiss. His father had had a coronary the previous year, and he described his relationship with his father as strained: "He'll have a fit—he's always felt that Tara has a stabilizing influence over me—I know he won't understand." David also feared the anticipated reaction of Tara's parents: "There's never been any divorce in her family—they'll rally completely to Tara's side and completely reject me."

What are some of the issues here for the man who is unhappy and who has more or less concluded that his marriage is over but has not yet actually separated? What are his fears and conflicts? Why is it so difficult to just get on with it and to begin the separation process? Why are these men so resistant to marital therapy and to the idea of working on their marriages with their wives?

I'll answer the last question first. They resist marital therapy, as conventionally defined, because they are beyond it. It's too late. They no longer possess the motivation, the drive, the interest, the feeling, whatever you call it, to work with their wives and a professional with preservation and enhancement of the marriage as a goal. In this regard, these men must be distinguished from the much larger group of unhappily married men whose marriages are not over but who also resist marital therapy. Their resistance is different and usually based in male gender dynamics (a need to be self-reliant and self-sufficient, a need to deny the seriousness of the problem, a need for privacy, and so forth) or simple ignorance about the process of marital therapy and its benefits. Many men in this latter group work very hard in marital therapy once they get started.

Men whose marriages are essentially over but who remain with their wives are usually struggling with a sense of duty and responsibility as men. The more traditional the marital role assignment, the more they will feel this sense of obligation. Some see themselves as guardians and caretakers of their families and therefore suffer variable amounts of guilt about separation and divorce. And this feeling will be magnified when they assume more than their fair share of responsibility for the marriage failing or are made to feel solely or primarily responsible for the marriage ending. Not only do wives, children, extended family, and friends sometimes contribute to this guilty feeling, but we therapists do as well if we don't adequately assess the individuals and couples who come to see us. In other words, we may inadvertently blame a husband for not engaging in marital therapy (thereby reinforcing his wife's position) when he is morally unable to do so because for him the marriage is no longer viable, and marital therapy is a sham.

A married man with a highly developed inner sense of responsibility who is contemplating separation may blame himself in many ways. He may chastise himself for not being able to stick it out and honor his commitments. Or he may blame himself for living a lie, that somehow, in some magical way he should be able to will himself to love, to regain something that is gone, or to rekindle a fire that has died. He may also chide himself for desiring personal happiness or longing for love that he no longer feels with his wife. He knows that marital passion wanes with the passing of years together, but he queries if what he feels and longs for is normal and common to all marriages of the same duration.

These same men feel guilty for not loving their wives as they once did. And this is made worse in those marriages where the wives' love for their husbands has not altered or if it has, not enough to make them want to end the marriage. One of the most common laments that I hear in my practice is: "Why don't I love her any more—she seems to love me, she's still attractive, she's bright enough, she's an honest woman, faithful, and she's a terrific mother." Logic and rational thought do not adequately explain the ache of the inner sense of loss.

Because the stage before actual separation is such a perplexing and disorienting time, these men do not completely trust their own perceptions of what is happening to them. One part of the man wants to be reassured that this is just a phase that he will pass through and that he will begin to love his wife again soon; another part of the man has considered that possibility and has rejected it. This is the part of him that knows that his perceptions are real, authentic, and need to be respected. What I do is validate what the man is saying and feeling and also interpret any change in his behavior that seems to jibe with the change in feeling. These men are often quite reassured by this type of therapeutic intervention.

Coupled with a strong sense of responsibility and a proclivity for guilt is a fear of being thought of as selfish for leaving a marriage. In the vernacular of the 1980s, these men fear being labeled as "narcissists," as "wanting it all," as being a part of the "me generation." Some of this attitude and feeling is a projection of their own unresolved and prejudiced feelings about those who divorce. As one man said to me: "I've always lost a bit of respect for the men I've known who are married a few years, have a couple of kids, and walk out on their wives—and I'm even more riled up if there's another woman in the wings. Now here I am doing the same thing myself." Therapists can be helpful by educating these men with a self-percept of selfishness about the complex emotional dynamics that characterize marital separation. They may then be able to see that their view of others and themselves has been unduly restrictive—and naive.

Another issue for men considering separation but not yet physically separated is the fear of being on one's own, that is, of living alone in one's own place, and the anticipated fear of loneliness. For many men, this may mean the first time they have ever lived alone (without parents, siblings, or roommates), for at no time did they establish a separate residence by themselves before marriage. For those men who have lived alone before they married, some may have done this so many years previously that they will have forgotten some of its good points. Others who lived alone before may not have favorable memories of that period in their life and dread a repetition of that experience, not giving themselves any credit for maturing or changing over the intervening years. Many of those men who anticipate loneliness once they separate may not realize, or be fully in touch with, how lonely they already are in their marriages. Asking them if they feel lonely, or interpreting to them their actions that may be masking loneliness, may be very therapeutic for them.

Separation for some men is not so much a fear of what's ahead but a fear of leaving what's behind them. Leaving the family home and all that that symbolizes may feel overwhelming. It is more than the house itself and all its trappings, although this cannot be underestimated when one considers the goals and aspirations of most American men—to save for and to own one's home—as one measure of having "made it" in our society. Most men are also mourning the family (who define the "home") and what once was the family or what was to be the family (a fantasied notion of family based on dreams of the future).

Other men who are further along in the process of psychological separation will feel less attachment to the home and the image of family. In fact, "home" for them is no longer happy or comforting or sustaining; it may be quite the opposite—depressing or tension-filled or empty. They may dread going home or may feel detached and no longer a part of the home and the family routines. For these men, having their own place to look forward to is exciting and challenging and serves to offset any fears they may have of being lonely. They look forward to the independence and privacy of their own place. It may feel like a refuge after the storm.

Bob was aghast when his wife, Ann, announced that she wanted a separation. He was stunned and told me that he went into a state of shock. He accused her of playing some type of sick joke on him. Ann, however, persevered and went on to tell Bob that she wanted him to be the one to leave and find an apartment, while she remained in the family home with the children. Bob was indignant and furious.

Weeks passed with neither Bob nor Ann making an effort to move out of the home. As the tension and distance between the two of them heightened, their feelings for each other deteriorated further. Ann began to go out more on her own in the evenings and on weekends. She also made plans for the children completely unassisted without consulting or informing Bob. She was clearly making more of a life for herself and the children.

Throughout the course of this, Bob went from denial that there was any marital problem whatsoever to panic, then to outrage, and then to bitterness. He was desperate to get some marital therapy, but Ann consistently refused. On developing many abdominal symptoms that were suggestive of duodenal ulcer, he went to his family physician who referred him both to a gastroenterologist and to me for a complete assessment and treatment.

After a couple of visits with Bob, I requested to meet Ann and to see her alone. She agreed to this, and in her session with me she strongly emphasized that she felt the marriage was over. Further, she remained firm in her resolve to separate. She was happy that Bob was seeing me, and she felt that his sessions with me were helping him to defuse his anger and to slowly come to terms with the marriage ending. Indeed, this is what happened. In time Bob was able to accept the inevitable, and as he became more in touch with feelings of unhappiness and defeat, he almost welcomed the separation. This was largely the way he felt when he moved out 3 months later, but he continued to state that he felt the separation was morally wrong, unnecessary, and a mistake.

Bob's resistance to recognizing a marital problem of several years' duration and his outrage at Ann's rejecting him became obvious as the dynamics unfolded. His father had "ruled the roost" and completely dominated his mother, who had committed suicide by taking an overdose of sleeping pills when Bob was 16 years old. After his mother's funeral, there was little more said about her death: "We just all carried on and got busy with our lives." Bob casually dated many different young women until he met Ann. They dated for 7 years before getting married! Problems of Bob's frequently being unemployed as well as his emotional and financial dependence on Ann led to a lot of tension and fighting. Bob refused marital therapy on several occasions, so Ann sought treatment on her own. She told me that this is what gave her the strength and self-confidence to ask Bob for a separation. Several weeks after the separation, Bob was able to see the connection between Ann's leaving him and his mother's "leaving" him when he was a teenager. This insight led to his working through of many unresolved aspects of grieving over his mother's death as well as a greater understanding of the possible dynamics of his parents' unhappy marriage. His use of denial as a major defense mechanism greatly diminished as he began to look at his problems of immaturity, dependency on others, passive–aggressive manner, feelings of inadequacy as an adult man, and fears of depression in himself (and death by suicide).

The termination phase of Bob and Ann's marriage is not an uncommon type of marital separation. Increasing numbers of unhappily married women are initiating separation and divorce, and many of their husbands are dumbfounded and/or furious that this is happening to them. Although I will elaborate on this theme in Chapter 7, let me just mention and emphasize at this point how traumatized these men can be. As therapists, we have to be careful not to underestimate the shock to the man's psychological equilibrium and his whole way of being. Men in this category vary tremendously in how quickly or how easily they come to accept the reality of the impending separation.

What are some of these variables? The husband's age and level of personal maturity must be considered. How much separation–individuation has he achieved thus far in his life? What stage of life is he at? What stage of marriage is he at? The man's measure of personal resourcefulness is another important factor. How educated is he? Is he employed, and if so, how satisfying is his work? What are his economic resources, and how will separation affect these? The amount of psychological support available to him and his readiness to use it are also critical. Are family members nearby and potentially helpful? Does he have friends whom he can reach out to? Does he have both male and female friends?

On a broader scale, what is his ego strength like? How much of a balance of dependency and autonomy has he achieved thus far in his life? Do his personality assets outweigh the liabilities? What is his capacity for acceptance, for change, for growth? How has he adapted to earlier losses in his life? What is his capacity for hope?

Although not quite as relevant so early in the separation process, the man's object relations with women are important for the therapist to try to assess. How healthy have these object relations been earlier in his life with key female figures, and how were they in any previous heterosexual relationships? How much previous experience has he had with women, and what was the degree of comfort? Having some information about this enables the therapist to have a better empathic understanding of the range of symptoms and feelings in the about-to-be-separated man. And for female therapists, it helps enormously to understand the transference manifestations in the patient–therapist relationship.

There are at least two other variables to keep in mind when assessing and treating these men. Whether or not there are children (or even the fantasied wish for children) is one of these. The age(s) and the sex of the child(ren) are specifically an issue for some men. The overriding fear—and this has been repeatedly documented in the divorce literature—is loss of the children, either partially (depending on the custody and access determination) or completely (irrational or rational fear of access being denied or of their estranged wives relocating geographically). The second variable is related to religion and religious attitudes (both intellectual and emotional) toward marriage and family life. Many men who are not religiously affiliated at the time of separation have grown up in a religious environment, and that history may strongly shape and color their immediate feelings about separation and divorce. For some men, this will dovetail with their ethnic or religious customs and values, no matter how assimilated they may feel in their marriages. Most will struggle with feelings of failure and disappointment in their own eyes and those of others. Some will feel ashamed and fear shame by others close to them, especially certain family members.

Clinical Presentation

How might men manifest symptoms or behavioral change when they present to clinicians as they grapple with impending separation? Most will experience some anxiety, either subjectively felt as anxiety (worrying, fearfulness, tremulousness, insomnia, and so forth) or manifest as physical symptoms (abdominal discomfort, diarrhea, frequency of urination, backache, and so forth). Men who already have a history of a psychophysiological disorder—such as migraine, asthma, ulcerative colitis—may get a flare-up of the illness. Some will approach their family doctors with a host of physical symptoms—vague aches and pains, persistent "colds" or "flu," headaches, listlessness, loss of appetite—that over time may begin to add up to the picture of a clinical depression, especially if there is a serious mood change, weight loss, marked guilt, severe insomnia, or impaired concentration. If these men have had a previous bout of depression or if there is a family history of depression, then an assessment by a psychiatrist is certainly indicated. Some may become suicidal and require hospitalization; others won't be as depressed but may still require antidepressant medication.

Occasionally men come to clinicians with classic symptoms of a panic disorder—recurrent and sudden attacks of shortness of breath, dizziness, tachycardia, trembling, sweating, fear of dying, fear of going crazy, and so forth—and they have no idea whatsoever about psychosocial stressors that might be contributing. Careful evaluation often reveals that there has been a recent change in marital functioning. The man may have a history of separation anxiety going back to childhood. I have seen a number of married men referred to me by their family doctors for either a panic disorder or generalized anxiety disorder who are actually in the early stages of marital separation but don't consciously realize it. If there has been some open discussion about separation at home, the gravity of the situation has not clearly registered. They may be using a lot of denial, intellectualization, or rationalization about their marriages and are not connecting their panicky feelings at all with the assault of impending separation on their personal and marital equilibrium. In some instances, their wives have pulled back emotionally and physically, have moved out of the bedroom, are going out frequently in the evening and staying out very late, and are obviously seeing another man. When the woman disowns any change in the marriage or is not being honest, clear, and direct with her husband, this makes his panic disorder worse and heightens his feeling of "going crazy" because none of it makes any sense to him.

Sometimes associated with anxiety and depressive symptoms are a variety of behavioral changes that can occur in men whose marriages are ending but who have not physically separated. In the face of threat to one's personal level of functioning and adaptation, most people regress to less mature behavior. Men who have been quite dependent on their wives will become even more dependent or will transfer this dependency onto someone else. They will cling or feel helpless or paralyzed. They may panic, become impulsive, and feel like dying or committing suicide. However, these feelings are usually short-lived and evanescent. These men are more apt to threaten suicide or to make gestures, as opposed to the more serious idea of suicide and acts of suicide in the clinically depressed I mentioned before.

Men who are passive–aggressive in personality or who have passive–aggressive personality traits will react in characteristic ways to the idea of separation. They will not express any direct anger, frustration, or outrage, which are normal feelings to have about marital breakdown. They may become petulant, withdrawn, emotionally and physically remote, or sarcastic. They may refuse to communicate at all. Some will become self-pitying and martyring victims who attempt to mobilize common friends and extended family in alignment with themselves against their wives. They will stubbornly refuse to discuss the important mutual concerns of separation such as finances, legal counsel, the children's needs, and whether to seek separation counseling, or they will pay lip service to these concerns and then not follow through. Examples include "forgetting" to call to make appointments, breaking appointments, arriving late, or canceling at the last minute, not returning phone calls, not opening mail, staying out late, and so forth. Not only are behaviors like these extremely frustrating and infuriating for their wives as well as their children, but in some cases they are sadistic. These women are being punished for wanting out, they become worn down, and some will capitulate to their husbands because they can't bear it any longer. It is easier to give in.

Other men are not passive–aggressive at all but are openly aggressive about impending separation. They may be verbally and physically abusive. Men who have battered their wives throughout their marriages will become even more violent in response to separation or the threat of separation. In these marriages, it is quite understandable why there is little open discussion about divorce. Classically, the husband comes home to an empty house—his wife and children have secretly found a new place or have moved in with relatives or friends temporarily or are in a shelter for battered women. These men can be extremely dangerous—to their estranged wives, children, themselves, and society at large. Once again, in Chapter 7, I will have more to say about overtly aggressive and violent husbands.

Men who are alcohol and drug dependent are another problem group. Often the chemical dependency has contributed to the marital breakdown. Their wives worry that their husbands' dependency or addiction will worsen with separation, and they are usually right. These women feel guilty about pushing for separation, but usually it's a matter of survival by this point—both for them and for the children. At this juncture, some of these men will, for the first time ever, agree to seek treatment. They suddenly realize how serious their alcohol or drug problem is now that their marriage is at stake. Their complicity with treatment represents a desperate attempt to ward off the separation. For many couples it is too late; even if the man stops drinking or using drugs, his wife has had it.

In the face of separation, some men develop paranoid symptoms or paranoid behavior. This can range all the way from a heightened sense of vigilance and suspiciousness about their wives' motives and actions to frank and fixed paranoid delusions of infidelity. The latter are more common in men with a personal history of paranoid disorder or schizophrenia or a family history of paranoid illnesses. Some men with paranoid delusions are psychotically depressed. Men who abuse alcohol and drugs are also more prone to delusions of infidelity throughout their marriages—delusions that are only heightened with impending separation. At the opposite end of the spectrum are many men who have minimal insight into themselves and their shortcomings as husbands *vis-à-vis* marital functioning, health, and growth. They also usually have very naive and simplistic notions about marital breakdown. When their wives wish to separate, these men can see no other reason except another man. They feel completely out of sorts and totally perplexed that their wives simply wish to be on their own. Many confess to an inner conviction that their wives are not being truthful.

Some men whose wives have initiated the separation are so hurt and so angry that they deliberately and immediately go out and become involved with someone else. Sometimes this is no more than a one-night fling. Their motives vary. Some men know they do this to bolster their damaged self-esteem—both their emotional and their sexual self-esteem. Some men are aware that they do it to taunt, to hurt, or to punish their wives ("you hurt me, so I'll hurt you"). They hope in their minds that their wives will be jealous and maybe reconsider the desire to separate. I have also seen several men over the course of my years in psychiatric practice who have lied to their wives about meeting new women and starting affairs in the face of impending separation. To quote one man, a 36-year-old computer salesman: "It was my pride that made me do it. I was blown away by her wanting to leave, to be on her own. I see myself as a good husband, 'a good catch' as women would say; I take care of my appearance. I work out and keep fit. I had to concoct a story of me with other women to prove to her that I was still worthy of a woman's love. I almost believed the lies myself. I couldn't have done anything sexually with another woman; I was so upset and so diminished, I couldn't have gotten it up no matter how hard I tried."

In treating the not-yet-separated man, I strongly recommend patience. The therapist must give the patient time to come to terms emotionally with what is happening to him. This applies whether the man is initiating the separation, his wife is, or the two of them are jointly. Inexperienced therapists tend to become impatient and frustrated, then judgmental, which only alienates the patient who may drop out of therapy. It is important to remember that there is enormous variation in how all humans adapt to change, especially grief, and as therapists, we must become comfortable with broad parameters of normality. I think the more that we communicate to separating individuals our willingness and commitment to being there as they find their way, the better. Most need the reassurance that they're doing fine and that it takes time, because commonly they are berating themselves for not feeling better sooner. We mustn't push or rush them (or allow ourselves to be manipulated by the spouse to do this—the spouse has often already mourned the marriage, weeks or months or years earlier, in anticipation of separating). We must let them vent their feelings of rejection, anger, hurt, guilt, and so forth. We must expect denial, bargaining, and desperate attempts to forestall the inevitability of separation. And we must expect mood fluctuation as the weeks and months pass.

Men Who Are Childless

What about men whose marriages are ending who don't have children? Up to this point in the chapter, I have talked about men in general terms or, more specifically, men who are fathers. Is there anything unique about men who are childless and who are not yet separated?

Fifty percent of divorces occur in couples without children, and understandably these divorces tend to be less complicated psychologically, economically, and legally. Most of these couples are comprised of younger individuals who didn't have to get married because of pregnancy or who consciously put off starting a family until they were a bit older and more mature, had completed their education, or had good jobs and some financial security. These are also couples whose marriages are shorter; that is, they divorce within 5 to 7 years of marriage. Because both individuals are still quite young at the time of divorce, their remarriage rates are high. In fact, many are aware of this and therefore feel less pessimistic about themselves and their futures in terms of new relationships. Divorce is not just sad or frightening—it can be liberating and empowering for both parties.

Despite these potential advantages, however, there are exceptions to this rather monolithic stereotype, and some men who are childless and about to separate do not find it easy at all. Several examples come to mind. First, some couples have been childless by choice. Therefore, not only might they be older and married longer when they approach separation, but their marital dynamics are often very different from those of couples who are their age, who have been married as long as they have, and who have children. These men can feel very isolated and very anxious about impending separation in that they are "losing" their whole family, not just a part— they have neither the comfort nor the continuity of a relationship with children after divorce. These men, as they project into the future, do not always feel optimistic that they will meet another woman who, like them, does not desire children.

Although not common, some childless men facing separation are infertile from a variety of medical causes. They may or may not want children at some time in the future. Some may also be struggling with unresolved conflict associated with their gender identity—their subjective sense of maleness and masculinity—and this conflict may be greatly enhanced by the specifics of their marriage ending. Has this infertility contributed in any way to marital estrangement? Is his wife involved with another man? Men in this category may need very careful assessment of their mood to rule out severe depression and suicide risk. Others may massively deny any assault to their sense of themselves as men and adopt an aura of braggadocio, or a hypermasculine mien. They may be hard to reach clinically if their behavior is unsettling and provocative. Privately, they feel flawed, second rate, and unworthy.

Another group of men in this childless category, and this is a very large group, is comprised of men who had definitely anticipated having children with their wives. This, in fact, was a significant and central issue in their relationship. To have to abandon this wish, this expectation, this plan on top of trying to accept becoming separated from their wives can be almost unfathomable in the early stages of beginning to discuss separation. This was poignantly illustrated in the response of one of my male patients to an interpretation I had made to him. I said something like: "This must be so hard for you—you're trying to come to accept your wife's wanting to leave the marriage—but you must also be mourning the fantasy of having children with her." He cut in angrily and emphatically: "Fantasy?! . . . It's no fantasy, man . . . it's as real as real can be! . . . I'm sick about it!"

In this group of men are some who are not strictly childless but only childless in this marriage that is ending. They have been married before and have a child or children from that marriage. However, they are not actively involved or involved at all in a fathering capacity. The reasons vary: they have shown no interest, they were young and immature at that time, they moved away, their wives moved away, or they lost visiting rights. Some have seen this marriage as an opportunity for a second chance of becoming a father or becoming a better father. Hence, their anger or forlornness at the marriage coming to an end. The most upset are those men, and I have only treated a handful of them, who had had their earlier vasectomies reversed planning to have children again, only to have their marriages break up before pregnancy occurred.

There are several issues that may arise in men whose marriages are ending and where there are no children. If the man is more desirous of separation than his wife, he may feel very responsible for her and her anticipated welfare. This may be more worrisome for him if they're new to a city, and she's not near family or friends, or he is more established in work than she is, or if he is working and she is a student, or if she is quite dependent on him financially and emotionally, or, finally, if there is quite a substantial age difference—he is much older—and their relationship has many father–daughter dynamics. If his wife has really wanted children, or if the marriage ends when she's trying to become pregnant, the man may feel even worse. He feels torn, anxious, and guilty while she feels resentful and rejected. For women in their 30s who are concerned about their "biological clock," this type of separation is even more disturbing. They fear the possibility of never having a child and struggle with depressed feelings about that.

In this type of failing marriage, when there is an issue around starting a family, things can become confusing and chaotic. I have seen several couples whose marriages have ended abruptly or at least very quickly once the husband began to voice his doubts about the marriage continuing. Because he simultaneously decides not to have children, he either withdraws sexually or wants to begin using birth control again. This not only frightens his wife by raising the possibility of her marriage and anticipated family ending but also hurts and infuriates her. If the two of them are not communicating well or never have been able to do so, he just retreats more; she in turn provokes more, and a vicious cycle ensues. The man becomes very mistrustful sexually and fears that his wife will try to seduce him into bed and deceive him regarding her menstrual cycle or use of contraception. He fears that she is so desperate to have a child that she will do anything. In some cases he's right, and there is a deliberate and conscious attempt on his wife's part to become pregnant despite his protestations. Some of these wives are using faulty judgment, which they can only see in retrospect once they are feeling better again. In other words, they see themselves as having been so panicked and destroyed about their marriages ending that they were out of control. Other women openly ascribe to other motives— if they become pregnant their husbands might reconsider and not leave the marriage. More commonly, though, the drive to become pregnant is so intense, especially if the women are a bit older, have postponed pregnancy, and are more independent occupationally and financially, that they are quite prepared, if not eager, to become a single mother. They do not expect and do not demand anything from their departing husbands.

One final comment about the not-yet-separated man who is in a childless marriage. Although these men and their wives don't have to worry about child custody and access matters, many own pets, and their feelings of attachment to their animals are strong and intense. Consequently, matters of who remains in the home with the pets and who leaves, or whether the pets go with the person leaving or indeed should be separated, all need to be decided. Feelings can run very high over these very pragmatic issues that are pragmatic only on the surface. Underneath what is happening is that a family that once existed is being disassembled, and the feelings of hurt and anger and sadness are just as intense. I find that childless couples with pets who are in separation therapy need reassurance that their therapist understands and respects these dynamics. Too often these individuals are embarrassed about their feelings for their pets and/ or put themselves down for reacting so strongly and sharply to their impending separations.

Men with Another Woman

What about the man who has not separated yet but is intensely involved with another woman? Not only is this phenomenon common in our society, but it is also a common presenting complaint in married men who consult therapists. He is confused and stuck. He doesn't know what to do and feels indecisive and paralyzed. In an attempt to come to some resolution of his state, he finds himself obsessed with comparing the relationship he has extramaritally with that which he has with his wife. He realizes the folly of this and also finds that he's no closer to deciding what to do. He asks himself one question after another. Is this merely infatuation or is it genuine and true love? Is this merely an affair or the beginning of a serious and committed relationship? What are the costs of this—is it worth breaking up my marriage over? Should I give up my "girlfriend" and work on my marriage? Or should I leave my wife and continue the relationship with my "girlfriend"? Should I end both relationships and be on my own for a while? If I decide to leave my wife, should I live alone or with my "girlfriend"? Am I seeing things clearly or does my marriage only look dismal because we've been married a long time and I'm now in a new, exciting, and intoxicating relationship? How do I sort all of this out?

When these men come for treatment, some have told their wives about the outside relationship and some have not. Also, some of these men come alone for treatment, and some come with their wives. Of those who come alone, many have not told their wives about their decision to seek individual therapy. Eventually most do tell their wives once they feel better about coming and as they feel clearer about their motives and the issues that are troubling them.

The task for the clinician is to assist the man in feeling less muddled and ambiguous. This may take time, and it helps the patient to be told this. The clinician also must watch for a mood disorder—especially depression—that may be coloring the man's judgment and impairing his ability to make reasoned and sound decisions. This mood disorder may be completely unrelated to the marital dynamics or may be a result of marital discord or a result of his strain trying to juggle a marriage and an outside relationship. Being depressed makes one's marriage look worse because everything looks worse when one is depressed; being depressed can actually make the marriage worse too, because there is no energy, vitality, or creativity being put into the marriage and so the spouse becomes demoralized as well.

The therapist must carefully attempt to differentiate the man who is acting out in his marriage by becoming involved with another woman from the man whose marriage is clearly or nearly over and who becomes extramaritally involved just before separating. In the former, the acting out is a cry for help—something isn't working in the marriage that needs correcting. Unconsciously, the man is getting needs met outside the marriage that he wants met in his marriage. The marriage is viable, and he doesn't really want to end it. Cross-sectionally it may be difficult for the clinician to tell these two situations apart because it isn't unusual for both types of men at the beginning of treatment to be extremely positive about the outside relationship and very negative about their marriage. Only in retrospect some months down the road, as these men in the first category look back on that period in their life, are they able to see that they were very vulnerable and "ripe for an affair."

The men in the second category are usually able to describe a long period, often years, of marital unhappiness or dysfunction that they have tried hard to deny, rationalize as normal, or just not think about by keeping extremely busy. Some of these men, though, have been very aware of their unhappiness and estrangement; however, they had made a conscious decision to tough it out and not rock the boat, especially when there are young children. When these men meet another woman, which is usually serendipitously, they then find themselves overwhelmed. They have met someone else after a long period of distancing from intimacy, and it is then and only then that they consider or reconsider separation. The feelings that are stirred up, almost apocalyptic in some men, plus the desire to pursue the outside relationship are what force these men to confront their marriages.

As clinicians, we have an enormous amount to offer these men. I am always struck by how isolated and dammed up they are. Usually they have spoken to no one other than their wives or "girlfriends" about their dilemma—and even then they may not have discussed much about how really torn up inside they are. Usually it is the man's wife and/or "girlfriend" who suggests that he seek professional help. Both of them are aware that they are so personally and emotionally invested in his life that they can't really help him sort things out. I also find that many of these men do not know how very common their situation is, or if they do, they know it only intellectually or remotely. They've never talked with another man in the same predicament. I also find that many are ashamed of their position and project feelings of self-loathing and rejection onto me. They anticipate that I will judge them, think less of them, or feel they are being immature, silly, and selfish. They are puzzled by their roller-coaster emotions, their inability to make decisions, their feeling one thing today and another tomorrow. Others are alarmed that they can't sort it all out logically, cognitively, and rationally. Many have never before felt so ruled by their emotions or so exclusively at the mercy of their feelings. And most of them have a lot of misconceptions about the impact of divorce on family matters, both the positive and the negative effects.

Men Who Refuse Professional Help

I want to focus briefly on the not-yet-separated man who refuses to accept professional help. Most often this is a group of men whose wives want the separation, whereas they do not. It is usually their wives who want them to accept help, either with them or individually. Their wives want the assistance of a therapist to help the two of them to discuss practical matters such as who will move out and when, interim money matters, what and when to tell the children, visitation of the children, and so forth. They also want their husbands to have the supportive counsel of a therapist because they know, usually correctly, that their husbands are usually not talking with anyone and, if they are, they are not getting unbiased assistance. Some worry about their husbands' mental health in response to the anticipated separation, especially his mood (Is he depressed? Is he suicidal?), his behavior (Is he drinking more? Is he violent?), and his judgment (Is his business activity O.K.? Is his decision-making ability O.K.?).

Some men have gone with their wives for marital therapy some weeks or months earlier. If in the course of this therapy it becomes clear that their marriage is not working or is no longer viable and that separation is necessary or inevitable, this may be impossible for the man to accept. Although his wife wants to remain in therapy as they come to terms with this very serious decision, he refuses. It is too much for him, too crushing to consider, and too upsetting. Further, he may become quite angry and disappointed in the therapist. He may blame the therapist for their separation or accuse the therapist of initiating it or inciting it or simply of giving up on them as a couple who can live together healthily and happily. Because his wife may be more accepting of the separation or perhaps has felt all along that it may become necessary, he may feel one down, left out, and rejected, a feeling that will only be heightened if he senses that his wife and the therapist are basically in agreement. Disgruntled, disillusioned, and demoralized, he bolts from therapy at this point.

The reasons why men refuse professional help are legion. Sometimes it is simply ignorance, naiveté, or misinformation about the benefits of supportive psychotherapy. Sometimes it is pride and honor: it is very difficult to have to reach out to someone else for assistance or to lean on someone temporarily. Sometimes it is denial that one is not coping well and is in need of professional help; here, the individual underestimates his symptoms or his change in behavior. It may even be willful stubbornness, a resistance or refusal to give in or to cooperate; in his mind, to seek professional help is tantamount to surrender, to giving up, or to losing a battle. The need to be autonomous and self-reliant is another common reason why men refuse to seek therapy. Fear is yet another reason—fear of the power of the therapist or the mystique of therapy or the subtleties of therapy (that is, a mistrust of a process that is very foreign to one's familiar and habitual way of going through life). Some men who are fathers may simply be egocentric and can't see beyond themselves—they can accept that they personally don't want or need any help, but they refuse to accept that their involvement in one or two sessions would benefit their children. And finally, some men have had one or more previous experiences with mental health professionals that were negative—one of his parents might have had a psychiatric illness, he might have seen a therapist when he was a child, he might have had couple therapy in a previous marriage, and so forth.

Not all men who haven't separated and who have refused professional help are men whose wives want to separate. There is another group of men who no longer truly love their wives and who behave as though they want to separate. However, they never mention to their wives the desire to separate, nor do they admit to their wives that they'd like to separate if their wives bring up the subject. These are men who are out a lot in the evenings, gone on weekends, and who are doing virtually nothing with their wives and children. Most are closed and secretive about their conduct and whereabouts, which is highly suggestive to their wives that they're having affairs. When confronted, most deny that they are or evade the question. Other husbands may be quite indiscreet about their extramarital liaisons or openly flaunt them. Another group of men are not extramaritally involved, nor are they out a lot or away from the home; but they are completely detached from their wives (and children perhaps) in the home and take no part in family functioning and activities. Some eat their meals separately and retreat to another part of the house like the workshop or a basement room. Some have withdrawn into alcohol and no longer communicate about anything with their wives.

A few words about men who have withdrawn sexually from their wives. These men may be out of the home a lot or may not go out at all. Their sexual withdrawal becomes a puzzle to their wives, who, in their attempts to explain it to themselves, begin to wonder if their husbands might be gay. Most of these women have had absolutely no reason whatsoever earlier in their marriages to suspect this of their husbands, but they can think of no other explanation for the sexual avoidance. A few wives do ask or confront their husbands about homosexuality; their husbands are usually shocked or outraged at the allegation, but this reaction is rarely reassuring for their wives. Indeed, a few wives develop a conviction, a delusion, that their husbands are gay, and this belief is not altered with attempts on the part of their husbands to refute their wives' ideas about them. If the two individuals remain together indefinitely with no movement toward separation or divorce, they may eventually each require a psychiatric assessment and possibly medication.

As one can see, it is quite understandable why women married to men who are detached or isolative would suspect that their husbands want to separate. These are women who come to their family physicians and to therapists because they are worried about their marriages and don't know what to do. Some are completely bewildered or feel they're going crazy because they never get a clear and straightforward response from their husbands. Or they get a series of mixed messages. Most do not want their marriages to end despite their frustration and fury at their husbands. Some are also quite worried about their husbands' health, and rightly so. Many of these men are abusing alcohol, some are paranoid, many are depressed, and some are hypomanic. Although these men have not sought help at their own initiative and have refused help at their wives' suggestion, many will come in for a consultation visit, and possibly treatment, when the physician and/or therapist extends the invitation.

In this chapter I have discussed many of the issues that arise for men who are contemplating a separation that they want and also those issues that arise for men who are facing a separation that they don't want, that is, separations that are initiated by their wives and that feel imposed upon them. This stage before actual physical separation is extremely stressful. Individuals are frightened, full of self-doubts, and mistrustful of their perceptions of things. It is a time that is often remembered by divorced people as far worse than the phase of beginning to live apart. I have tried to emphasize common themes and what is specific for men because so much of what happens at this stage determines what happens later.

CHAPTER 4

The Newly Separated Man

I define a man as newly separated if he has been living apart from his wife anywhere from a day to a few months. The two main themes of this chapter are the giving up or relinquishing of something that once was and the acceptance of and adaptation to something that is new. Both are processes and thus, by definition, include the concepts of doing or action, moving forward or progression, and passing or lapsing of time. When the newly separated man is viewed in this broader and dynamic context, as opposed to a more restricted and fixed context, the therapist begins to obtain a more accurate and richer appraisal of his/her patient. This perspective not only enhances the therapeutic work with the man himself but also enables the therapist to explain "the inexplicable" to the man's wife and children when the newly separated man is not a patient or refuses assistance.

Giving Up What Once Was

In the previous chapter, I talked a lot about the psychological aspects of coming to terms with one's marriage not working and beginning to consider the realities of living apart. For most newly separated men, this process begins weeks or months, and sometimes years, before the point of actual physical separation. It is a giving up of something that the man once had, or thought he had, or thought he would have in the future had his marriage continued as he had hoped and planned. I use the word *hope* because this is the word I hear used a lot by my patients as they talk about their separations: "I began to lose hope for my marriage about 6 months ago"; "All my hopes and dreams for the two of us are shattered— owning our own home, starting a family, not having to work and save so much, traveling together—all gone!"; "I'm still hoping we can turn it around. . . . Cathy has no hope at all"; "I hope we can still be friends despite the divorce"; "You can't have a marriage without hope . . . and I lost mine a long time ago . . . and it's never come back"; "I sure hope you can help us, Doc."

Giving up or letting go of what once was is one aspect of mourning, and this is precisely what people are doing who are preparing for separation. Even when men are not in touch with their feelings of grief, they will show it in their behavior, especially the denial and protest. Later they will display signs of bargaining and eventually sorrow as they come to accept the inevitable.

One of the tasks for the therapist who is assessing the newly separated man is to determine where his/her patient is at regarding his letting go of the marriage. How much grief work has to be done? Has he done any? Some men who are recently separated are using complete and massive denial, for example, "My wife and I are just taking a little break from each other, we'll be back together in no time." An even more extreme statement is: "Our marriage is perfect . . . we just wanted to experiment with my having my own apartment for a month or two and my wife having the house and kids to herself . . . I think all couples who have been together for a while shouldn't be afraid to try new things." Other men have mourned completely. Typically, they respond with "I did all my ranting and raving, and crying, and struggled with my guilt and my fears of the unknown months ago . . . I'm fine now . . . It feels good to be living on my own." Most newly separated men are somewhere in between—they have had a bit of time to work through some aspects of the marriage but by no means all. This applies to those men who actually want the separation and have initiated it as well as those men who want no part of it but have come to realize that their wives are serious, and they must begin to cooperate. It is harder, though, for the latter group of men, and if they have had relatively little time to accept that their marriage is ending, they will be more symptomatic and more likely to seek therapy (or be forced to seek therapy) shortly after separating.

Men who are not particularly psychologically minded may be prone to somatization of their distress, and they also may use the language of the body as opposed to the language of feelings or psychology. Examples might include: "I've got this pain in the left side of my chest" (instead of "My heart is aching"); "There's something wrong with my breathing" (instead of "I sigh a lot"); "I think I might be getting an ulcer" (instead of "I've got so much anger on board I feel I could explode"); "I've gained 15 pounds in the past month, and I don't know why" (instead of "I've gained pounds in the past month . . . I'm so starved for love and affection since my wife and I separated that I just stuff myself with food").

Some men will deny missing certain individuals of the family, either their wife or children, but will talk in terms of missing inanimate objects or things that are all symbolic of family. Examples include: "I remember putting the back deck on the house and how it took me so long to do it that summer had passed, and it was almost Christmas before I got the stain on it"; "I miss my workshop"; "I miss coming home to an evening meal being served to me"; "I miss pulling into the driveway and feeling proud of owning such a beautiful home"; "I feel sort of guilty saying this, but I don't miss seeing my kids on a daily basis. . . . I do miss Morgan [the family dog], though, greeting me after work and walks with him in the morning."

Shame and feelings of failure are not uncommon in newly separated men, as illustrated in the following example:

Mr. D, an architect, came to see me several months after he left his wife. He was 53 years old and had been married for 23 years. While recounting the early weeks of his separation, he told me how self-conscious he had been during that time and how socially handicapped he had felt. The first time that he went to the local supermarket to buy groceries, he found that his eyes were burning and that he couldn't see clearly. He was exquisitely aware of being on his own and of shopping for one. He was reluctant to look at the other shoppers in the store for fear that they might have been staring at him. "I felt like a real loser and that everyone else who was shopping was either with someone or rushing home to have a meal with someone. All around me were sounds of families." Mr. D also recalled how difficult it was for him to go for walks on the beach even though he had walked alone on the beach almost daily throughout his marriage. "I just couldn't do it— except at dusk when no one would be able to identify who I was—I just felt too conspicuous—too obvious."

Mr. D was not depressed. He did, however, have a long history of awkwardness and shyness in interpersonal situations, suggestive of social phobia. He had blushed a lot when he was a child and was very anxious when called on to answer questions in the classroom. He avoided being the center of attention at all cost. Dating was difficult for him as a teenager; he spent hours rehearsing how he would ask a girl out before actually calling her on the telephone. He responded nicely to supportive and insight-oriented psychotherapy. He could easily see the connectedness between the incident in the supermarket and a similar experience he had had in college when alone at a basketball game after he and his girlfriend had broken up. His eyes were burning then too!

Adaptation to What Is New

This is the second part of the process of adjustment for men who are newly separated, and it doesn't necessarily have to follow in sequence the mourning of the marriage. In fact, in most cases the processes go on simultaneously even though the giving up and letting go of the marriage begin first. Both processes take a long time, and by the time the man has adapted successfully to being separate, he has accepted that the marriage is over. My emphasis here is on the word *successfully* because there are certainly many men who would claim that they have adapted to separation but have not forsaken the possibility of an eventual reconciliation with their wives. My question then is: How successful is the adaptation to separation—or is it more of a resignation to separation?

Most men who have separated have left, or have been asked to leave, the family "home." This is especially true for men who are fathers and whose wives are the primary caretakers of the children. Their moving out of the home, whether they originally desired the separation or not, is felt to be the simplest or most convenient means to get the separation underway. Their wives then do not have the psychological burden and economic stress of trying to find a place for themselves and the children, and the children do not have the additional trauma of being dislodged from a familiar home, neighborhood, and school. Many of these men are moving "down," at least temporarily, to a smaller and less substantial dwelling and a different neighborhood. Separations for childless couples are different—many wives are the ones to move out, sometimes both the husband and wife are moving out into new places, and not infrequently the man is moving "up" given the general disparity in income between men and women and the economic advantage for men in our society.

For those men who have moved out into their own place, learning to live alone is probably their greatest challenge. It doesn't seem to matter much whether they have ever lived alone before or not, except for those few newly separated men who were bachelors for many years and then were married only very briefly—for them, living alone is a preferred way of being. Most men beginning to live alone feel isolated and lonely. Many do not spend much time at home; commonly, they pass time in the evenings eating out in restaurants, going out to bars and clubs, playing sports with male friends and acquaintances, or working overtime. Dating may become haphazard and frenetic. Their way of coping with aloneness is active, which is positive in some ways but also negative if the man can tolerate absolutely no time alone and is constantly suppressing or running away from any unpleasant feelings.

In the early weeks of separation, especially when it is not clear whether the separation might be temporary rather than permanent, some men will live with friends. This may be another man who is single or divorced, a group of men who are all living together, or a married couple with a spare couch or bedroom. This kind of living arrangement can be very supportive in the short term because the man has someone to talk to, someone to do things with, and often someone to guide him in the early days and weeks when he's most in need. However, it can enhance his distress if he doesn't move on in due course or if his friends can't appreciate the ambivalence and indecisiveness of people who are newly separated. For example, they may become impatient and frustrated with his mood swings and contradictory statements about his wife—he badmouths and is furious with her one moment and is praising and loving of her the next, or he wants to divorce her today, whereas he wanted a reconciliation yesterday. This type of feeling and thinking is common and normal, but sometimes friends don't appreciate this, or if they do, they become weary after a while.

Some men, when newly separated, return to their families of origin, usually parents (or a parent, if widowed or divorced) or, less commonly, a sibling. Many of these situations are not just temporary or short term until the man finds a place of his own. There is an interlocking of needs on both sides; some parents want or need or enjoy their son's living back at home again. This type of separation with divorced adult children living at home again has become increasingly common in the 1980s. It is still too early to be studied longitudinally, but the proponents of this type of arrangement attribute it to economic reasons (it's expensive living alone; why not pool resources?) more than anything else. All parties, after a period of adjustment, benefit psychologically in having each other's company, assistance, support, and so forth. Its critics see this phenomenon as regressive and neurotic, a retreat to an earlier state of differentiation and separation where individuation is lost for all parties. Family members cling together in an insular way and do not move on or beyond to meet new people and form new adult age-appropriate relationships. Cultural factors are important here as well—what is normal in one cultural group would be considered deviant in another.

Another group of men separate and begin living with a woman. Usually this is someone they were involved with toward the end of their marriage and someone they have known for months or even a few years. If they don't officially begin living together at the point of marital separation, many are spending most of their time and overnights together. Other men may separate and meet a new woman partner within days or weeks of being on their own and quickly thereafter begin living together. What my point is is that these men are never really on their own for very long, if at all. They have moved so quickly into a new relationship that they don't allow themselves much of a period of mourning or a period of regaining (or constructing for the first time) a healthy measure of self-sufficiency. The women they are now involved with may really have their hands full, so to speak, when these men struggle with regrets about leaving their wives, battle over the children, regress into child-like behaviors, get depressed, and so forth.

The early months of a new relationship like this can be very difficult. As the novelty and glow of the first few weeks begin to wear off a little, some of the unfinished business of the man's marriage (and hers too if she's also recently separated) begins to surface. This might include ambivalence and self-doubts about leaving the marriage, resentment at his wife for leaving the marriage and abandoning him, mistrust and anxiety about women being loyal and steadfast, financial pressures and debt associated with separation, pining for his wife regardless of how much he loathes her, conflicts with his wife over visitation rights and custody of the children, and unrecognized and unexpressed fantasies of reconciling with his wife. In fact, many of these men secretly see their wives or contact them by telephone without their new partner's knowledge. Often this is only transitory, nonthreatening, and part of the process of unraveling a relationship and becoming unenmeshed. Few of these men will actually reconcile, but the pull to see their wives or to think about getting back together is very strong and all part of the attachment of marriage, especially enduring marriage. Having some contact with his wife frequently dispels this feeling of needing to reunite, and the man begins to feel fine again and reaffirmed about the decision to end the marriage. These thoughts and the

urge to carry them out are greatest during the early months of being physically separated.

Underdiagnosing

The most common error made by family doctors and therapists
in treating newly separated men is underdiagnosing their distress.
If the physician is too biomedically skewed, he/she will miss the
psychosocial determinants of the patient's symptoms and focus too
exclusively on an extensive, and sometimes very costly, medical investigation. I am not saying that patients with headaches, with
back pain, with cramps and diarrhea should not be thoroughly and
carefully evaluated. They must be, but they also must be asked
about their divorces and how they are managing. They must be listened to and allowed to talk about their feelings and difficulties.
Many doctors are very good at this, but some doctors do underestimate how stressful divorce can be and how much it can make
people sick.

Beginning therapists may underdiagnose the newly separated
man who is covering up a lot and who is not being honest about the
way he's feeling. Sometimes it's male pride and bravado—he wants
the therapist to think he's doing well, that he's not "weak," and that
he's fairly independent and self-reliant. At other times, the patient
is not being honest with himself; he is indeed not feeling well but
represses these feelings or actively suppresses them in order to convince himself that he's O.K. For these men, not being in control or
strong is a very frightening notion and can make them very panicky. One needs to read between the lines then and encourage these
individuals to continue in treatment until they truly feel back on
track.

Some therapists unintentionally enter into a conspiracy of si-
lence with their newly separated male patients. Both therapist and
patient avoid talking about the very painful emotions and issues associated with separating and concentrate too much on cognitive
strategy. I have treated men whose previous therapists were pushing them to socialize and meet new women when they were in no
way ready. Other men were literally told to buck up and be tough,
that their behavior, although understandable and real, was unbecoming of a man. I have also seen men who were shamed by their
previous therapists and made to feel guilty—they were accused of
feeling sorry for themselves (or it was strongly implied) if they were
despondent and mired. And finally, I have seen many men whose

therapists verbally attacked or rejected them if they began seeing their wives again after having been separated for a while. These men ended up feeling even worse. They already had a strong sense of failure; now they felt that they had failed their therapist.

One patient of mine, who had been separated for about 6 months, went to his family doctor already feeling guilty (he had initiated the separation from his wife). He told his doctor that he had done a lot of soul searching and was considering approaching his wife about "dating" with a possible reconciliation in mind if all went well. His doctor chided him: "You can't have it both ways—you've hurt her too much already. I think you should just leave her alone and accept your life as it is." This man did listen to his doctor for a while, but the feelings of wanting to make contact with his wife did not go away.

This type of approach ("I know what's best for my patients") is inappropriate. The man was well aware that he had hurt his wife and didn't want to hurt her more. He didn't need a wrist slapping or lecture from his doctor. I allowed him to explore with me both the reasons why he wanted to contact his wife as well as the feelings he still had for her. He tried to sort out how genuine these feelings were, especially the feelings of still loving her. He tried to determine whether he was merely lonely and somewhat nostalgic for his wife or whether he indeed still truly loved her enough to try again. In the course of doing all of this (three visits over a 3-week period), he met someone else, and because of his interest in pursuing this new relationship, he decided not to contact his wife. This was the last I heard on this issue in the course of his psychotherapy with me.

Routes to Treatment

In Chapter 1, I highlighted some of the gender differences in divorce and mentioned that, unlike women, men do not tend to consult their family physicians early in the separation process but often do later. This is at a time when divorce is more a certainty or actually in process. They also tend to come with more serious, sometimes life-threatening complaints. Morbidity and mortality rates for divorced men are higher than for divorced women.

Many of these men first appear in Emergency Rooms with a variety of ailments. Panic disorder is one of these. The man is seized with sudden chest pain, shortness of breath, rapid heart rate, and sweating—he is certain he is having a heart attack. Attempted suicide is another. A high percentage of men with drug overdoses, wrist slashing, self-inflicted gunshot wounds, carbon monoxide poisonings, and hangings are men who are recently separated or divorced. Many of the alcoholic patients who come into emergency rooms with DTs, alcoholic paranoia, and alcoholic hallucinosis are men whose recent separations have exacerbated their underlying and pre-existing alcoholism. And many of the lacerations, abrasions, fractures, and bruises in young men are a result of fights, alcohol abuse, and marital separation.

Some newly separated men end up in jail. A few of them are wife-batterers who have been charged with assault. Shoplifting is sometimes a response to marital breakdown. Street fighting is common, as is disturbing the peace. Impaired and reckless driving is another. Trafficking in drugs and breaking and entering also occur with some regularity. These are rarely crimes that arise *de novo* in the average newly separated man; almost always there is a history of antisocial behavior that has been reactivated by the marriage breakdown.

Another segment of newly separated men go directly to psychiatrists or nonmedical psychotherapists. Sometimes this is a decision they have made entirely on their own, but more commonly it is at the suggestion of family or friends, especially women friends. They have become symptomatic—anxious, depressed, insomniac, restless, and drink too much—and this worries their family members and friends. Commonly these men have underestimated the magnitude of stressfulness of marital separation so that even though they are aware they don't feel well, they don't always attribute it to their separation. They feel inadequate and erroneously assume that other people cope much better with separation than they seem to be coping. The therapist's perspective of how common and reversible their symptoms are and the reassurance that they will get better are extremely helpful. Many of these men benefit simply from talking to someone who is objective, yet interested in their welfare.

The clergy are frequently consulted by men who have recently separated, and it is at this time that men may return to the faith in which they were reared or embrace a new religion. Many men are helped and feel better talking to their minister, priest, or rabbi even when that person is a complete stranger to them. They are seeking permission to be separated from their families, and they need supportive affirmation in making the decision to be living apart from their wives and children. They need to know that they have tried hard to make their marriages work, including marital therapy in many cases, and that nothing has worked: it is therefore all right to be separated. Other men may have specific religious matters to discuss: their religion's position on divorce, a request for dispensation or annulment in the Catholic church, information about the granting of a *get* in Judaism, and so forth. Some men may request their religious leader's opinion and counsel on reconciliation therapy.

The Delayed Reaction

There are some men who come for professional help who are not technically newly separated but have all the characteristics of someone who is newly separated. I am referring to men who have a delayed reaction to separation and who don't feel its sting either before or shortly on separating. Some have been using a lot of denial that their separations are serious and permanent. For example, one man who came to see me more than a year after he and his wife had separated said: "I had no idea that Karen actually wanted a divorce even though she said that over and over from the beginning—in fact, I really still don't accept it. I see our living apart as just taking a little break from each other." Some men sublimate by throwing themselves into their work, sports, or projects of some sort. One man, an obstetrician married for 20 years and separated over 2 years, told me: "I guess I can't push it away anymore—I used to be able to—I've been working like a madman for the past 2 years so I wouldn't have to think about getting divorced. Now that Peggy's living with someone else, I just have to bite the bullet whether I like it or not."

I think the most common type of delayed reaction is seen in those men who are intensely involved with another woman before they leave their wives, but the relationship ends after a few months. These new relationships are powerful, compelling, and passionate. They have a tendency to begin suddenly and forcefully and to end in much the same way. Frequently the man's judgment is impaired, and his thinking and his behavior before, during, and after separation are driven by intense emotion. He has become highly egocentric, insensitive to others, and his actions are out of character for him. Some of these men have been subclinically depressed for some time before meeting the other person, but this has not been recognized or understood.

What happens then is that these men suddenly find themselves alone and bereft somewhere down the road after separation. At this point, they begin to confront for the first time their feelings about living alone, adjusting to this, and their marriages not working out. If he is a man who has few friends or who has alienated his friends and family by "suddenly" leaving his marriage, then he might be quite isolated and panicky. A high percentage of these men run back to their wives, who receive them with mixed feelings of welcome, nurturance, hurt, rage, and fear. Some immediately reconcile, but most give reunion some consideration by gradually and cautiously seeing each other over several weeks or months on a trial basis. Eventually some couples will resume living together, but many don't; in time they will go on to divorce.

Men with these kinds of separations are often racked with guilt and repentance and are highly motivated to accept professional help alone or with their wives to see things more clearly. Many still love their wives with varying degrees of ambivalence. A smaller number no longer love their wives much at all but miss their children, the idea of family, material comforts, and so forth. Plus, they detest living alone and refuse to work at it. They would rather return to a loveless—but familiar—marriage.

A variation of the delayed reaction in a newly separated man is the man who, although not involved with another woman *before* separating, does become involved immediately *upon* separating. This may be involvement with one woman or several, at the same time or in succession. My point is that this activity with women is another way of running away from the painful feelings of being separated. Consequently, this phenomenon is not uncommon in that group of men whose wives have initiated the separation and have left them. These new relationships lack depth and commitment and are really a defense against intimacy and loss. True mourning may not actually begin until several months after physical separation, when these men tire of these new relationships and the inner drivenness to keep up the pace.

Sometimes these men will staunchly deny that separation is difficult for them or that there are unresolved feelings about their wives. But they belie their stance by continually bringing up their wives in conversation or by referring to their wives in the present tense as if they weren't even separated. I recall this in one of my patients who had been separated from his wife for 18 months and who was already living with another woman. He was telling me about an argument that he and this woman had had after attending a play the night before a session with me. He added: "My wife and I *love* the theatre—we never *fight* like this when we *go* to plays." Some separated men describe examples of how they have embarrassed themselves and hurt their new partners by slips of the tongue, such as calling one's partner by the name of one's estranged wife.

I am struck by the almost exclusive and persistent use of the words "my wife" by men who are separated and have been for some time. Not only do these words suggest ownership and possession but they are usually uttered with an inflection or intonation suggestive of that. Plus they imply: "I'm not ready to let go of her yet." Many men do not even attach a first name and say "my wife, Sarah," so I find myself asking "Can you tell me your separated wife's first name?" From that point on, I try to be careful to refer to her by her first name as opposed to "your wife." I find that they can then begin to look at their feelings more accurately and definitively.

Ethnic and Racial Factors

All men who are newly separated cannot be fully understood out of their sociocultural context and hence must be assessed and treated according to the norms of their reference group. The feelings of loss, anger, fear, and so forth are universal and cut across all cultures, but how men manifest these feelings and their behavior as a consequence of or in association with these feelings may be culture-bound.

Tony was a 42-year-old Italian construction worker who was referred to me by his family physician, Dr. X, for assessment and treatment of a possible mood disorder. Dr. X told me that Tony had been in his office at least once a week for the past 4 months with various physical symptoms: loss of appetite but no loss of weight, headaches, dizzy spells, intermittent chest pains and shortness of breath, upper abdominal pain and gas, low back pain, frequent urination, constipation, and burning pains in his legs at night. The symptoms came and went, but most of the time he complained of some combination of symptoms. Dr. X had examined Tony on most visits, had ordered many laboratory tests, and had referred him to several different specialists. No one found anything except that they found him "excitable and nervous." Dr. X felt that many, if not all, of Tony's symptoms were related to his wife's leaving him just before he became symptomatic. He had been in perfect health prior to the separation.

When I saw Tony and was able to complete a thorough psychiatric assessment, I agreed with Dr. X. Tony had emigrated from a small town in Italy with his family when he was 10 years old. He had married his wife, Maria, also an Italian immigrant, when they were both 24 years old. They had three children aged 16, 14, and 10. When I tried to obtain a clearer picture of his marriage and the reasons for his wife (and children) leaving, Tony seemed dumbfounded and terribly perplexed. He became increasingly anxious, then tearful, and muttered something about his being a good worker and father and "not a man who runs around." He also stated that Maria wanted more freedom, and he attributed this to the "bad influence" of the divorced women Maria had met at a small garment factory where she worked part time as a seamstress. He stated that all he wanted was to be back living with her and the children and told me that he prayed every night for this.

At his second visit with me Tony told me that he had called Maria and informed her that he had gone to see a psychiatrist. He told me that she was very happy about this and might be interested in working toward a reconciliation. Quite understandably this made Tony happy. He said that she wanted to come in to speak to me. I asked Tony how he felt about this, and he had no objections. The visit ended with my asking Tony to have Maria call me, if she was still interested, and set up an appointment. She called while I was in session with my next patient!

Maria's visit with me was enlightening. She was extremely ambivalent about reconciliation and was leaning much more toward permanent separation and divorce. She hadn't proceeded with this because she still cared a lot about Tony and his welfare, she felt guilty about leaving and taking the children, and because she was Roman Catholic she was reticent about divorce. Her reason for separating did not surprise me because I had not felt that Tony was being completely open and frank with me: she was a battered wife. Tony first struck her before they were married, and this violence had continued intermittently through their entire marriage. He was also violent with the children and irrationally strict in his discipline, especially when he had been drinking. Over the years Maria had been treated many times in hospital emergency rooms, but, like many battered women, her shame prevented her from revealing the true nature of her injuries, whether the doctor queried her or not. The night that she separated from him with the children she fled to a woman's shelter after he had raped and beaten her. She was now living in a small apartment with her children, and although she missed her home, she was enjoying the peace of mind and feeling of safety. Tony was not coming around, nor was he harassing her.

I commended Maria on how well she was doing on her own with the children and supported her in her determination to remain separated unless she felt that Tony had indeed truly changed his controlling and aggressive conduct. I continued to see Tony alone to gauge his ca-

pacity for insight into his role in the separation dynamics. I suggested a group for battering husbands—he dropped out after two visits. Likewise, he stopped taking the antidepressant that I had prescribed for him, as well as his visits with me once he realized that I was not prepared to begin reconciliation therapy with him and his wife.

In this example, we have a separated man who is anxious, somatizing, depressed, and seemingly bewildered about what has happened to him. We have a separated woman who is fighting for her life and that of her children, not to say her pride and self-respect, but who feels guilty and responsible in some ways for her husband. Theirs has been a very traditional marriage with rigid sex roles; an attempt on the woman's part to "change the rules" has heightened his sexism and aggravated his tendency to control through violence, coercion, and intimidation. Although this type of marriage and the underlying dynamics can occur in all ethnic and racial groups, it is more common in particular groups, and therefore therapists have to be alert to this possibly occurring with certain patients. Therapists must be able to work constructively in this framework and to tailor their approach accordingly and appropriately. The greatest challenge for the therapist is anticipating and coming to terms with the massive countertransference feelings that are aroused in working with newly separated individuals. And these emotions arise not just with individuals from vastly different ethnic or racial groups than the therapist but also with individuals of the same ethnic or racial affiliation as the therapist.

I don't want my comments here to be misunderstood as white, middle-class, and supremacist. Newly separated men from all walks of life exercise power over their estranged wives. In the "Introduction" to his edited book *The Making of Masculinities*, Harry Brod emphasizes the importance of distinguishing personal from institutional power (Brod, 1987, p. 15). He refers to the common cliché in our culture that white, middle-class men are less sexist than third world or working-class men. This cliché is reinforced with institutional power, which is merely camouflaged power, because men appear more personally congenial the higher up they are on the economic ladder. They may appear congenial, but they are exercising the institutional power that is responsible for women's lower status. In contrast, men who have only their personal power are more conspicuous when exercising their power. As clinicians working with a range of patients, we are wise to keep abreast of these and other reconceptualizations of race, socioeconomic class, and ethnic contrast.

Premorbid Personality

By premorbid personality, I mean the pre-existing or underlying personality of an individual before he became symptomatic. In other words, what was the man like before he separated or before the marriage became nonworkable? What were his strengths and assets? What were his weaknesses and liabilities? How developed was his usual ability to cope with stress and adversity? How sociable, outer-directed, and interpersonally integrated is he normally? Some newly separated men can easily articulate the difference between the way they are feeling and functioning now as compared to the way they felt before separating. Others are not good at it, and this is where collateral information from a family member or close friend can be very helpful.

Having an understanding of the man's premorbid personality greatly assists the therapist in knowing how much of the symptomatology is acute and stress-related and how much is longstanding and deeply ingrained. The former is treatable and reversible, whereas the latter is not (except with psychoanalysis in some cases of personality disorders). There may be an underlying serious psychiatric illness such as schizophrenia or bipolar affective disorder. When men with these illnesses are newly separated, they may have a recurrence of their illness such as a psychotic relapse if they've been in remission or an exacerbation of their symptoms if they've been chronically ill. Symptoms might include inappropriate and bizarre behavior including various kinds of hallucinations (especially auditory) and delusions (of persecution, of grandiosity, of guilt, of sin, of poverty, and so forth). Men with pre-existing personality disorders may manifest a worsening of their personality problems when they separate. For example, a schizoid man will be even more isolative and indifferent to others; a dependent man will not be able to function at all without leaning on many others; an obsessive–compulsive man will be even more orderly, perfectionistic, and indecisive about his affairs; an antisocial man will be more nonconforming, aggressive, impulsive, and manipulative.

The "Immature and Irresponsible" Stereotype

I present this newly separated man as a stereotype because I hear this description so often by newly separated wives. These are their words, not mine, and these are not words that the men would use to describe themselves. The men are usually fathers of young children. This description of their husbands' behavior is uttered by women in the early weeks and months of separation more commonly than when more time has passed, but this description is not restricted to newly separated men. These women are angry and know it. Their anger is not just the diffuse anger that is part of a stage of separating and accompanies all separations; it is anger borne out of frustration and exasperation with their husbands. They try to get their husbands to share the responsibility of the children, but they are constantly thwarted. These women feel overburdened and exhausted, and indeed they are.

Sue, a 30-year-old former teacher, was at home full time with her two daughters aged 3½ years and 9 months when she and her husband, Frank, separated. They had been apart 6 weeks when she came to see me. She was depressed, irritable, not eating well, not sleeping well, and very fearful that she would harm her children. She described her husband as "useless and out of touch." What she meant by this was that he didn't see the children very often, and when he did, it was only briefly. Her attempts to try to arrange a predictable and regular visitation schedule were unsuccessful—he couldn't and wouldn't commit himself, arguing that his work schedule was too erratic (he was an articling student in a legal firm). Although Sue knew and acknowledged that Frank was indeed working long days and many weekends, she also knew that he was able to find time to date and socialize. She and the children had run into him at a local festival with another woman after he had called earlier in the day to cancel his plans with the children stating that he had to go into the office. Her words captured her feelings: "He's such a jerk . . . I don't care if he doesn't give a shit about me, but I do care that he's so selfish and insensitive to the girls and their needs at this time. When he comes to see them, or takes them out, he always makes me feel that he's doing me a favor . . . as if they're my kids rather than our kids. And he's so self-righteous about it—whenever I try to tell him I want him to see the kids more often, especially our older, he gets defensive and attacking. I sit on my feelings because I'm sick of fighting in front of the kids. They have a wonderful time with him and really look forward to seeing him—and I love the break—(beginning to cry)—I need that break. What am I supposed to do?—force a man to see his children more often?—shouldn't it just come naturally?"

Any therapist who does a lot of separation and divorce work or who sees a lot of women patients will find Sue's words very familiar. In my work with newly separated fathers, I find that many of them grossly undervalue their importance in the lives of their children, especially in the early weeks and months of separation. This is the time in the separation process when the children need the constancy of their fathers the most (Jacobson, 1978). Not only do the children benefit but usually the father does too *vis-à-vis* his own psychological adjustment to separation (Hetherington et al., 1976; Greif, 1979). It has been argued that some newly separated fathers avoid seeing their children because they are not adjusting well, and it hurts too much to see the children. They may withdraw into themselves or throw themselves into overwork, sports, and dating. This may account for the behavior of some separated men, but what about the rest? As one woman (Barbara) said to me: "I don't think Mike's suffering that much—I have trouble feeling sorry for a man who's making twice the money I am, who just bought a new sports car, and who's out with a different woman almost every night of the week. Gimme a break. Is hedonism the 'new suffering' of the '80s?"

Much of the literature on fathering describes contemporary fathers as men who are finding their way. They want to be more involved with their children than their own fathers were. They want to be more expressive of their affection and to be more nurturing. Some also want their children to have more, in the sense of material comforts. The course of fathering is not always easy because of a lack of, or vastly different, role models in earlier generations of fathers. The literature also emphasizes that one can't predict the nature of post-separation fathering. In other words, some closely involved fathers before separation do not remain that way after separation, and some uninvolved fathers before separation become model fathers after separation. However, as a therapist, and especially as a male therapist, I find that these ways of explaining and attempting to understand the way that some recently separated men behave do not always hold up. They sound defensive and apologist of men. They do not make women like Sue and Barbara feel better or reassured.

I want to conclude this chapter by re-emphasizing that newly separated men are struggling with at least two issues—giving up or relinquishing something that once was and accepting and adapting to something that is new. Cross-sectionally, an individual at this moment may be very different a year later or 2 years later. He will be much further along in the divorcing process, and many of his conflicts will be attenuated. There may also be new conflicts and challenges. I want to turn now to the specifics of divorce occurring at various stages and ages in a man's life, the subject of the next chapter.

CHAPTER 5

Divorce at Various Ages

Divorce occurs throughout the life span despite the fact that most divorces occur in the early years of marriage of young adults, generally people in their 20s and 30s who have been married 5 to 7 years. With increasing longevity, fewer children, liberalization of divorce laws, and greater employment opportunities for women, more divorces have been occurring after several years of marriage in mid- and later life. In this chapter, I have made an arbitrary division of divorces into four age groups—young men in their 20s, men in their 30s, men in their middle years, and men in their retirement and later years. My purpose here is simple: I want to alert the clinician to the centrality of age in assessing and treating divorcing men.

Young Men in Their 20s

These men are a mixture. Some have been married only a couple of years, whereas others married as teenagers and may have been married 10 years or more. Most of the men who marry in their teens and many who marry in their early 20s are expectant fathers at the time of marriage. Therefore, a high percentage of men in their 20s who are divorcing are fathers of young children; in some cases their wives are pregnant at the time of separation. Although those men who are fathers may have more complicated and difficult divorces, it is important not to underestimate how traumatic some divorces are for young men in their 20s who are not fathers. There is a tendency for health care workers to see these latter marriages in a somewhat elementary fashion, that is, that they were a mistake from the start, impulsive and immature relationships, that both husband and wife are better off without each other, and that they are young and resilient. The clinician who takes a detailed history of the man's developmental years and who has a good understanding of the dynamics of the marriage will have a greater appreciation of the man's difficulties with the divorce.

It is a common assumption that the longer the marriage, the more upsetting it is for the partners that the marriage is ending. However, Weiss (1975, pp. 62–63) found in his Seminars for the Separated that once a marriage was integrated into the individuals' emotional and social lives (a period of about 2 years after marriage), additional years matter little. In other words, the impact of separation is just as great after 3 years of marriage as after 30 years. Goode (1956, p. 191) found that a small segment of respondents who had been married 4 years or less said that their separations had been highly traumatic.

Because teenage fathers are sexually active at an early age, it is assumed that they are more knowledgeable about sexuality and reproduction than most teenage boys. This is a myth (Robinson & Barret, 1986, p. 173); sexual naiveté is extremely common in adolescents, and there is a pressing need for continued sex education, especially about contraception and the responsibilities of parenthood in our society, before teenagers become sexually active.

There is no typical profile of young men who are divorcing, but there are similarities. Many married their "childhood sweetheart" or their first love, someone they began dating in high school, occasionally even in elementary school. Others may have done a fair amount of dating and may have had brief relationships but have never been as serious or as committed as they've been in their marriages. A lot of men, if not most, who marry at a young age lack separation–individuation from their families of origin and have not had a significant period, if any, of living on their own. Some may have moved out of the family home, say, to attend college or to travel, but they are not wholly or perhaps even partially self-supporting. Those whose wives are pregnant at marriage are literally moving from a family or origin to a family of procreation overnight. Their seeming maturity is really pseudo-maturity; it is tremendously difficult for many of them to appreciate fully the responsibilities of marriage and fatherhood, to delay immediate gratification of their own personal needs for those of others, and to have the self-confidence and inner security to allow their partner to evolve and function healthily within the marriage.

Todd was a 20-year-old married man whom I was asked to see in psychiatric consultation. He had been brought into the Emergency Room of the teaching hospital where I work after he had taken an overdose of aspirin tablets. When I came to talk to him he was medically cleared. Todd told me that he took the pills because he was fed up. "I don't want to live any more. I'm sick of being married to a bitch who doesn't give a shit about me and who thinks of no one but herself." He told me that he and his wife, Alice, had been married for a year and had a daughter who was 11 months old. They had met in grade 10 when they were 16 years old. They began living together the following year just after they both quit school. Todd was enrolled in a mechanics' apprentice course, which he had been enjoying, until recently, when he and Alice began fighting a lot. Because of his temper outbursts and physical threats toward her and the baby, Alice had begun to spend increasing amounts of time at her mother's and a woman friend's home. This only made Todd angrier and more disillusioned with marriage. He did not see his relationship with his daughter as separate from his relationship with his wife. He told me that he really "wasn't into kids anyway" but that Alice wouldn't even discuss abortion when she became pregnant. I interviewed Todd and Alice together in the Emergency Room and scheduled a return visit for the two of them the following week. Only Todd came to that visit. He told me that Alice moved out the day before. When pressed, Todd admitted to striking her in the middle of an argument. Alice called to tell me that she would not be returning to Todd and the marriage was over.

Todd had come from a unhappy background. He was the youngest of seven children, most of whom had been married and divorced at least once. All of his four sisters were pregnant when they got married. His father had been married once before and had "three or four" children by his first marriage; Todd did not know these half-siblings at all. When Todd was born his father was 65 years old, and his mother was 45. Todd described his parents as "always at war" as he was growing up. "I survived by staying away from home as much as I could get away with," was Todd's description of family life.

Todd only came for two visits and then dropped out. Although he was no longer suicidal, he remained upset and angry that Alice wanted to remain separated. She refused to see him and threatened a restraining order. I urged Todd not to attempt to see Alice again until he felt better and more in control of his temper. I also urged him to refrain from alcohol, since he was always more impulsive and emotionally labile when he drank. I also encouraged him to accept his older brother's reaching out to him and to talk openly about his feelings with him. Although Todd denied it, I felt that part of his separation distress was compounded by the sudden death of a boyhood friend 1 month before his overdose.

Many young husbands have enormous underlying anxiety about being alone and being self-sufficient. They require a lot of affirmation and companionship from their wives, an amount that may be stifling for many young women. These same men become jealous and possessive when their wives wish to be active on their own or with their women friends. Their husbands respond with openly expressed anger and control mechanisms or with covert anger, like petulance, self-pity, and other passive–aggressive maneuvers. Autonomous wishes and actions on their wives' part are very threatening for these young men unless these needs are explained and thus understood as healthy and necessary in marriage, not unhealthy and destructive.

Some of these young men give histories of growing up very quickly. Some have been fairly responsible and serious about life from an early age. They have had part-time, after-school, and weekend employment for years, and they have been frugal with their money. They have taken jobs after completing their education and are loyal and steady workers. In marriage, they take their responsibilities seriously—they are faithful to their wives, work hard at being fathers, they pay their rent and other bills on time; they may have bought a home when their peers were still single or, if married, were renting. These men may be very happy with their marriages, which on the surface look great; unfortunately, this is not always the case underneath. It is their wives who are unhappy and frustrated—they find their lives orderly, secure, and predictable, but dull. They respect their husbands but find them boring and usually controlling.

These men have not had an extended period of "crazy youthfulness" when they were teen-agers. There has not been a phase of youthful abandon, of self-centeredness, of normal instability, and of exposure to the world outside of the neighborhood where they've grown up. For middle-class and upper-class youths, this usually means traveling, often to foreign countries, on their own or with male friends. For inner-city and ghetto youths and new immigrant youths, there is still a longing and a dream of visiting and traveling to other places, even when there aren't the economic means actually to do this. The first few years of marriage may be fine and relatively trouble-free, but many reach a point where they become restless and feel confined by their marital responsibilities. As they become increasingly unhappy, resentful, and envious of their single friends, some of these men blame their wives and children for their feelings of entrapment. Their wives can't help but feel defensive and unjustly accused—some fight back in self-defense; many take on the blame and feel guilty. Marital communication and intimacy rapidly deteriorate, and soon the young husband is acting out—going out more with "the group," drinking excessively, having extramarital affairs, and so forth.

By the time these men come to clinicians, things are usually pretty miserable at home. They are behaving in a morbidly egocentric manner by being away from home a lot, neglecting their wives and children, overworking, overdrinking, possibly using drugs, and seeing another woman or many women in a sexually indiscriminate manner. Because their personal and social behavior is usually seen as "bad" rather than symptomatic of underlying unhappiness and confusion, many of these men do not come directly and willingly for medical and/or psychiatric help. Some are persuaded to seek help or are brought in by their wives, family members, and friends. Others are responsive to professionals who reach out to them in a nonthreatening, nonjudgmental, and invitational manner. But most fall between the cracks and become objects of social condemnation more than anything else as they pass through the period of their marriages ending and separations beginning.

There is a subgroup of these young married men who are more or less doomed from the beginning. I am referring to those men who have grown up in unhappy, tension-filled, or chaotic family circumstances. To be more specific, one or both parents may have been alcoholic, they may have been victims of physical or sexual abuse, there may have been marked emotional, economic, and nutritional deprivation, there may have been many geographical moves, and there may have been successive losses of parents and stepparents through multiple marriages, divorces, and remarriages (or common-law unions). These young men enter marriage with a lot of immaturity and few adult life experiences that have been happy and stimulating of their growth. They have had a lot of life experience, but this has almost always been traumatic and has occurred at a time when they were far too young to cope with it. These men therefore enter relationships with a very fragile sense of self-worth and lovableness. They are emotionally needy and demanding, no matter how much they try to deny it. They are bound to feel disappointed in their marriages and to feel angry with their wives, especially if their wives are busy with a child (or children) and part-time employment. Not infrequently, their wives also have come from similarily deprived backgrounds, and they as well come to feel let down and unhappy in their marriages.

There is a familiar ring to the oppositional dynamics in these marriages. Under stress these young men become irritable, domineering, and dictatorial in their behavior toward their wives in an effort to regain control and mastery. Most of them are quite traditional in their ideology about sex roles and sex-role behaviors in marriage. Many are jealous and possessive of their wives, and any threat to the integrity of the conjugal bond may precipitate hypervigilance on their parts, mistrust and accusations of infidelity, physical violence, and paranoid rages. Their sexual overtures become increasingly frequent, more demanding, coercive, and insensitive. In its most severe form, this rapidly escalates into repeated acts of marital rape.

The tragedy of all of this is that it tends to be a cyclical and repetitive process that passes from one generation to the next. These young men have not had good male role models who demonstrated, or taught, them how to be a husband or a father in a healthy, honest, and consistent fashion. Often their fathers (if they've known their fathers) and/or stepfathers haven't had this kind of male modeling either. They are really on their own, sometimes influenced for better or for worse by the marital role behaviors of older siblings, peers, and workmates. Their male sexism in marriage is reinforced also by how men are depicted in the media, again for better or for worse. And their attitudes toward women and sexuality, including any violent sexual conduct with their wives, is certainly reinforced by the pornography industry. When the clinician takes a detailed personal and family history, going back at least two generations, and constructs a family genogram, the dynamics of how these young men come to be who they are become self-evident.

Some clinicians, especially married male clinicians, may have difficulty appreciating how controlling, jealous, and traditional in their male role behaviors these men are during their marriages or become during their separations when their anxiety is heightened. Usually the male clinician's marriage has been formed and maintained differently: he married later, when he was older and more mature; he is more highly educated; he has been exposed to more facets of life; and he may have had more personal experience with relationship breakdown and loss before marriage or in an earlier marriage. All of this leaves him with more flexibility and a greater ability to channel life's stresses into meaningful tasks such as work, sports, and leisure. Because of his intuitive interest in the psychosocial sciences and his training in psychotherapy, he is also more verbally articulate and better able to communicate his needs, wishes, and frustrations in both his personal and professional relationships.

By way of contrast, most men who married young and who are divorcing young do not have this in their backgrounds. More of their needs and frustrations are communicated through action. For example, most young men in marriage regard frequent and regular sex, especially sexual intercourse, as central in their lives as a couple. They are young individuals with a healthy sexual drive and capacity. A lot of their sexual urgency then can be explained on a purely biological basis alone, but there is much more to it than that. For them, sexual expression also documents their sense of marital health and stability. Their inner voice says "As long as we're having regular sex, we're O.K.," and this reassures them. There is much less emphasis on the quality of their love-making and how much pleasure their wives receive. Most young couples are not able to communicate easily at this level or to appreciate fully the importance of communicating verbally about sex. Consequently, there can be tremendous misunderstanding by these men about how happy or unhappy their wives are, not just in the bedroom but in many aspects of the marriage. The clinician must recognize that many young men who are married and are separating from their wives lack the education, maturity, and verbal skills to express their fears and frustrations openly and directly. How they behave sexually can be tremendously revealing.

Another hurdle for many young men who are divorcing is their lack of financial autonomy and what this represents to them in terms of their masculinity. Not all men are bothered by this; some unashamedly walk away from financial obligations to their estranged wives and children and transfer this to others, even, at times, with an attitude of entitlement. Others are quite affected and feel embarrassed and guilty to be on social assistance or to lean temporarily on the good will of their friends or sometimes their fathers. In fact, for some men who work for their fathers or who have been financially dependent on their fathers in some capacity all through their marriage, this may have been a contributing factor in the marriage's breaking down in the first place. Such marriages often suffer from not enough separation of generational boundaries in the marriage, too much parental interference, too much parental control, and not enough privacy and marital independence. This is usually felt most sharply by the man's wife first, and, because she feels unsupported in her complaints, this contributes to her unhappiness in the marriage. Her husband, typically, feels caught in the middle of two conflicting loyalties, and this contributes to his unhappiness.

Not a lot has been written about the impact of an adult child's divorce on his/her parents and how the parents' reaction in turn affects the adjustment of their child. Indeed, parents never stop having an intergenerational concern for their children, just as children retain loyalties—both visible and invisible—to their parents throughout the life cycle. Hyatt and Kaslow (1985) have described the reactions of parents to their children's divorce, which include anguish, grief, sense of failure, humiliation, self-blame, self-examination about their own marriages, and occasionally elation. When a man has married at quite a young age, there is a greater likelihood that his parents see his choice as "all wrong," and it may take them a long time to give unconditional support, if they ever do. If their son is divorcing, some parents who are unhappy with their own lives look forward to his return to add some meaning and excitement to their lives. Other parents may resent the added financial or emotional burden of a divorcing son. If they are unhappily married and feel trapped, they may be jealous of his ability to separate and build a new life. On the other hand, when parents are happy with their own lives and when parent–child relationships are healthy, then the man's parents are there for him with empathy and support.

In an interesting study of divorcing children's perceptions of their parents' behavior, Lesser and Comet (1987) noted that 40% found their parents' reactions purely positive, 20% as purely negative, and 40% as a mixture of supportive and nonsupportive. They interviewed both men ($n = 12$) and women ($n = 18$) whose ages ranged from 19 to 55 years and whose marriages ranged from 2 to 28 years in duration. Helpful behaviors included five general categories of support: emotional, financial, child care, good rational advice, and allowance for autonomy or regression. Unhelpful behaviors were punishing the child for divorcing, repossessing the child and intruding, denying the divorce, holding onto the divorcing child's spouse to effect a reunion, rejecting the divorcing child's spouse, bypassing the divorcing child and overconcern for the grandchildren, and parental personalization—the parents make the divorcing child feel guilty and responsible for their well-being.

Two final points about young men who are divorcing. First, many of the men who are fathers, or their estranged wives, will underestimate the importance of regular and frequent paternal visitation (in maternal custody situations) and the maintenance of child-support payments. I find that many separated young fathers I see in my practice need both confrontation and support about how emotionally and financially essential they are to their children—not only for the mental health of their children but also for their own mental health. This needs to be explained and re-explained until it is clear if we are ever going to see universal change in the irresponsible and self-centered behavior of many newly separated young men. Second, a certain number of men who are divorcing are more distressed than meets the eye. They must be assessed very carefully for associated psychiatric illness such as a major depression, panic disorder, drug and alcohol dependence, suicidal thoughts and behavior, and many other disorders. Others may have homicidal fantasies, and they need to be watched closely over time in order to appreciate fully the degree of severity and risk. Suicidal and homicidal ideas are not uncommon in many separations and divorces. Most are momentary or fleeting, but they must always be taken seriously.

Men in Their 30s

In Levinson's terms, men who are divorcing in their 30s would include men in the "age thirty transition" (Levinson, 1978, p. 71) and men in the "settling down period" (Levinson, 1978, p. 139). During the "age thirty transition," the provisional, exploratory quality of the 20s is ending, and a man feels a greater sense of urgency. Life is becoming more serious, more restrictive, more "for real" (Levinson, 1978, p. 85). For many men, this is a painful transition, and they experience an age-30 crisis, which may include separation and divorce. At the end of the "age thirty transition," men enter the settling down period: the early settling down period includes finding one's niche in society and maintaining a stable life structure (Levinson, 1978, p. 41), and the late settling down period involves becoming one's own man (Levinson, 1978, p. 144). Independence and affirmation by society take primacy at this time as life tasks. A man is so outer-directed during this time, especially regarding his career and making a name for himself, that his marriage may suffer.

Building on Levinson's work on adult development, Berman and Lief (1975) have described how marital and individual development are interrelated, especially how critical stages in the marriage are intimately connected with critical stages in the individual life cycle. For example, couples during the "age thirty transition" may have marital conflict if one of them is in doubt about his/her choice of marital partner or if there is unresolved stress over parenthood.

There may be increasing distance and less intimacy as they make up their minds about each other. There may also be competitive vying for power and dominance in their communication. The marital boundaries may be broken by extramarital affairs on one or both parts. Later, during the "settling down period," the husband and wife may grow apart if they have different and conflicting ways of being productive; there may be less intimacy, and their patterns of decision making, dominance, and power become entrenched.

Brad and Sylvia came to see me for marital therapy because they were fighting all the time at home, their sexual relationship was deteriorating, they were worried about the effects of their tension on their children, and Brad was becoming depressed and not functioning as well at work. Brad was a 31-year-old attorney, Sylvia a kindergarten teacher who was not working outside the home when I saw them. They had two sons, aged 5 and 2 years, and had been married 7 years. My initial impression was that they were overstressed, demoralized, and fatigued and that they mainly needed support and assistance with communicating more honestly and effectively. Not so. At the beginning of the third conjoint session, Brad announced that he wanted a divorce and couldn't continue in good faith coming for marital therapy when his heart wasn't in it. He told Sylvia that he had felt ambivalent about the two of them continuing as a couple for at least 4 years. She actually knew this and agreed that things had been unhappy at home for several years. She had wanted to get marital help much earlier, but Brad had refused. Their second son was not planned, and because their relationship was so tenuous, they had both considered abortion when Sylvia learned she was pregnant. They decided against this course, and things actually improved for about a year but then deteriorated again. Six months before beginning marital therapy with me, Brad had begun an outside relationship with another woman, Joanna, a former classmate in law school, and they were now quite seriously involved with each other. She was also married but had no children.

I continued to work with Brad and Sylvia in divorce therapy, both conjointly and individually, until both of them were feeling better and more settled in their personal lives. This was more complicated for Brad, and he continued to see me in individual treatment for about 2 years. He had a number of unresolved issues from his childhood that had never been addressed—having been born with a physical deformity of his right arm, the death of his brother when he was 11, his parents' divorce when he was 13, the death of his father 2 years later, and a longstanding and misdiagnosed learning disability. Also, his relationship with Joanna had not worked out after she left her husband, and that was another hurdle for him. At the conclusion of our work to-gether, Brad was quite happy to be on his own, doing a bit of dating but not seriously involved with anyone. His main satisfactions were his sons, with whom he was a superb father, and his work, at which he was extremely successful and highly regarded in his community.

Here is another example with marital dynamics that are different.

Tom was a 38-year-old building contractor who came to see me 1 month after he and his wife had separated. He had moved out of the family home with a great deal of ambivalence and resistance. Tom told me that he had been aware that their marriage was in trouble for a couple of years but that he hadn't appreciated the seriousness of it un-til his wife, Mary, announced one evening that she no longer loved him and wanted him to leave. He was hurt and outraged and at first refused to even consider moving out. He wanted her to get marital counseling with him, but she refused, stating that it was too late. He told me that Mary had been in therapy with a women psychologist for about 6 months, and he blamed the therapy "for putting 'I want to be me' ideas into her head." Mary insisted Tom leave within a few weeks; she told him that she would leave with their three children herself "if he dug his heels in the ground."

When I asked Tom what he felt the reasons for Mary's wanting a divorce were, he told me that it boiled down to one issue—his work. He worked day and night virtually 7 days a week, especially during good weather for building. If he wasn't out of the home meeting with trades-people and clients, then he was in his office in their basement conduct-ing business on the phone or doing paperwork. Mary's efforts to get him to slow down, to hire an assistant, and to spend more time with her and the children fell on deaf ears. "I'm a Type A workaholic—third generation actually—and I've been on a roll for the past 5 years. My business has grown by leaps and bounds. Mary just doesn't under-stand that I'm doing all of this for her and the kids" were his words—words that are classic for many men in this age bracket.

When I saw Tom he was actually quite symptomatic. He was rest-less and agitated and felt terribly guilty and regretful about his life. He was sleeping poorly, awake a lot at night and up very early in the morn-ing because he couldn't sleep any longer. He had become preoccupied with work matters, was becoming forgetful, and was losing his high level of confidence in conducting business. His appetite was off, and he had lost 10 pounds in the previous month. He hated his apartment and hardly spent any time there. Alarmingly, he was barely seeing his chil-

dren and his parents who lived in the same city where he lived and worked. He had told no one that he was separated. Although he was not suicidal himself, there was an extensive history of bipolar affective disorder and suicide in the family. I treated him with an antidepressant and psychotherapy. Tom began to realize how much difficulty he had getting close to people and showing his feelings. He also gained some insight into how controlling he had been in his marriage and how controlling he was in his relationship with his children. He had certainly felt controlled by his demanding, strict, and workaholic father during his own growing up years and even then, as an adult man. I helped Tom organize a visitation schedule that gave him quite a lot of time with his kids; although he had to cut back on his work, he was happier. The children were happy, and so was Mary.

Tom was a textbook example of a man in the late "settling down period" of his 30s (becoming one's own man). Until his marriage ended, he had everything by our society's standards—a very successful business, lots of money, a beautiful home, the "right cars," a sailboat, a ski cabin, an attractive wife, and three children in private school. He had tremendous job satisfaction and truly loved his work. Like so many men on this kind of trajectory, he was unable to see that his life lacked balance: he gave everything to his work and nothing to his family except substantial material comforts. And also, like many men, he didn't "hear" his wife's complaints about the marriage or pay heed to her unhappiness until it was too late.

What are some of the conflicts for men in their 30s who are unhappy and are making plans to leave their marriages or already have left? In the early stages of this period of recognition that one's marriage feels over or of concluding that one no longer loves his wife, there is usually a lot of guilt. The degree of this guilt and its duration vary tremendously from one man to the next, but it is always there to some extent. The reasons for feeling guilty also vary, and some men have multiple reasons: they feel guilty for no longer loving their wives, they feel guilty for living a lie ("my marriage's a sham"), they feel guilty for continuing to be sexual with their wives, they feel guilty for leaving, they feel guilty for putting their children through a divorce, they feel guilty for being more financially independent than their wives, and sometimes they feel guilty for being stronger emotionally then their wives (whether this is true or not is highly subjective and open to conjecture—many men certainly proclaim that they are stronger emotionally when what they actually mean is that they are more *controlled* emotionally).

The man's guilt and sense of responsibility will be colored by his perception of his wife's strength and coping ability. How independent is she now and was she in the past? How young are the children? Is she a full-time mother, wife, and homemaker or is she partly or fully employed outside the home? How much does she earn compared to him? Does she have a supportive family and a network of friends to "lean on" through a separation and divorce? Does she have documented psychiatric illness that has required treatment and possible hospitalization in the past and may be precipitated again by the stress of a separation? Has she ever been suicidal? If there is a background of psychiatric vulnerability in his wife, a man who is leaving his marriage may feel less guilty and fearful if his wife already has a psychiatrist. If not, he may try to engineer this in a somewhat strategic way before leaving. Several years ago a husband literally gave me his wife to look after within the first few minutes of their second conjoint session with me. He told her that the marriage was over, that he was moving out that day, kissed her on the cheek, wished her well, and walked out of my office!

Men who know or feel that their wives still really love them also have a lot of guilt about leaving. They will also come to doubt their own feelings of unhappiness in the marriage and then question their judgment about wanting to leave. Their feelings become ambivalent again for a while, only to be replaced later by a returning conviction to leave. They commonly talk about an inner sense of confused feelings that can be summed up in one sentence: "I can't tell whether I still love my wife or just feel guilty." Like all individuals whose separations are not mutual but are singly initiated, these men frequently state a variation on the following: "You know, it would be so much easier to leave my wife if she were a real bitch . . . or if she was sleeping with my best friend . . . or if she was 100 pounds overweight . . . or an alcoholic . . . whatever . . . but she's a nice person, a good person, I like her . . . I just don't want to be married to her anymore."

Fathers contemplating divorce feel a strong sense of responsibility to their children's emotions: they don't want to put their children through a separation. If they must, then they want it to be as smooth and pain-free as possible. Depending on the ages, sex, and temperament of the children, most fathers have a range of ideas and feelings about their children and how they will manage. It is common to hear statements like the following: "I worry most about Jonathan—he's 11 years old and really sensitive—and he keeps it all inside"; "Melanie will be O.K., I think, because she's only 9 months old, but I'm concerned about Andrea—she's 4—and how to explain all of this to her"; "I don't worry about Patrick and Frank— they're 17 and 19 and about to leave home—if anything, they've been damaged already with this lousy marriage—they'll probably be relieved to see us finally separate. But Bart's the one I agonize over—he's only 13, and he's always been different than his brothers—he has a very strong sense of family and family loyalty—he even won an award last year at his school for an essay he wrote on divorce and the family in the 1980s. I'm going to have to spend a lot of time with him on this because I know he'll see me as just walking out on him and his mother—as one big cop-out."

Men who themselves come from "broken" homes may have a flood of memories and surge of feelings of how it was for them when their parents divorced. They can identify strongly and easily with their own children. But they can also misidentify or overidentify and fail to realize that in many respects their separations may be very different. For example, a father may be temperamentally quite opposite to his son or daughter, who may be more resilient, more outer-directed, more resourceful, and better integrated and socialized with siblings, extended family, and friends. Likewise, he is probably approaching his separation with more knowledge about the psychological aspects of divorce for various family members than his father did a generation ago. The fact that he has consulted a psychotherapist is at least one measure of that, and having this and other facts pointed out to patients is very reassuring and guilt-reducing for them. Most contemporary fathers who are facing divorce also plan and expect to be much more directly and intimately involved with their children after separation than they feel their own fathers were with them when they were children. In fact, many lament that they never really knew their fathers either before or after the divorce.

These and other concerns that fathers have for their children and how they might react to divorce weigh heavily on their minds when they contemplate whether to leave their marriages or not. Most men in their 30s who have children reject their early ideas of separating in the hopes that things may still improve and divorce will not be necessary. If things don't improve, many men will try to live with an unhappy or unfulfilling marriage in order to spare their children, and themselves, the pain of separation. Ways of coping include spending more time at work, socializing with the children alone, taking up individual hobbies and interests that exclude their wives, cultivating friends of their own, avoiding one-to-one time with their wives, and socializing only with other couples and groups of friends. These avoidance maneuvers work, at least for a while, even if they don't address the basic marital flaw of disappointment, unhappiness, and loneliness. For many men this is only a stopgap measure; eventually, they leave the marriage, often having met someone else.

There are many other internal dialogues that men have before and during separation that are common and play a part in their decision making. These are not all confined to men in their 30s but can occur at any age. One voice is telling the man that he has a right to be happy and free, especially if he has been unhappy in the marriage for a long time. This voice also tells him that he only lives once and that he's not getting any younger as the years pass by. An opposing voice reminds him of his responsibilities, first to his wife ("you married for better or for worse") and second to his children ("you don't shirk your responsibility as a father"). Men who have an extramarital involvement with another woman, especially if it is quite serious and of some duration, will also feel a strong sense of responsibility and caring for this woman. They worry about her and her welfare as the following illustrates: "If I remain with my wife, how long can my girlfriend put up with and live with this. If I break it off with her, how will she be? How fragile is she? Will she collapse? Will she be vindictive? It's unfair to just drop her—plus the guilt I feel is horrible. If I left my wife and pursued things with my girlfriend, then I would feel awful about that too—guilty for leaving my marriage and not ready to commit to another relationship just yet."

Some men have inner dialogues with their parents. A man may fantasize that his parents will first and foremost be disappointed in him, that he's failed, and that he hasn't lived up to their expectations of a mature and responsible son who is a good husband and father. Frequently, this is a projection of his own sense of failure and disappointment in himself. In fact, his parents might be quite supportive and understanding, not condemning. He may also fear that his parents will side with him too much against his wife, that they cannot help but be emotionally biased and more sympathetic toward him. This is a realistic fear in that it is extremely difficult for many parents to be neutral, fair, or objective. This will depend a lot on the specific dynamics of the parent–son relationship before and during the marriage as well as on the specific nature and dynamics of the separation itself. The closer the relationship that the parents and daughter-in-law have had throughout the marriage and

the more they are in communication during the separation, the easier it will be for the parents to keep a balanced perspective on
things.

Men in Their Middle Years

The middle adult era stretches roughly from ages 40 to 60 according to Levinson (1978) and includes the midlife transition, the entering of middle adulthood, the age-50 transition, and the culmination
of middle adulthood. The man has to end his early adulthood, review it, and reappraise what he has done with it. He has to confront
middle adulthood, his present, and the future. For some men this
includes marked external change: divorce, remarriage, occupational change, and change in upward social mobility. Midlife individuation occurs at this time too, as men struggle with coexisting
polarities within themselves: young/old; destruction/creation;
masculine/feminine; and attachment/separateness (Levinson, 1978,
p. 197).

During the middle years, husbands and wives may perceive
"success" differently, and this may lead to marital conflict (Berman
& Lief, 1975). Depression and acting out are not uncommon during
the middle years when there are concerns about losing one's youthfulness, and different directions of emotional growth may occur in
the marriage. Aging threatens intimacy in many marriages, as does
the familiarity of many years together. When children leave home,
intimacy may be increased or decreased, and there may be increased conflict and power struggles in the marriage at that time.

*George was a 50-year-old bank manager who had left his wife of 25
years 4 months before our first appointment. He told me that he had
three children—two sons aged 21 and 19 (both away at college) and a
17-year-old daughter living at home with her mother. Within moments
of mentioning his children, George became tearful and was not able to
continue talking. He told me that he was embarrassed about losing his
composure and went on to tell me how close to tears he had been most
of the time the past several weeks. As he talked on, I learned that he
was actually quite depressed. He had lost some weight, he was eating
poorly, he was not able to do his work well, his sleep was very disrupted, and he was drinking much more alcohol than usual. He had a
lot of guilt about leaving his wife and daughter (because his sons were
away and older, he had less immediate worry about them) but did not
regret his decision. He knew it was right—and inevitable. He was liv-*

ing alone but was spending a lot of time with a woman with whom he had begun a relationship about a year before he and his wife separated. This relationship was not going well—he swung from pushing her away one moment and clinging to her the next. What prompted his coming to see me was that he had felt acutely suicidal the previous weekend after another angry and tearful episode with the woman at her home. As he was driving back to his apartment, he seriously considered driving his car off the freeway. He was so afraid of giving in to this impulse that he pulled over, called his brother, and asked him to pick him up.

I give this example of George not to discuss the specifics of his particular problems but as a springboard to elaborate on general issues for men in their middle years as they face divorce. What are the challenges, the fears, and the obstacles that men face in "starting over" at this time of life? First and foremost, they must confront loss—loss of what once was or loss of a fantasied dream of what might be or could have been. This includes the loss of a standard or image of themselves in a marriage. There is loss of a role— the role of husband and, for some men, the role of father (this is rarely an absolute loss, but many men mistakenly believe they lose their role as father when in actuality what they lose is being an everyday father). Another loss is "stability"—one loses the predictability, the sameness, the order, the routine of everyday life that one has had with the same person over many years of married life. Because most men are the ones to leave, either by desire, convenience, default, or order, they are also coming to terms with the loss of material goods. This may include the home, the furnishings, and treasured and emotionally cherished possessions. These are usually only short-term losses, and after several weeks or months there is a fair division of assets. The house may be sold, and when this occurs, all family members must mourn their home. And most significantly, there is loss of contact time with loved ones when a man divorces in his middle years. He loses time with his wife (the part of his relationship with her that is conflict-free and loving), the children, the pets, in-laws, friends, and neighbors.

The fear of being alone is one of the obstacles that men in their middle years must overcome if they are to make a successful adjustment to divorce. I discussed this at some length in the previous chapter when I described the issues for newly separated men. Some divorcing men will be living alone for the first time in their lives; others have not lived alone in many years. They must establish and maintain their own apartment or home including decorating, cleaning, marketing, cooking, and laundry. Some will learn these tasks if they don't know how; others will hire help. When a man is happy with his own company and can be content at home most of the time, he is ahead of the game. But many men aren't. They get lonely, bored, restless, and find themselves eating out in restaurants a lot and hanging out in bars. This can lead to an alcohol problem and significant weight gain, both of which make the man feel worse about himself than he does already. Most divorced men, in the early stages, are also trying to adjust to a lower standard of living in a small apartment with meager furnishings and less disposable income. Their plaintive query is well known: "Is this all I've got to show for all those years of hard work and struggle?" This contrasts with Weitzman's study of men who are down the road a bit after the divorce is finalized, whose standard of living is higher than their wives' (Weitzman, 1986).

Learning how to socialize is another task or challenge for the divorced man in his middle years. "How do I meet new people?" "Where do I go to make some new friends?" "Where do I meet other people who are also on their own—in their 40s and 50s?" "I need some new hobbies and interests. Maybe I should take a course in something." These are common concerns. Meeting women and dating can be extremely difficult and very awkward. Most men who are separated and are trying the bars and clubs to meet women say the same thing: "It's a whole different world out there than I'm used to or than when I was single many years ago." They often have outdated values and expectations that don't jibe with the times, and these range from ultraconservative to ultraliberal. At this moment in our social history, everyone is worried about AIDS, but there are lots of other worries too, which include fears of being rejected, fears of intimacy, and fears of commitment to and the responsibility of a new relationship.

Most men in their middle years are also conscious of aging, and this consciousness is often heightened by their being on their own and not in a relationship. They are painfully aware that they do not look as youthful as they once did and that they have less energy, less hair, and more pounds on board than they once had. Most do not feel as fit as the younger men around them, and they know that they are not as sexually vigorous. Increasingly men are keeping in shape by working out in gyms and playing sports on a regular basis. In addition to this, some men are consulting plastic surgeons. In a *Time* magazine (*Time*, Sept. 14, 1987) article on cosmetic surgery, one 46-year-old man, Michael, is quoted as saying after his three operations: "I had a body by Michelangelo and a face by Goya. . . . No matter how much exercise I did, the face didn't respond."

Men in Their Retirement and Later Years

Individuals who are 60 years and over are at a stage in life where they are trying to deal effectively with aging, illness, and death while simultaneously retaining a zest for life (Berman & Lief, 1975). As married individuals, their task is to support each other in their struggles for fulfillment and productivity in the face of aging. They try to remain intimate with each other despite fears of sexual failure, desertion (by death or divorce), and loneliness. Both are struggling with loss as family members and close friends move away or die. Their physical environment also changes as they move from the family home into an apartment or from a multi-aged residential neighborhood into a retirement community.

Although being divorced in the older years is still relatively uncommon (the proportion of older persons divorced or separated is only slightly over 5%) (Uhlenberg & Myers, 1981), the population of the United States is "graying," and therefore the numbers at risk for midlife and later-life divorce are increasing (Lloyd & Zick, 1986). Since most people who divorce in their younger years do remarry, many of the people divorcing in their later years will have been married once or twice before; remarriages are more prone to end in divorce than first marriages (Uhlenberg & Myers, 1981). Because there is a greater social acceptance of divorce nowadays, and there is some liberalization of divorce laws, it is expected that people will continue to use divorce as a solution to an unpleasant marriage. There is also greater economic independence for women now. More women are in the paid labor force for longer periods of time, and there is more legislation for women to receive their fair share of social security and pension benefits earned by their former husbands. Finally, with increasing longevity, fewer unhappy marriages will end by death before old age; more of these may end in divorce. Men who are widowers have a higher frequency of remarriage than widows do, and when these marriages are hastily conceived they are at greater risk for divorce.

Some couples who divorce in their later years have been miserable together for as long as they can remember. Unlike many of their peers whose distressed marriages improved once the children matured and left the family home, their marriages remained static

or actually worsened as time passed. Their efforts to remain together by sheer will, determination, or habit have not been
successful, and divorce becomes inevitable. There may or may not
be a third party, and when there is, it is more common that the
man has met and become involved with someone else. As in divorces that occur earlier in life, the person who initiates and who
wants the separation usually feels guilty and responsible for the
other's welfare. This means that he/she will want to ensure that
there is plenty of support—both financially and psychologically—
for the spouse. Frequently the one who wants to leave the marriage
is optimistic and forward-thinking in disposition, is keen to approach his/her remaining years with gusto (rather than resignation),
and enjoys good health. The spouse may be the opposite in temperament and attitude.

*Dr. W was referred to me by his family physician who was worried
about his mental state, in particular his judgment. He wondered if Dr.
W might be "hypomanic or going senile" because of his persistent desire to leave his marriage. Dr. W was an 82-year-old retired dentist and
university professor who had been married for 59 years and who had
five children, all married and out of the home. I conducted a careful
and thorough assessment of Dr. W over a series of appointments that
included a detailed personal and family history, marital history, medical evaluation, and mental status examination, especially of his cognitive and affective functioning. Dr. W was in superb physical and
mental health—but he was indeed unhappily married and had been so
for a long time. I had only to listen to him with an open mind (and an
open heart, I might add) as he gently described his subjective sense of
sadness, loneliness, and restlessness to begin to appreciate his dilemma. His words were poignant: "It's terrible to be thought of as having a screw loose because you want to leave your marriage at 82 years
of age. If I were 40 years younger, no one would bat an eye. I admit
I'm being selfish, but I have only a few years left on this earth, and I
still have a lot to accomplish. I can't do these things if I remain
married." Dr. W did separate, and this was eased by my working not
only with him but also with his wife and his children for several
months.*

*I interviewed Mrs. W shortly after Dr. W told her that he was leav-
ing but before he actually moved out. Her husband's decision to leave
did not come as a complete surprise, since he had spoken about separation at many points over the years. She too was unhappily married
and had many complaints about her husband but never seriously considered leaving herself. At one level she was relieved, since she had felt*

"on hold" for a long time. But she also admitted that she was nervous about being on her own (she was fearful of intruders in her neighborhood and fearful that if she became sick, no one would be immediately available to help). A private woman, Mrs. W had many concerns about what to tell her friends and what her neighbors might think about her husband's departure.

Dr. W adjusted quickly to the separation. He began traveling a lot, became more active at his community center, enrolled in a creative writing course, and did volunteer work. I only saw him a couple of visits. On the other hand, I saw Mrs. W for several months. She attended a psychiatric day program for a couple of months, and that was helpful for her. It alleviated her sense of rejection and isolation. On two occasions, I met with her two daughters. They were very angry at their father. I think it helped them just to ventilate about the loss of family.

Mrs. W coped remarkably with the separation, but this is not always the case, as all clinicians know. Many spouses do not do well at all when the separation is not mutual; they feel acutely rejected, discarded, and abandoned. Indeed, for some, becoming separated by divorce may be the last straw—it is the last in a series of losses (health, friends, family members dying, or moving away) and becomes too much to bear. They may become severely depressed and dangerously suicidal when they can see no reason for living. And some struggle with shame that has become overwhelming. I will never forget the words of one 79-year-old woman whom I saw in consultation after she had awakened from an overdose of tranquilizers: "You can't know how ashamed I feel inside . . . the humiliation of being a separated woman . . . I expected to be on my own at this age . . . but as a widow . . . not as a . . . as a . . . as a divorced woman."

It is not unusual for older persons who are separated not to want to divorce at all, unless they or their estranged spouses wish to remarry. I think there are many reasons for this—social stigma, the many years spent married, a desire not to completely erase the possibility of getting back together—but one of the most common has to do with morals. I have heard many patients, some separated for years, say that they are still married to their spouses and are content to leave it at that. In some cases their spouses have been cohabiting with another person for some time as well. These same individuals would never consider socializing as a separated person or dating "because that would be immoral." They are still married. Sometimes it is hard for their adult children to appreciate their reasoning, and they pressure their mother or father to proceed with divorce and/or attempt dating other people.

I want to say a few words about the adult children of men and women who divorce in their later years. Many of them can benefit from the services of professionals who work with older people who are divorcing. They need to know how important and necessary they are to their parents as they go through a separation. Their support, patience, understanding, and nonjudgmental stance are critical. But because they are family members and closely invested with their own personal dynamics, their ability to assist and be there for each parent will vary tremendously from family to family and within families. Some children will find it easier than others to be objective. Some will be raging at one parent and wholly sympathetic with the other. Some will do all the caretaking and supporting; others will do none. And some may become exhausted and burned out if a parent's physical and mental health becomes severely affected by the divorce. It is well known now that stress, bereavement, and depression affect the immune system (Calabrese, Kling, & Gold, 1987) and render individuals more susceptible to infections, rheumatoid arthritis, coronary artery disease, hypertension, and some cancers.

It is also disconcerting for the adult children of divorcing parents when or if their aging mother or father wants to remarry someone else quickly. They feel worried about the opposite parent and the profound sense of hurt and sensitivity that that parent feels. They may worry about the judgment and mental state of the parent who plans to marry someone else. They may find it impossible to meet and to get to know the other person, let alone approve of and support the marriage. They may feel terribly divided and caught in a maelstrom of conflicting loyalties regardless of what they do. If this person is younger and "from a different station in life" (as one of my patients so diplomatically put it), they may seriously question his/her motives. In other words, they may fret for that parent's financial position and economic security. Ultimately, they worry about themselves and attempt to safeguard their potential inheritance as sons and daughters.

Conclusion

In this chapter I have described some of the factors that affect the dynamics of divorce throughout the life cycle. My division of men into four different age groups—young men in their 20s, men in their

30s, men in their middle years, and men in their retirement and later years—has been somewhat arbitrary. Many men do not fit neatly into such age categories based on their chronological age; their divorces may have features of those of men younger or older than themselves. Also, men who are divorcing from a second or third marriage may not necessarily fit into an age bracket that is based solely on how old they are. I will say more about men who have been divorced before in Chapter 8. My purpose here has been to emphasize the comingling of both life-stage issues and marital-stage issues when men are contending with divorce. Understanding this gives the clinician a richer appreciation both of the struggle divorce presents for these men and of their symptoms.

The next chapter discusses divorcing men with younger women.

CHAPTER 6

Divorcing Men
with Younger Women

There is an invariant pattern across most societies for men to marry women younger than themselves (so-called hypergamous marriages) (Rossi, 1987, pp. 40–41). Although the age difference is not that great in first marriages in western societies, there is an increasing age difference in remarriages. Consequently, there is a much greater probability that women will live out their elderly years alone, whereas most men still have wives when they die. Among young American adults between ages 20 and 24, there are roughly 60 unmarried women for every 100 unmarried men; by ages 50 to 59, the ratio is more than 250 unmarried women for every 100 unmarried men! This also means that a much larger proportion of men than women will be parents of children separated by a generation in age, with children in their 20s from a first marriage and a child or two born after a second marriage to a much younger woman (Rossi, 1987, p. 43).

Why Do Husbands Leave Their Wives for
Younger Women?

In searching for answers to this common phenomenon, I was alerted to the research on differential parental involvement of mothers and fathers in child rearing (Lamb, Pleck, Charnov, & Levine, 1987, pp. 114–115). Sociobiologists, stressing the principles of natural selection, point out that the goal of any organism is to maximize the representation of its genes in future generations. This means high levels of fertilization and rearing of one's offspring to reproductive maturity. Here there is also a sex difference. In mammals, females must invest much time in the intrauterine maintenance, delivery, and postnatal care of their offspring. During this period, males are free to mate with other females and maximize gene survival through multiple matings rather than parental investment. By evolutionary principles, one might expect sex differences in human parental involvement, with women being more involved in child care than men are. This argument dovetails with the proximate (hormonal) argument, which proposes that women are hormonally prepared for pregnancy, parturition, lactation, and ultimately nurturant child-care tasks. Men can but do not "need" to participate in child care.

These arguments only go so far. There probably are biogenetically determined sex differences in behavioral propensities, but these same propensities need not be deterministic, mandating female involvement in parenting and precluding male involvement. Indeed, men can parent just as well as women can (Pleck, 1984). This fact dispels simplistic notions of biological determinism and supports the plasticity of the "biological" model. As interesting as this behavioral ecology paradigm is to explain why males leave females for other females, it seems like a quantum leap for this model to explain why husbands leave wives for other women. Furthermore, it doesn't explain at all why childless husbands leave or why the new partners are so commonly *younger* women who *may or may not* bear children.

Helen E. Fisher, a research associate in the Department of Anthropology of the American Museum of Natural History, thinks that our divorce patterns are a reflection of our evolutionary heritage (Fisher, 1987). By synthesizing and analyzing data on the mating and bonding habits of nonhuman mammals, on the marriage patterns of peoples throughout the world, and on the history of marriage and divorce trends from Roman times until the present day, she theorizes that the human-pair bond originally evolved only long enough to raise a single child through infancy. The so-called 7-year itch, recast as a 4-year human reproduction cycle, may be a biological phenomenon. Furthermore, there may have been biological advantages to changing mates during the reproductive years: males would have had the opportunity to pick a younger "spouse" more capable of bearing and raising babies, and females might leave one mate to "marry" a better provider for themselves and forthcoming children. The cultural advantages to serial monogamy, as opposed to life-long bonding, in early human groups would have extended their ties to and associations with other groups just as divorce and remarriage today have created the "new" extended family of stepparents and other steprelatives.

Turning to the sociological literature, it is helpful to look at the research on divorce at mid- and later life. Lloyd and Zick (1986) have noted that one of the reasons given for divorce at this stage of life is the perception of other partners being more rewarding than one's current partner. Herein lies a major gender difference that characterizes men. There are twice as many unmarried females than males for the 55 to 64 age group and three times as many unmarried females as males for the 65+ age group (Brubaker, 1983). Also, men have a greater pool of eligible partners because of the marriage gradient; men can marry much younger women (Hagestad & Smyer, 1982). By way of contrast, women at midlife and beyond are more apt to leave their marriages because of a perceived opportunity for a more rewarding life style. This fits with the increased assertiveness and increased desire for self-sufficiency characteristic of women at this stage of the life cycle (Zube, 1982).

What are some of the social and cultural factors that help to explain older men entering subsequent marriages with younger women? One of these is the unquestioned cultural assumption in our society of male superiority in marriage, namely, that men must be superior or at least equal to their mates in education and in income (Chodorow, 1986). This is very common when older men marry younger women. There is also a major difference between men and women and how they are defined as desirable commodities on the marriage market: women are defined by their ascribed characteristics, especially beauty and youth, which decline with age, whereas men are defined by their achieved characteristics such as income and prestige, which increase with age.

Using a psychoanalytic perspective, Chodorow argues that the phenomenon of men marrying younger women and women marrying older men provides for each partner a psychological solution to recurrent tensions in heterosexual relationships. Let me attempt to summarize her analysis. She describes asymmetries in the relational needs and capacities of males and females that occur because primary parenting is performed by mothers, and fathers are relatively absent in the normal nuclear family. Hence men, because of their development, are led to fear dependence on and connection to the mother (and women, who come to represent the mother), and they are then apt to deny and repress relational needs in themselves and others. Love for women, insofar as it represents love for the mother, constitutes a basic threat to selfhood and masculinity and therefore leads to ambivalence in masculine heterosexual commitment.

For women, the father (and men) represents an escape from exclusive maternal involvement, and the father also represents power and distance through his familial authority and cultural role. This translates into women looking up to men in heterosexual relationships. At the same time, though, women want to re-experience the intimacy and nurturance they had with their mothers. But because men have grown up with so much ambivalence about their own needs for intimacy, they are likely to be intolerant of these desires in women and to fear the intimacy that women want.

For men, a relationship with a younger woman is less likely to engender such a fear of intimacy and nurturance from women because of the power disparity in the relationship; a younger woman is less likely to represent the maternal threat than a woman of equal age. For women, a relationship with an older man is more likely to meet their needs for intimacy because older men are more tolerant of and more capable of intimacy with women than their younger counterparts. Chodorow concludes that this psychological solution to tensions in heterosexual relationships is only an apparent solution, a pseudo-solution. What it does is perpetuate in adult life early developmental conflicts instead of fostering growth beyond these toward satisfying mature relational desires in women and men of all ages. This type of relationship also presumes superiority and power on the one side, as the price of adequate male nurturance, and a relative immaturity and lack of equal adulthood on the other.

When Mr. and Mrs. O came for marital therapy, they were on the verge of separating. Mr. O was a stockbroker, and Mrs. O was a salesclerk in a women's clothing store. They were both 48 years old and had been married for 25 years. Only the youngest of their four children, a 16-year-old daughter, was still living at home. When I asked the two of them what their concerns were, Mrs. O replied: "I'll go first—it's very simple—my husband's having a male menopause (beginning to cry)—*he's got a girlfriend; she's half my age, and I don't know what to do—what do you do when you're my age and your husband doesn't love you anymore?" Mr. O then spoke: "My wife's right, I am involved with someone else, but this isn't a male menopause. Our marriage has been the pits for years. I'm not surprised that this has happened. And it's not true that I don't love my wife anymore. I'm not sure about anything anymore."*

The two of them went on to describe a marriage that had been stormy from the beginning. Mrs. O was pregnant with their first child when they got married, and they were never certain whether Mr. O was the biological father or not. This was because they had broken their engagement several times during their courtship, and each of them had taken up with an ex-boyfriend and ex-girlfriend. When Mrs. O became pregnant, they married immediately, as abortion was not an option for either of them. There were financial problems for years, since they had not anticipated having as many as four children, and Mr. O did not always have steady work. Over the years, Mrs. O had seen several psychiatrists for depression. She was always treated with individual psychotherapy and medication; her marriage was never assessed and treated. Although Mr. O admitted that he did not believe in marital counseling, he was never invited in to be interviewed and evaluated by his wife's psychiatrists. When her last therapist made a pass at her, Mrs. O bolted and never sought help again. The oldest three children had been a strain over the years—all had had academic and behavioral problems at school, one was alcoholic and attending AA, one had almost died after a serious car accident 2 years earlier, and none was fully self-supporting. Mr. and Mrs. O had separated three times over the last 10 years, the longest separation for 6 months. Each of them had had "brief affairs" over the years, but with "no one really serious."

Because their situation was so complicated, I used a combined approach of conjoint and concurrent therapy with the two of them. They did separate after 2 months, and Mr. O continued his relationship with his 24-year-old "girlfriend." Mr. and Mrs. O divorced a year later, and Mr. O quickly remarried. Mrs. O did not remarry, nor was she dating anyone when my work with her ended.

Any experienced clinician would probably agree that the above case example, or some variation thereof, is not uncommon in his/her practice. Mr. and Mrs. O came for help together; both were motivated for therapy, and both continued in individual treatment with me for several months after the separation until they were largely asymptomatic. Although some older men who are extramaritally involved with younger women request professional help on their own initiative, it is far more common that their wives do. Usually their wives get help on their own before, during, and/or after separation because of the range of symptoms that this type of separation generates. Not only do they feel "discarded" after so many years of marriage, they also feel enraged that their husbands are leaving after the hardest years of the marriage and when they are just on the threshold of having time to relax together and beginning to enjoy each other again. Also, it hurts tremendously to be "replaced" by someone else so quickly, especially someone half one's age.

On the surface, what is it that a man in his 40s or 50s finds so appealing about a woman 20 years his junior? Some men admit to being drawn to physically attractive and youthful-looking women. This is in part a reflection of the emphasis on youth and definition of beauty in our society—that women must have trim figures, must be in shape, have no stretch marks, have firm or taut or large breasts, and so forth. In addition to these physical attributes, some men use other adjectives and expressions to describe their younger women: refreshing, naive, adventuresome, friendly, ambitious, independent, likes a man to fuss over her, "looks up to me," sexually liberated—the list seems endless. Many of these men, in almost a checklist fashion, compare these idealized younger women with their wives. It is interesting that this comparative perspective is frequently denied ("I'm not comparing her with my wife, but she really is a completely different person") or, if uttered aloud, is rationalized ("I know I shouldn't be comparing her with my wife, but what other yardstick is there?"). Because these men often feel guilty about leaving and being with someone new and still feel loyal to their wives, many do not realize that for every positive statement they make about their younger woman friend their vocal tone implies a negative statement about their wife. For example: "Sally's a lot of fun [stated] . . . my wife's boring [unstated]"; "Cathy doesn't give me any hassle [stated] . . . my wife bitches a lot [unstated]"; "Geri loves sex [stated] . . . my wife hates sex [unstated]"; "Tanya's got a body that just won't quit [stated] . . . my wife's fat, frumpy, and sexually unappealing [unstated]."

In her book *Some American Men*, Gloria Emerson asked five men, all 45 or older, why they remarried women significantly younger than they were (quoted by Kimmel, 1986). The men do not mention the words "love" or "sex" but instead describe their wives' admiring appreciation of them and their wives' willingness to give up something for them. One man describes his wife as agreeable; another marvels at his wife's lack of bitterness. These are anecdotal comments; Emerson makes no attempt to analyze her findings, although her subjects are from a wide range of occupations and geographical settings within the United States.

It is significant that a higher percentage of men who become involved with much younger women are in their 40s and 50s. They have often been married for 15 to 20 years, and there are specific personal changes going on in their lives and their wives' lives. Men at this time of the life cycle are becoming increasingly nurturant, affiliative, or family-directed after many years of career building and being outer-directed. By way of contrast, their wives are becoming increasingly busy with their own lives after so many years of being husband- and family-centered. Their children are grown, and now it is their turn to re-enter the paid work force, to return to school, or to take on community projects. These activities become exciting and compelling and, for many women, empowering. Some men are threatened by these changes in their wives and do find themselves drawn to younger women—women who adore them, who give them attention, who make them feel younger (and perhaps sexier), and who are relatively less independent than they see their wives becoming.

There have always been women who are more attracted to older men than to men their own age. These women find older men more secure, both personally and professionally, and indeed they are usually more settled *vis-à-vis* job or career. Compared to younger men in their fields, they are already defined as successful as opposed to having the promise of becoming successful. Some are wealthy, and this appeals to some women who not only enjoy being indulged and feeling financially at ease but who do not want the experience and challenge of building up an economic base with a man their own age. Other adjectives commonly used to describe older men are mature, charming, debonair, urbane, worldly, calming, and so forth. These traits and attributes of the older man are brought out and reinforced by the traits and attributes of the younger woman that I described earlier, and vice versa. It is this interactive and dynamic process that gives these relationships their unique cast, to say nothing of the societal reinforcers: popular novels, movies, fantasy, and plain gossip about the "older man–younger woman" dyad.

These are surface and conscious matters. What are some of the unconscious dynamics that may be operative? As I mentioned above, the older man being with a younger woman may suggest that he is having a problem with aging. Dating or marrying a woman in the prime of life makes him feel younger physically and sexually. There is always a certain amount of ego gratification being with a young and attractive woman, to say nothing about the competitive strivings that exist in men in relation to other men. That is, the man feels secretly superior to his male peers (friends, acquaintances, and work associates) whose wives, *in his eyes*, are not as attractive. In some social and work settings, he may fantasize (or it may be factual) that he is the center of attention or the object of envy of other men, especially those men who are unhappily married.

Men who hold traditional values and expectations of marriage will need to have the upper hand, so to speak, in their relationships with women. With a younger woman, this type of man is more assured of having and retaining the bulk of the power in the relationship, for although she has youth and beauty on her side, these attributes pale in comparison to his achievements. For example, he is more mature, wiser, and more articulate. He has had more life experience, is more worldly, and knows a lot of people, often from many walks of life. Most important, he has more money, property, and possessions—all of which symbolize power in relationships. Most younger women wouldn't even attempt to compete with or to challenge these matters; they are much more likely to be impressed and dazzled by it all, which in turn feeds his self-image (even if it is largely a veneer) of brilliance, competence, and success. In the early stages of the relationship, she feels powerful by association and identification. Only later does she comprehend the enormous power disparity and her relative powerlessness as a woman in this type of relationship. Those couples who cannot talk about these concerns and work toward more egalitarianism in their being together will not do well and may need to separate.

The father–daughter dynamics in some older man–younger woman dyads stand out in bold relief. I said earlier that men in their middle years and beyond are much more capable of being caring and nurturing to others. Those men who themselves have never had a daughter may establish a relationship with a younger woman of promise, especially someone who is looking for or desperately needs this type of influence. He believes in her and her potential, he wants to get her going in life, he may want to protect her (especially if she has suffered a great deal already in her personal and family life), or he may want to spoil her. There are many examples of this in the business world, politics, academia, and the arts, where the more senior person becomes the benefactor, the teacher, or the mentor to the student, the mentee, or the prodigy, where the personal merges with the professional development of the individual. Once again, as the young woman matures and becomes more secure in her own sense of self and identity, her needs will be different. Unless her partner can begin to let go and not feel rejected or threatened, she will feel hemmed in and unhappy.

The motivating factor for some older men to be with a younger woman is to have a second chance at life. These are men who married quite young the first time, and their wives were either pregnant before marriage or immediately afterwards. Typically, they have assumed adult responsibility from an early age, have worked very hard, and have been unhappily married for many years. They see their lives as self-sacrificing and serving others. Now they have reached a stage in life where they feel it is their turn to be self-indulgent and to enjoy themselves more. Many of these men welcome, or at least are not adverse to, starting a second family with their new and younger wives. They may indeed feel more care-giving and succoring now. As they reflect on their first marriages, they recall being so obsessed with work, so rigid in their male sex-role behavior, or so young themselves that they missed a lot of their children's babyhood and growing-up years.

How much is the symbolism of youth and youthfulness a central dynamic when older men are with younger women? The youth of our society do represent the future and a sense of hopefulness. One conjures up a sense of renewal, of rebirth, of new beginnings. Many men may need this, although this need is rarely conscious, especially at the beginning of a relationship with a younger woman. I am referring to men who have become more weighed down by their responsibilities and undertakings than they have realized. Their jobs, debts, wives, children, homes, mortgages, and community involvements have made them tense, irritable, and weary. Some are mildly to moderately depressed but don't realize it, and some even have medical symptoms that are purely stress-related. These are not men who deliberately and consciously seek out a new relationship with a younger woman. In fact, most do not even know that they're unhappy at home or not as close with their wives as they once were. They're too busy to know this, or they quickly suppress any such feelings. Serendipitously, they meet someone new and become intensely involved very quickly. The feelings are powerful and compelling. They feel refreshed and carefree. The relationship is defined as a pick-me-up, a tonic. As one man, a 52-year-old surgeon, said to me: "I feel like a kid again—I haven't laughed so much in years."

Finally, what about social conditioning as a contributing factor when older men are with younger women? There does seem to be a certain amount of social sanctioning of this kind of relationship, and indeed there is a precedent in our society that has been in place for generations. Despite the jokes about the older man–younger woman couple as well as the sympathetic outpouring of sentiment for the abandoned older wives of these men, the behavior continues. Has it now become normative? Its opposite, the older woman and younger man relationship, is certainly far less prevalent and more taboo in our culture. Once considered titillating and suspect—he is judged as being an opportunist and exploiting her, especially for her money, and she is judged as a sexually wanton woman or as using him for her own narcissistic needs—there is some evidence that attitudes are changing (Toufexis, 1987). Many of these couples are of the upper middle class and design their marriages along egalitarian lines. It will be interesting to chart the course of age-discrepant relationships and how they are viewed as our sex-role norms, values, and expectancies continue to evolve.

I want to move on now to discuss three groups of men: men who begin an extramarital relationship or "affair" with a younger woman, men who begin dating younger women on separating from their wives, and men whose next marriage is to a younger woman. These categories are somewhat arbitrary and not mutually exclusive; I want only to highlight some of the dynamics that may be specific for each group.

"Affair" with a Younger Woman

All clinicians who do marital and family work know how common extramarital relationships are as a presenting complaint when people seek therapeutic help. In most cases, a serious outside involvement is symptomatic of an intrinsic, and often unrecognized, problem in the marriage. By serious, I mean any relationship of sufficient intensity or duration to affect the psychological equilibrium of the involved parties, whether there is sexual expression or not. Thus, I am including here all those men who are still with their wives but who have become significantly involved with a woman much younger than themselves. The men may come for help alone, or with their wives, or not at all. In some cases, only the man's wife or his "girlfriend," or both, are the ones who seek professional help.

The underlying reasons for the "affair" vary from one couple to the next and often include a mixture of intrapsychic and interpersonal determinants, many of which I've already mentioned: difficulty coming to terms with aging, unrecognized and undiagnosed depression in the man, underlying marital dysfunction (causing unhappiness, tension, boredom, loneliness, anger, and isolation), anxiety about declining sexual interest and "performance," and the attraction and appeal of a young and exciting woman. No matter how serious the outside relationship and how dismal and dysfunctional the marriage, most of these marriages do not end at the time of the marital crisis, if they end at all. It is critical that clinicians, especially inexperienced clinicians, know this so that they can be most effective in their therapeutic work. There are many possibilities: the "affair" may end quite abruptly or wind down slowly over weeks or months while the man remains in his marriage; the marriage may be strengthened, stay the same, or worsen; the man and his wife may eventually separate, but many do not, regardless of the state of the marriage; if the outside relationship continues, the man and his wife may separate but often only on a trial basis to see what happens; after separation, if the new relationship gathers momentum and increases in intensity, the couple usually remains separated and eventually divorces; rarely, both the "affair" and the marriage end abruptly and simultaneously so that the man is completely on his own.

Let me just say a few words about the older man who becomes involved with a younger woman and shortly thereafter separates from his wife, precipitating the end of the marriage. I am referring here to those marriage breakdowns that not only are fairly common in the middle and later years but that also generate much social disapproval and public outcry. "He dumped her for a younger woman" is the statement that we hear so often (if we don't utter it ourselves) as friends, acquaintances, and relatives try to understand what happened to a couple they have known. Although people realize that it's never as simple as all of that, that they as outsiders never really know what truly happens in other people's marriages, and that there must be extenuating circumstances, they are still left with very angry feelings toward the man and his "girlfriend" and very sad feelings for his wife.

As clinicians, we are accorded the opportunity to examine these relationships much more closely, to get to know the individuals more completely and intimately (not just the "parts" that they reveal to friends and family), and to call on our "compassionate neutrality" to understand and assist. We know that with the exception of those men who have personality disorders or who are psychiatrically ill and perhaps psychotic (either depressed, manic, paranoid, or organically impaired), most older men do not just up and abandon their wives for a younger woman. Most have been unhappily married for quite a while, if not for several years, but have maintained a facade of contentment and harmony. Sometimes their wives know this and try to live with it, or they may be equally unhappy themselves. Her husband's meeting someone else is alarming and painful but not totally unexpected. Unfortunately, many men camouflage their marital unhappiness exquisitely well, not only from their wives but also from themselves. When they meet someone else and pull away from the marriage, it is extremely hurtful if not overwhelming in intensity for their wives.

It is also wise to remember that the relationship that the man has with the younger woman merely serves as the catalyst to the separation. In other words, he doesn't simply leave his wife for the other woman. Many men admit that they never would have left their marriages were it not for there being someone else nearby who offered incentive, assistance, and a lot of support as they made the transition from a long marriage to being separate. These comments are made by men who remained with the woman they met before separating and whom they went on to marry. They are also made by men whose relationship with the other woman did not survive the long and difficult process of separation and divorce.

"Dating" Younger Women after Separation

This group of men comprises individuals who do not become involved with younger women when they are married but who do become involved after separation or divorce. Many of the underlying dynamics, especially the reciprocal meeting of the older man's and the younger woman's needs, are the same. What is different is that the man has negotiated the pre-divorce period, and often much of the divorce period proper, on his own without the assistance and complications of a new relationship. In this regard, when he begins meeting and dating women, he is further along in adjusting to his divorce, is more independent, more stable, and more healed.

Over and above the biological and psychological determinants of older male–younger female pairings, are there sociocultural factors that are operative here? Are younger women actually more visible, if not more available, in the settings where men are? We know there are huge numbers of young, single women in the workplace, and many men and women who begin relationships first meet at work. Other settings in which people meet after work include sports and leisure activities, bars and clubs, service groups, political organizations, and through mutual friends. These are all settings in which young women and somewhat older separated and divorced men come in contact with each other.

It is interesting to compare these settings with those in which the older man's former wife spends her time: the home, the garden, the supermarket, the suburbs, parent–teacher meetings, various volunteer groups, and many places connected with their children's activities—playing fields, hockey arenas, swimming pools, concert halls, orthodontist offices, and so forth. Although the numbers of married, separated, and divorced women in the paid work force are at an all-time high (indeed, many separated and divorced older women are visible in the workplace), many are working only part time because of the responsibility of young children. If they are working full time then they are not available for after-work leisure activities in the workplace because they are rushing home to "latchkey" children, to nannies going off duty, or to the daycare center. With the exception of those joint custody situations in which each parent has the children 50% of the time, most working mothers are the primary parents and bear most, if not all, of the responsibility for their children. In other words, while they are rushing to make dinner, to drive children to and from lessons, to supervise homework, to monitor bedtime activities, many of their former husbands are working out at the gym, playing softball on the team from work, or having drinks and dinner with men and women colleagues from work.

When divorced women in their 30s or 40s sample the singles' scene, they usually find it upsetting, lonely, and depressing. What they find, and I hear this complaint quite often in my office, is that the men who are in their age range and of potential interest to them are attracted to and are socializing with women 10 to 15 years their junior. Needless to say, most of these older women have no desire to expose themselves to this kind of experience again. As one of my female patients summed up her evening at a popular night spot for the "over-30" crowd: "I'm having enough difficulty accepting being on my own, I don't need to wear a neon sign."

This is one of those times when there may be significant gender factors in the therapist–patient relationship that affect transference and countertransference, especially when the therapist is a man. It may be difficult for a woman patient to tell her male therapist about the behavior of divorced men, which she finds so objectionable and unbecoming of men. If she knows nothing about her male therapist's marital status and personal life, she may suppress her anger at her former husband or men with younger women or men in general. She may fear that she'll upset her therapist or put him on the defensive, for she doesn't know if he's divorced himself or not, or whether he himself is with a woman much younger than he. Similarly, it may be upsetting for the male therapist to listen to what his patient has to say about the conduct and values of other men. He may feel embarrassed and ashamed about how this group of men behave. He may feel guilty and scolded if he has behaved in a similar manner himself in the past. Or he may be angry at his patient and feel that she is bitter and overcritical, or stereotyping men as a group. If she senses his anger at her, or if he interprets her anger as hostility, they may clash.

Not all newly separated and divorced men continue dating younger women indefinitely. Sometimes it is just a phase that is connected with being out a lot and not having come to terms with being on one's own. Because these men hate being alone they spend a lot of time and money going to bars, restaurants, and partying where a lot of the women are younger and single. Some men, after a period of social and sexual experimentation with young women, or after a serious relationship with a younger woman, reject the entire process completely. They complain that they have nothing in common with the woman when there is such an age difference, that they feel "old" by comparison, that their values are too old-fashioned and traditional by today's standards, that there's no substance or intimacy behind the sexual attraction, and so forth. Although some of these men are just hurt and bitter because they've been spurned, or they are projecting their own problems with intimacy and commitment onto others, most of this group will settle into socializing only with women who are in their age group. These are women with whom they share many life experiences such as having grown up in the same era, having common tastes in music, having similar educational and work experiences, having been married and divorced before, and having growing or adult children.

Next Marriage Is to a Younger Woman

At several points in this book, I have alluded to the common phenomenon of one partner being involved with another person before he/she leaves the marriage. In this chapter I have thus far discussed the subject of older men meeting younger women both before and shortly after separation. Some of these men go on to marry the woman whom they met at either of those points once their divorce is finalized. I want now to discuss the situation in which a man marries a younger woman whom he meets much later down the road, 1 or more years after he and his wife have separated. For these men, many of the early and most painful emotions of separation and being on one's own have passed or at least have lessened in their severity.

One of the most common statements that I hear in my practice from older men who are engaged to and possibly living with a younger woman is a variant of the following: "If [name of the woman] and I could just be left alone in our happiness, life would be fine. But it's the disapproval we sense from our families, my old friends, her friends, and my kids that is so upsetting. I don't even like to imagine what my ex-wife thinks of all of this." I wonder then if there are shades of gray here: is our society more tolerant of or accepting of older men having affairs with younger women, that this is somewhat titillating and to be expected ("he's having a male menopause," "boys will be boys," etc.)? Does our society condone newly separated older men dating younger women, if it does not actually expect that they will ("it's only transitional behavior")? Is society more disapproving and condemnatory when older men actually marry younger women? Is it deviant? Is it a challenge to our norms of acceptable conduct? Does it make us anxious?

Most, if not all, former spouses have some feelings or reaction when the person they were once married to marries someone else. Their reactions are dependent on many factors: how long they were married and how long they've been divorced; how unhappy the marriage actually was; how much they wanted the divorce and how much they've accepted being divorced; their overall present state of well-being and level of adjustment; their present relationship with their former spouse, including the degree of comfort and respect; and who the new spouse actually is. Age can be a complicating factor here when there is a significant age difference between the man and the woman he is marrying. Here are the words of a 39-year-old woman, divorced for 4 years:

"When my marriage ended, yes, I felt hurt and rejected, and sad. I expected from the beginning though that my husband would marry again. I thought I was over most of my pain until I learned that the woman he's marrying is 15 years younger than I am. That news has opened up old wounds for me—I feel even more discarded and useless than I did when we separated. Even though I'm outwardly a cynic and can be very sarcastic about men with younger women, I'm terribly hurt and lonely deep inside."

When there is very little age difference between the man's children and his new wife (his children are older adolescents or young adults, and his new wife is in her 20s or early 30s), all parties may need to make an allowance of time for adjustment. Indeed, there may be quite a lot of discomfort and awkwardness, both personally and socially, until the children have come to know their father's new wife and vice versa. This will be even more complicated if there is an expectation of her becoming a stepmother to the children, depending on their ages and whether or not they actually live in the same home as their father all of the time or part of the time. This expectation of being a stepmother may stem from within the woman herself, from her husband, or from the children. It is imperative that they all recognize and discuss this openly because there will be many periods of tension, misunderstanding, and unhappiness when these expectations are not clear or are unrealistic.

Adolescent or young adult daughters often perceive and/or feel a threat to the close, confidante relationship they have with their father when he remarries a younger woman (Ahrons & Rodgers, 1987, p. 190). Indeed, the man's new wife may view his relationship with his daughter as competing with her own role as his partner and confidante. Increased friction will also occur between the man's daughter and his wife if the daughter begins now to identify more with her mother, especially if her mother has not entered another relationship and is quite isolated. They may consciously or unconsciously collude in their feelings of anger, hurt, and rejection.

The situation for adolescent or young adult sons may be a bit different, although they too will feel a loss of the father's time spent together in recreation and other activities when he remarries. Because of a narrow age difference between themselves and their father's new wife, they may find themselves struggling with powerful and confusing feelings for her. Affectionate feelings may become sexual feelings, which produce a lot of inner conflict. Although these feelings are rarely acted out, I have treated one remarried family where the man's 36-year-old third wife was emotionally and sexually involved with his 26-year-old son from his first marriage. One of the central dynamics in this family was that all of the individuals had a plethora of needs that were not being met by the appropriate other—the son felt unloved by both his mother and his father, the wife felt unloved by her husband, and he in turn felt unloved by her (he was extramaritally involved with someone else when I first assessed this family).

Marriages of older men with younger women are not without their own intrinsic problems, or propensity to problems, that are purely secondary to the age difference between the partners. I have written about this elsewhere (Myers, 1988b) in describing the remarriages of male doctors, but many of my observations are more general than that and apply to a range of older men, not just doctors. The most common fears of the man are, first, not being able to continue to meet his wife's sexual needs because of aging and waning sexual drive and/or sexual functioning; and second, losing his wife to a younger man whom he imagines his wife would find more appealing (better looking, more fit, sexier, more dynamic, and so forth). When the man is conscious of these fears and can verbalize them directly to his wife there is much less friction and tension. Unfortunately, this is not always the case. What happens instead is that the man becomes anxious, preoccupied, possessive, and jealous (if not frankly paranoid), which angers and alienates his wife. As she pulls away, he becomes even more anxious or demoralized, and a vicious cycle ensues. This then connects with a common concern of women who are married to older men, the sex-role rigidity of their husbands and their inability to move beyond traditional norms and expectations of women in marriage. This is a subject that makes these men very defensive because they often pride themselves on how modern and contemporary they are in their ideas and values about women as compared to their male peers. This may be true, but in the eyes of their wives and other women of the younger generation, they often seem like dinosaurs!

In this chapter, I hope I have shed some light on the common phenomenon of older men being with younger women. I do not consider my analysis to be complete by any stretch of the imagination. Rather, I hope it is a beginning to a broader and more complete understanding of the biological, psychological, social, and cultural factors that bring these men and women together.

CHAPTER 7

Abandoned Husbands

"Man Chased after Killing of Ex-Wife"
"Squabble Ends in Death"
"Wife-Killer Jailed 15 Years"
"Missourian Shoots Children"
"Man Slays Ex-Wife"
"Jilted Husband Jolts House"
"Wife-Beater Jailed"
"Machete Killing of Estranged Wife Charged"
"Father Murdered Children He Loved"
"Wife Tells Inquest of Night of Violence"
"Wife's Exit Said Killer's Last Straw"
"Man Weeps as Killings Recalled"

These newspaper headlines have been culled from my news clippings over the past year. They are a vivid, and chilling, documentation of the violence that accompanies many of the divorces in our society. All of these headlines introduce articles about separated men who have gone to the homes of their estranged wives. They have then physically assaulted their wives, or murdered them, then murdered their children, and in several cases have then committed suicide. I believe that an overwhelming subjective sense of abandonment, at least in part, accounts for the desperate and frenzied behavior of these separated men. In this chapter, I want to concentrate on abandoned husbands (not all of whom are as distraught as these men but nonetheless are significantly distressed) as a distinct subgroup of men coping with divorce.

Background

Although the initiator role (the one who initiated the separation) has long been felt to be a significant factor in adjusting to separation, there has been little focused attention to this variable in studies of separation and divorce. In their study of 144 men and women interviewed on three occasions after their separation, Pettit and Bloom (1984) found that initiators consistently perceived more benefits to the separation, especially the female initiators. This is noteworthy when it is coupled with the fact that women are more frequently the initiators of marital separation anyway, especially women who are less traditional in their marital sex-role orientation. They also usually have a stronger social support network in place at the time of separation (Bloom & Hodges, 1981). Thus, not only are men increasingly the noninitiators of their separations (that is, often they are the "rejectees"), but they also do not perceive benefits to separation, and they are more isolated. These factors have important implications for mental health practitioners.

In a study of responses to marital separation in 205 individuals who were interviewed soon after their final separation, Spanier and Thompson (1983) also found that there was a higher level of reported distress in those individuals who were recovering from a spouse-initiated divorce. This included both men and women. In an earlier study, Spanier and Casto (1979) found that timing was an important factor: those individuals who had considered divorce for a longer period of time were less disturbed at the time of separation than those whose separations came without much forewarning. This is certainly borne out clinically, since the vast majority of those men who feel abandoned by their wives perceive their separations as "coming out of left field." Their wives argue that their marriages have been in trouble for years and that their husbands have consistently refused to recognize that fact and to join them in seeking professional help. Thwarted in their desire to work on their marriages, these women give up and begin to prepare psychologically to end their marriages.

Attachment is ubiquitous in people who are divorcing, and in one study of 177 men and women in suburban Cleveland, Kitson (1982) found that 86% indicated some signs of attachment to their ex-spouse. Greater feelings of attachment were likely when the decision to divorce was recently made and when the spouse had asked for the divorce. Attachment was felt to be the primary cause of the subjective distress experienced by the divorced, and males were more likely to be attached than females if the impact of distress was removed.

What is attachment? John Bowlby (1975) defines attachment as "the propensity of human beings to make strong affectional bonds to particular others." It is a persistent, learned behavior that begins to develop in infancy (Bowlby, 1969). His attachment theory (Bowlby, 1980) postulates that affectional bonds or attachments between child and parent (and later between adult and adult) evolve during the course of normal development. These bonds are not confined to childhood but continue actively throughout the life cycle. Intense emotions arise during the formation, the maintenance, the disruption, and the renewal of attachment relationships. Threat of loss precipitates anxiety, and actual loss arouses sorrow; each situation is likely to give rise to anger. In adult life, the characteristic ways in which an individual's attachments are organized will be determined by the experiences he/she had with attachment figures during infancy, childhood, and adolescence. Attachment theory provides perhaps the fullest explanation for the anomalous situation in divorce in which an individual is apparently grieving over the loss of someone of whom he/she is often simultaneously glad to be rid (Kitson, 1982).

Once established, attachment may continue to a significant degree even when a relationship is no longer rewarding. This is because the predictably familiar is preferred over the strange (Kitson, 1982). The changes produced by the decision to divorce induce the need for the familiar and previously comforting attachment of the former spouse. However, with loss of the spouse, the bonds of ease, comfort, and security are gone, and this loss produces separation anxiety or separation distress. Attachment behavior in separating adults and the "separation distress syndrome" have been described by Parkes (1972) and amplified by Weiss (1976). There are symptoms of physical and mental health disturbance, including preoccupation with the lost person, guilt, restlessness, hypervigilance, and difficulty sleeping.

Anger is a common emotion in abandoned husbands (Halle, 1982; Myers, 1986b), and it is one of the stages in the coping response to divorce—denial, mourning, anger, and readjustment (Kressel, 1980). Dinnerstein (1976) explains male anger and dominance as a possible adult reaction to the small, helpless son and large, all-powerful mother dyad. Also helpful for understanding the anger in abandoned husbands are Adler's (1980, p. 32) concepts of psychological inferiority and masculine protest. In the cultural context of defining masculine as valuable, strong, and victorious, abandoned husbands feel the direct opposite.

To what degree are the abandoned husband's rage, retaliatory fantasy, or propensity to violence defenses against narcissistic injury? This will vary with the level of the individual's premorbid personality integration and the peculiarities of the marriage itself, in particular unresolved power and autonomy issues between the man and his wife. Psychoanalytic theory argues that exaggerated, hypermasculine behaviors are rooted in unconscious anxiety about psychologically feminine parts of a man's personality. These feelings of emasculation, impotence, and passivity are very common in abandoned husbands. Pleck (1981) argues for sex-role strain theory; that is, men are homophobic and misogynistic because they are socialized to hold these values. They in part adopt exaggerated male role behaviors because of actual social rejection and ostracism they receive if they deviate from the traditional male role.

It has long been known that separated and divorced men have higher morbidity and mortality rates than separated and divorced women (Bloom et al., 1978). More recently, Kiecolt-Glaser and associates (1988) have examined immune function in men following marital disruption. They studied 32 separated or divorced men and 32 sociodemographically matched married men. As expected, the separated/divorced men were more distressed and lonelier and reported significantly more recent illness than married men. They also had poorer values on two functional indices of immunity (antibody titers to two herpes viruses) but did not differ significantly from the married men on quantitative indices (percentages of helper and suppressor cells and their rates). Those men who had separated within the previous year and had initiated their separations were less distressed and described themselves as less attached to their ex-wives. They also had lower antibody titers to one of the viruses, Epstein–Barr, than those men who had not initiated their separations. The data from this study suggest a confluence of increased distress, poorer immune function, and a greater incidence and/or severity of infectious illness.

Subgroups of Abandoned Husbands

In an earlier paper (Myers, 1986b), I delineated five subgroups of abandoned husbands. I want here to expand on each of these groups of men and to give case illustrations.

Overtly Aggressive

The predominant emotion in these abandoned husbands is anger. They are fully in touch with this emotion, it is visible, and most will openly acknowledge feeling angry. These men are completely against separation and have been since the beginning, when their wives first broached the subject or announced they were leaving or actually did leave. If they have come to some acceptance of the inevitability of separation, it is only partial acceptance because their mood and behavior remain largely angry and aggressive. As time passes, usually their anger diminishes.

Most of these men have refused to go for marital therapy in the past. They mention this, somewhat regretfully, to clinicians at the time of impending or actual separation or some months after separation if they're considering reconciliation. Classically, their wives have wanted marital therapy months or years earlier; they recall that their husbands refused to recognize marital difficulty or played it down or were too frightened or embarrassed to go with them for professional help.

Overtly aggressive abandoned husbands are a mixed group of men, but they all have one characteristic in common: their wives are afraid of them. Some of these husbands are verbally aggressive—they shout, yell, scream, swear, or fly into rages that scare their wives and their children. Other men are more controlled but no less aggressive—they are verbally quick, articulate, sarcastic, venomous, and denigrating in their choice of words. Other men are psychological bullies—they intimidate and control their wives with their talk, threats, coercive maneuvers, and empty promises. Some men are wife batterers who use physical violence in response to threats of abandonment or actual abandonment. They slap, punch, bite, shove, and kick their wives. These same men commonly rape their wives—to teach them a lesson, to regain control, to punish them, or to prove to themselves "that everything's O.K. now."

When assessing these abandoned husbands, I have found it helpful to try to sort out how much of the aggression is characterological, longstanding, and actually present before the marriage. Some women will disclose that their husbands first assaulted them verbally, physically, or sexually when they were dating. They then go on to describe an intermittent or gradually escalating pattern or cycle of aggression and violence throughout the course of their relationship. Stressors provoke the violence at first, for example, pregnancy, toddlers in the home, job pressures, unemployment, financial worries, and so forth, but in many relationships the pattern develops a life of its own. Eventually, and partly because of the violence, the woman decides to leave the marriage. This in turn heightens the man's anxiety—the separation distress mentioned earlier—and he responds with renewed and heightened aggression.

The clinician is wise to remember that most overtly aggressive husbands who are struggling with abandonment will minimize or deny the magnitude of their aggression. Wife beaters notoriously downplay their actions, as do verbally and sexually abusive men. Their wives tell very different stories. When or if clinicians get an opportunity to speak to them, they have no difficulty appreciating the terror and humiliation these women, and their children, have endured.

As opposed to aggressive, character-disordered husbands, there are other men who are about to become separated or who are newly separated whose aggression is purely situational and *de novo*. These men are experiencing aggression in response to threat and impending loss as well, but it is symptomatic of their crisis and is more amenable to psychotherapy. For these men, the aggression is transient and will lessen with time. It is also more distressing for them to feel aggressive or to behave in an aggressive manner, as it conflicts with their underlying value system and more stable personality. When these men play down their aggression, it is more often because of shame or embarrassment as opposed to the characterologically disordered man who denies it, or lies to himself or others about it, or feels that it's his right or duty to lash out verbally or physically against his wife.

A corollary to anger directed toward their estranged wives in men who feel abandoned is anger directed toward all women. In other words, their anger is not focused or encapsulated but is diffuse. For some of these men, it is no more than a stage, a transient period in the process of separation. It is typified by the reflective, and retrospective, statement, which goes something like: "I was angry at my wife for a long time after she left me . . . in fact, I was angry at all women for quite a while . . . I was bitter, jaded, and mistrustful of them and their motives." The diffuse anger of other men is more suggestive of misogyny (hatred of women in general; it is longstanding and deep rooted and more common in men with severe personality disorders). These men bring barely concealed anger and mistrust of women into their relationships. This in turn contributes to their wives being unable to live with them and their need to leave for their own survival and sanity. Their husbands have no insight into this whatsoever and feel furious at their wives for leaving. Being "abandoned" by their wives reinforces the mind set of these men that women can't be trusted or depended on. Thereby they justify their anger at women in this circular type of reasoning.

There are other forms of overt aggression, or their behavioral correlates, in men who feel abandoned by their wives. Until some of their anger recedes, these men will not cooperate in any way with their wives. They will not be able to discuss separation details such as who will be moving out, when this will occur, where the person will be living, and so forth. They will not be able to sit down together and tell the children about the separation or be available together for support for the children. In fact, they may not be able even to discuss when, if, or how to tell the children anything about what is happening. After separation, they will not be able to discuss financial matters, division of property, custody, or visitation arrangements. Some husbands are so angry and hurt, they barely see the children or refuse to see them at all during the early weeks or months. Some women, if they have custody, refuse to let the children see their fathers (unless closely supervised) if their estranged husbands are acting erratically, hostilely, or in a threatening manner. While they are this angry, very few of these men will consider going with their wives to a divorce mediator to try to negotiate cooperatively on separation matters. Most are so angry and feel so aggrieved that they want their own attorney to represent them and to fight for what they feel is fair. The best divorce lawyers, and certainly the most ethical, are accustomed to working with angry clients—they know when to listen and be supportive and when to listen and take action.

The overt aggression of some separated men coming to terms with abandonment is also illustrated by what these men talk about in therapy. In addition to venting their rage, they also release feelings of hurt, rejection, and powerlessness about their situation. Themes of retaliation and retribution are not uncommon, including fantasies, dreams, and fears of maiming and murdering their estranged wives. The intensity and actual seriousness of these ideas have to be assessed very carefully by the clinician because of the potential dangerousness of the patient and the clinician's duty to warn (Stone, 1984). Most of the men who disclose these types of thoughts and fantasies, including those reporting dreams of such events, are actually quite anxious about them and feel relieved and reassured just talking to their therapists. They have no actual plan, their underlying personalities are quite stable and healthy, and their distress is purely situational, albeit severe. Very worrisome is the abandoned husband who has an unstable personality with poor impulse control, who is dependent on alcohol or other drugs, who is isolated, who has a previous history of depression, psychosis, or antisocial behavior, who has been denied access to his children, and whose separation is sudden and makes no sense to him.

Something else that occurs in overtly aggressive newly separated men is their desire for reconciliation therapy with their wives. As I mentioned before, usually their wives are beyond marital therapy at this point; they wish to just be on their own, maybe not permanently but certainly at the time of separation and for several months afterwards. Overtly aggressive husbands are so unable to hear or accept their wives' wishes about this, or become so obsessed with the fantasied benefits of marital therapy, that they become very manipulative. They attempt to bargain with their wives, or cajole, or shame them into "at least trying," which may be partly effective since most women, especially mothers of young children, who initiate separation do feel guilty and unsure of what they're doing. Therapists have to watch for this for many reasons. They have to guard against becoming an "agent" for the husband when reconciliation therapy is totally inappropriate, ill-advised, or at least premature. They have to guard against being unsupportive of the wife's need for aloneness, distance, and time out for healing and reflection. And they have to guard against disappointing the husband-patient—not by refusing to collude with his manipulative ploys but by missing and not addressing the hurt, the loneliness, and the desperation behind his manipulative behavior.

Mr. S, a 38-year-old journalist, came to see me with the following complaint: "My wife and I separated a month ago, and I'm not doing very well." He went on to describe a mixed array of anxiety and depressive symptoms including headaches, an upset stomach, restlessness and pacing, loss of appetite, inability to concentrate and to do creative work, and despondency on awakening in the morning. In fact, his sleep was terrible—he had trouble falling asleep, staying asleep, and getting up in the morning. His dreams were frightening and full of images of disease, violence, and death. He had many thoughts of wishing he was dead but no thoughts of suicide.

Mr. S told me within the first 5 minutes of our initial visit together that their separation was completely his wife's idea and that he had fought it from the beginning. He was living with his brother, having been ordered to leave the family home 1 month earlier by the police who were called by his wife after he struck her. He was charged with assault, and a restraining order was in place. His wife sustained a black eye that evening that required assessment in their local emergency room by an ophthalmologist.

Early in that first visit with me, Mr. S told me that he needed my help to get well and to get back with his wife. He realized now that she was unhappy with him and frightened of him. He said he wanted marital help desperately. He admitted that he would never agree to go for help before when his wife wanted it. He stated that separation was morally wrong and was killing his daughter, that separation is unfair to children. He said that he could only stay temporarily at his brother's home, and he had no desire to take a place of his own. He asked me if I would call his wife and set up a joint visit for the two of them later in the week. His words were: "I want her to know how serious I am about this, how much I love her and care about her, and what I'm prepared to do to turn things around." I gently refused Mr. S's request to call his wife and told him that I was more interested at that moment in working with him alone and understanding and assessing his distress.

According to Mr. S, their marital problems had been going on for about 2 years and were related to his losing a very good job with the city's newspaper. He was unemployed for 3 months, and although he had been working since, his work was not interesting or challenging, and he was not earning as much money. His wife had returned to full-time work as a nurse, and they were sharing the responsibility of caring for their 2-year-old daughter. This was new for Mr. S and although he enjoyed having more time with his daughter, he stated: "I've never been a new-age father; I'm not sure how I feel about it." He went on to tell me, angrily, that his former first wife was taking him to court for nonpayment of child support for his 14-year-old daughter from that marriage. He said that they had divorced after many years of fighting and growing apart. Mr. S had met his present wife at a party, and they had become seriously involved before he had separated from his first wife.

My questioning about physical violence didn't lead very far. Mr. S at first told me that this was the first time he had struck his wife, although he alleged that she had hit him several times before. He denied hitting his first wife or any women he had been previously involved with before marriage. He attributed striking his wife to her "stubbornness and insistence about wanting a divorce." Later, as our work together continued, and as our rapport with each other improved, he opened up more and more about other episodes of violence. However, he always rationalized his actions and never seemed that repentant. Several months after separating and still hoping for a reconciliation, he was told by his wife that she would not even consider dating him unless he did something about his temper and potential for lashing out at her. With this he was agreeable to joining a group for assaultive husbands, which he attended regularly and enthusiastically. He gained a lot from this group and learned new ways of understanding and venting his frustration and anger. He and his wife did see each other occasionally after that, but nothing came of it, and eventually they went on to divorce.

Passive–Aggressive

Abandoned husbands with passive–aggressive personalities (or personality traits) typically do not express their anger and feelings of aggression openly or directly. Indeed, many of these men are not even in touch with these feelings, which are unconscious and always accompany a subjective sense of being abandoned. Often these men have not expressed normal feelings of anger and frustration toward their wives throughout the course of their marriages. Classically, their wives describe them as cool, detached, pouty, sulky, or sarcastic in marital situations that would normally provoke anger. Behaviorally, they then withdraw verbally, affectively, and sexually for hours, days, or weeks. Their wives consequently feel punished for their openness, their anger, and their assertiveness.

Procrastination is common in these men and again has often been there throughout the marriage. They have put off doing things—chores, paying bills, making appointments, and following through on stated plans—and advance excuses when confronted. This infuriates their wives, which is the unconscious intent of these men, that is, to express their aggression at their wives for being "bossy" or "domineering." Other passive–aggressive maneuvers include doing a half-hearted job at some task they don't want to do, "forgetting" to do things after saying they will, and breaking promises that they make to their wives and children.

In the marriages of passive–aggressive men, the marital problems are usually felt, defined, and aired exclusively by their wives. When these women try to discuss their felt concerns and worries with their husbands, they either get no response of shared acknowledgment about the problems or get a "lip-service" type of response. Their husbands agree that there are problems and agree to work at changing and to continue more talks. Nothing comes of this. If they agree to marital therapy, they may cancel at the last moment with a lame excuse or not even show up. They may come to therapy for a few visits but not actively participate, or be duplicitous with the therapist, "forget appointments," or simply drop out.

Marital separation for these men brings out their passive–aggressive traits and tendencies. They see themselves as the hapless victims of circumstance because they dare not express their anger openly at being "left" by their wives. Friends and family tend to feel quite sorry for them and feel fury toward their wives, who are seen as harsh, selfish, or foolish for leaving "such a good man." Many of these men will defend their wives' actions to others while seething with rage and resentment inside. They also tend cleverly to mobilize the sentiments of family and friends too, but this is not always conscious. They seek out family and friends because they feel so alone, frightened, or despondent.

Some abandoned husbands are more obviously and consciously passive–aggressive. They refuse to negotiate separation issues and disputes with their wives. They may refuse to move out of the family home despite overwhelming tension and palpable hostility. In some cases, their wives are forced to move out into new or temporary quarters in order to preserve their sanity and the psychological welfare of the children. These men resist discussing impending separation with the children either alone or with their wives. If they do talk to the children about separation, they communicate verbally, or nonverbally, that they are "being kicked out" or that they "are not loved anymore." They manage to deny or negate their part in the marital disharmony and portray the children's mother as the villain.

When it comes to seeking legal counsel, passive–aggressive men are more apt to opt for the more traditional and adversarial approach to divorce as opposed to mediation. Indeed, when they engage notoriously aggressive divorce lawyers in their community, this action enables them to release even more aggression in a passive way because they don't have to do it themselves—they can say it's out of their hands or let a paid agent "do the dirty work." Indeed, some abandoned husbands will even complain to their wives, friends, and families about the ruthlessness of their divorce lawyers and yet not consider engaging someone else! Inside they're delighted.

Abandoned husbands who are fathers may use passive–aggressive means to discharge their aggression toward their wives and to get back at them. In a self-seeking and revengeful manner, they may fight for sole custody, not because they have the best interests of their child(ren) at heart but because they are so hurt, angry, and spiteful. Not only does this action handle their aggression but also it enables them to regain some control, which has been lost. For many abandoned husbands, their bid for sole custody is short-lived, a form of posturing, or a face-saving mechanism. Once they begin to feel better and less wounded, they soften on their single-minded quest to have exclusive possession of the children.

Some abandoned husbands behave passive–aggressively in other ways toward the children. They may refuse to see them, or they see them very infrequently. This is upsetting and emotionally damaging for the children as they pass through an already confusing time for themselves developmentally. It is of course upsetting for their mothers who, already feeling responsible and often guilty for initiating the separation, now have to try to explain to the children why their fathers aren't visiting them, calling, or taking them out. At times these women also have to endure their children's frustration and wrath as they blame their mothers for "leaving daddy" or "making daddy leave us." Sometimes these women are forced to go to great lengths pleading with their estranged husbands to see the children. This works sometimes; the children get to see their fathers, and their mothers assuage their guilt a little. But in my practice, I see far too many situations where women expend an enormous amount of time and energy trying to promote father involvement and not much happens. When these men do see their children, they may be late in picking them up (or not show up at all), they may demean their wives to their children or tell a very one-sided and inaccurate story about the separation, and they may be tardy in returning the children after visitation.

Mr. and Mrs. M came to see me for what Mrs. M called "a serious communication problem." They had been married for 10 years and had one daughter who was 6 years old. She stated that they had always had trouble communicating, right from the beginning, and she went on to give an example of a misunderstanding that had occurred during their courtship, which she described as "our prototype." Over the years, she found herself becoming increasingly frustrated, angry, and lonely in her marriage. She mentioned that she had had a brief affair 2 years earlier: "That was merely a symptom of my loneliness." Overtures on her part for the two of them to receive marital therapy were never accepted by her husband. He always refused. Finally, she entered individual psychotherapy a few months after her affair, and her work with her therapist ended just prior to the two of them coming to see me together. "I simply told Winston that we get help together or I'm leaving."

Mr. M sat quietly with a controlled nervousness as his wife spoke. I invited him to tell me how he viewed things in the marriage and to comment, if he wished, on anything Mrs. M had said. He didn't volunteer much despite a fair amount of assistance and gentle prompting on my part. He did say that he was quite happy in his marriage and loved his daughter very much (I noted that there was no specific reference to loving his wife in that comment). He denied any upset about Mrs. M's affair and stated, with a lot of intellectualization and rationalization, that it was probably therapeutic for her to meet another man because it did offset her problem with loneliness, at least for a while. His comment about Mrs. M's individual therapy was: "I was glad she went to a psychiatrist. She's always been very insecure. It's rooted in her parents' divorce. Her therapist really helped her." He said that he felt "fine" about accompanying Mrs. M to marital therapy, then added with a wry smile: "Besides, with a threat like that hanging over my head, I'd be a fool not to toe the line, wouldn't I?"

Our conjoint work together was slow, measured, and tedious. Despite some noticeable effort on Mr. M's part to be more attentive, communicative, and affectionate, Mrs. M was barely responsive to him and seemed more distant and closed off in the sessions. She acknowledged this, and this led to a discussion about her wish to separate. She wanted Mr. M to leave the family home and to take an apartment of his own. She said that she wanted him to remain very involved with their daughter, seeing her during the week and having her at his place on weekends. Mr. M expressed no feelings about this, stating only that he needed to think about it. I suggested that we continue to have more conjoint visits to discuss this more carefully and more thoroughly. They both agreed.

When they came 1 week later, they were not speaking to each other. Mr. M stated that he was not leaving and wanted to work on his marriage, not "throw it out the window." He accused Mrs. M of "copping out." She wanted to have a discussion of how and when the two of them should explain the impending separation to their daughter. She stated that she was prepared to leave the home if necessary, and this is what she did that very evening. I never saw the two of them together again. Despite my repeated efforts, Mr. M refused to return to see me alone for support during the separation process. Mrs. M came for several visits over a period of several months. She had enormous guilt. Mr. M cut off all direct contact with her and her daughter for almost 3 months. He didn't respond to her letters or phone messages. He didn't return the two calls I made to him. For several weeks he called his mother-in-law in another city, mobilized her love and support, and inflamed the already tenuous and strained relationship between her and her daughter, his estranged wife. In fact, Mrs. M's mother called me to ask me if I thought her daughter should be committed to a hospital! Mr. M paid nothing toward his daughter's support for several months after he began seeing her again. Mrs. M went to court about this, whereupon Mr. M made a brief bid for sole custody but changed his mind after a few weeks. He called me, very upset, requesting an appointment as soon as possible to discuss ways of negotiating a better visitation schedule so he could see his daughter more often. I scheduled a visit for him the following day during my lunch hour. He didn't show up, didn't respond to my phone messages, and didn't pay my fee for the missed appointment.

Depressed

Marital separation and divorce are well known to be major stressors in people's lives, and it is therefore not uncommon for individuals who are separating or who are separated to develop depressive symptoms or a full-blown clinical depression. As I mentioned earlier in this chapter, noninitiators have a much more difficult adjustment to separation. Thus, husbands who feel abandoned and rejected by their wives are prone to depression. This is especially so when they have not had much time to become accustomed to the *idea* of separation, let alone the *actual* separation itself.

At what point the man begins to perceive and accept the gravity of his marital difficulties and the seriousness of his wife's intent to separate are critical variables for the clinician to keep in mind. I say this because it is not uncommon for clinicians to underestimate the subjective distress of men who feel abandoned and to overestimate the length of time these men are taking to come to terms with their separation. As I have stated at earlier points in this book, most unhappily married women have been struggling with what to do about their situation for months or years before their husbands come to accept the presence of problems in the marriage. Often the complaints of these women are unheeded, no matter how unhappy they or their children are. Typically their husbands have refused to recognize or accept the need for marital therapy, so after many years these women conclude that nothing can be done. With or without professional assistance, they begin to prepare themselves psychologically for leaving their husbands and being on their own. This usually includes increasing disengagement at home, and it is at about this time that their husbands begin to recognize that something is different or changed. Then, and only then, do these men begin to realize that their marriages are in serious trouble, and it is this time of recognition that clinicians should inquire about and make a note of.

It is normal for husbands who see themselves as abandoned and who feel abandoned to be angry and depressed. Usually their depressive symptoms are mild and phasic and recede with the passage of time. Family physicians, internists, and psychotherapists see a lot of men with a range of mild physical and psychological symptoms who are adjusting to separation. However, there are other men who are abandoned husbands who are very seriously and severely ill. Some have a mood disorder (for example, bipolar disorder; they may become manic or depressed on separation), major depression (single episode or recurrent), or dysthymia (formerly called depressive neurosis) (American Psychiatric Association, 1987). Some have an exacerbation of an underlying problem with alcohol or drugs (psychoactive substance use disorders, dependence, or abuse). Some have an underlying personality disorder that worsens temporarily with the stress of abandonment (for example, paranoid, antisocial, borderline, avoidant, and so forth). Some become suicidal. Some even become homicidal.

Abandoned husbands who have suicidal thoughts must be carefully assessed by the clinician for the presence of a suicide plan and serious suicide intent. Men who make suicide threats, especially to their wives, also must be evaluated for suicide risk. It is not uncommon for these men to be simply dismissed as "manipulators" who are trying to play on their wives' sympathies or who are trying to coerce their wives into taking them back. This may be a partial dynamic in some men, but it is rarely the whole story; generally, these men feel panicky, desperate, and alone. Likewise, abandoned husbands who end up in emergency rooms after attempting suicide also need a thorough assessment of their mood, impulsiveness, and continued presence of suicidal thinking. Some will need admission to a psychiatric unit (possibly involuntarily) and intensive treatment; others will be able to be discharged with close follow-up and possible antidepressant medication. Any man with a number of suicide risk factors such as advancing age, alcohol or drug abuse, concomitant medical disorders, lack of social and family support, or a family history of mood disorder and/or death by suicide must be diagnosed and observed very closely.

Homicidal fantasies are not uncommon in men who feel abandoned by their wives. Fortunately, most of these thoughts are fleeting, intermittent, and not organized or carefully constructed into an actual plan. Likewise, most men are quite alarmed by these thoughts and either seek help about them or, if they are already receiving help, feel relieved just talking about them. The homicidal thoughts and feelings may be focal and restricted to their wives, such as "If I had a gun, I'd kill her; I'm so angry at her." Or, coupled with suicidal thoughts, the homicidal thinking may include their wives and children: "This isn't right, this separation . . . no one deserves to live . . . I feel like killing all of us . . . please tell me this feeling will pass." Some abandoned husbands have diffuse rage and more generalized thoughts of homicide: "When I was at MacDonald's last Sunday, I had to get out of there . . . I felt like throwing a grenade and blasting all of those happy families to bits . . . it just isn't fair!"

Most worrisome is the man whom the clinician deems dangerous because of serious and planned homicidal thinking. Psychiatrists and other mental health professionals have a duty to protect—the so-called Tarasoff doctrine (Stone, 1984). This doctrine has gradually evolved since 1974 to the point where psychiatrists today may be held responsible for protecting parties whom their patients seriously threaten. Where the threat is imminent, the patient may need to be hospitalized, either voluntarily or by commitment. In many states, the psychiatrist may also be held responsible for taking steps to protect the third party. This usually includes notifying the threatened person and calling the police department. Because these are such difficult ethical, legal, and professional matters for the practicing psychiatrist, most will obtain a consultation with a lawyer and their local medical society when faced with a dangerously homicidal abandoned husband.

Mr. and Mrs. E, both elementary school teachers, came for therapy in the midst of a marital crisis. Mrs. E was seriously involved with another man and had been for almost a year. She told her husband about 10 days before I saw the two of them together. During that initial visit, both Mr. and Mrs. E described a long history of mutual distancing in their relationship, which they described as a "professional marriage." Mrs. E stated, and Mr. E agreed: "We have our work in common and our children." They had three daughters, all in high school, aged 17, 15, and 13. They had talked about separating many times and actually did separate briefly for a month 3 years earlier, when Mr. E was involved with another woman. This relationship ended, and Mr. and Mrs. E reunited.

Both stated in that initial visit that they didn't want the marriage to end. Mrs. E, although admittedly in love with the other man, Mr. S, was making plans to end the relationship with him and to "work on my marriage." Mr. E was calm and relieved about this, admitting that deep inside he was hurt, frightened, and angry about his wife's relationship with Mr. S. I met individually with each of them and learned firsthand how seriously involved Mrs. E and Mr. S really were and, second, how desperate Mr. E was for his marriage to remain intact.

Within 3 weeks it was becoming increasingly clear that Mrs. E, despite her best intentions, was unable to disengage from Mr. S. Quite understandably, she was completely unable to work on her marriage. She was spending little time at home, and when there, she was tense and remote or in the bedroom crying. Mr. E was becoming increasingly anxious, angry, vigilant, and threatening. He became violent with her the night before one of their visits with me, and during that visit, with my support, they agreed to separate.

I will briefly summarize the events of the next several months. I continued to see the two of them after they separated, mostly individually but also conjointly to discuss living arrangements and the children. I met on a couple of occasions with the three daughters as a group and also once with the whole family. After the separation, Mr. E became increasingly depressed (there was a family history of depression, and his father had committed suicide) and required an antidepressant. When he became suicidal, I hospitalized him. He required aggressive antidepressant therapy and a 6-week hospitalization. One month after discharge he began to withdraw again and for the first time expressed ideas and ruminative thoughts about killing his wife and Mr. S. He dismissed them as "silly jealousy." Because I was concerned, I arranged to see him again briefly 2 days later. He was haggard and agitated, hadn't gone to work, hadn't eaten, and hadn't slept since my last visit with him. He had purchased a pistol (which he had with him in his briefcase), and he easily relinquished it to me. Because he refused to be readmitted to hospital, I committed him against his wishes and notified the police, Mrs. E, and Mr. S. He responded well to a different antidepressant and electroconvulsive therapy.

Sexist

I am using the word sexist here to refer to men who hold an attitude of superiority about their own sex and a devaluing attitude toward the female sex. Thus, the predominant emotions that sexist men feel when their wives leave them, or ask them to leave, are disbelief and outrage. Because controlling their wives has been a central dynamic in their marriages, to no longer have control is completely disorienting for them, and they can become quite panicky. Their aggression is often one way that they attempt to regain control over their lives.

Most sexist men have no insight into their inflated values about men and ideas of inferiority about women. Indeed, many bristle and become immediately defensive if charged with sexism. They will argue about how much they respect, admire, and love women, but when examined closely it becomes obvious they are talking about only certain types of women or those women with stereotypical female traits. In the language of the 1980s, they will profess that they like independent women (translate: women who keep their emotions to themselves, who don't cling, but are always available on hold), women with careers (translate: as long as she is self-supporting, doesn't earn more than he does, and doesn't put her own career before his), and women who are assertive (translate: as long as she's not "aggressive," a quality that tends to be defined differently by women and by men). Those men who do admit that they are sexist usually only have partial insight into the magnitude of their sexism. By admitting it, they expect to endear themselves to others, especially women, through being open or apologetic about it and by this maneuver are actually being sexist and controlling. Acknowledging sexism is not the same as saying "I'm unhappy or embarrassed about my negative attitudes toward women—I'm trying to do something about it."

Men who are quite traditional in their attitudes toward work and family may be also quite sexist in their beliefs toward women. They have set ideas about their own roles and responsibilities as men and the roles and responsibilities of their wives as women. These men work hard and conscientiously at their jobs, and they define themselves in terms of "what they do." Those in the professions are usually quite ambitious, striving, and competitive. Most of their energy is directed outside the home and toward the acquisition of money, power, and status. These men have a conscious or unconscious belief that their wives will create, organize, and run the home and family. Their wives, at least initially, also define themselves in terms of this role and its expectations. When everything goes well, these marriages can function very smoothly; the women are challenged by and enjoy what they do, and their husbands are appreciative, respectful, and proud of them.

The downside of traditionally defined marriages can be very problematic. Most of these men tend to take their marriages for granted either because they are so busy with their own working lives or because they don't want to be bothered or for a combination of factors. They will assume that all is well at home, and rarely do they have any complaints. Indeed, even if they have concerns, they may not air them directly (although they may begin to drink more, work longer hours, avoid coming home, or begin an affair). When their wives have complaints about the marriage or concerns about their own marital unhappiness or feelings of depression (which are endemic in women who have small children and who have no paid work outside the home), these complaints often go unheeded. These men dismiss their wives' worries as silly, exaggerated, or self-pitying because they have trouble fully appreciating what their wives are complaining about. They see themselves as the ones with the "big problems" and their wives' lives as "cushy." When professional help is sought, most of these women go alone because their husbands see the problem as hers and her inability to cope.

Sexist abandoned husbands then may be in tremendous turmoil. By the time they come for therapy, their wives have already decided to leave or have already left. These men present for help in a panic. They are either completely bewildered and disorganized or in a state of numbness, shock, or incredulousness. They make statements like: "I had no idea that she was so unhappy, she has her dream home, a beautiful car, two adorable children, a cleaning woman, and a husband who works his ass off to make it all work" or "It's that woman therapist she's seeing, she's a real feminist I hear" or "I should have known better, a lot of the 'girls' she hangs around with have left their husbands" or "She's making a big mistake, wait till she sees how many losers there are out there in that singles scene."

Not uncommonly, these abandoned husbands reveal an ambivalent mixture of overidealization and devaluation of their wives. They are solicitious, flattering, and ingratiating one moment and angry, criticizing, and rejecting the next. When threatened with separation or if their wives have already left, they may adopt lavish gift-giving behavior or may redouble their efforts at courtship. Usually their wives are not interested (because it's too late), and in turn they feel embarrassed, guilty, or simply annoyed at their husbands' behavior. When these men come for individual, marital, or divorce therapy it is very difficult for them: they find it foreign, awkward, frightening, and often humiliating. They are accustomed to handling problems on their own, usually very skillfully and successfully. It is very hard for them to appear so vulnerable (one man told me he felt "pathetic" in my office), both emotionally and behaviorally, with their therapists.

What follows is a case example from an article I wrote for family physicians a few years ago (Myers, 1984, p. 166) that reflects the disbelief of some abandoned husbands.

Arthur and Marilyn have been married for 20 years. They have three adolescent children all living at home. During an appointment, Marilyn expresses concern about Arthur's increasing difficulty with erections. You next see Arthur alone. A complete medical, neurological, and urological workup is negative. You then schedule a conjoint appointment at which you uncover several areas of blocked marital communication, including Marilyn's longstanding desire to separate. You refer the couple to Doctor X for counseling. Six months later, Marilyn makes an appointment to see you alone. She complains that they are still together, that Arthur dropped counseling sessions after three visits, and that she is very unhappy. He pressures her constantly for sex, which she refuses; she is now sleeping in another room. She has asked him to move out; he rejects the idea. She has tried to discuss the option of leaving the family home with the children; he will not talk about it. Last week she consulted a lawyer; Arthur refuses to see one himself. Yesterday, he booked a Caribbean cruise as "a second honeymoon" for the two of them.

Passive–Dependent

These are a group of abandoned husbands who are overdependent on their wives and have had problems of dependency in relationships throughout their lives. In fact, excessive dependency has often been a central conflict in their marriages and has contributed to the marital breakdown: their wives can no longer live with it. Although most of these men are younger abandoned husbands who married young, many are not. Some are in their 30s and 40s and have had an added problem of alcohol and drug dependency. Passive–dependent abandoned husbands must be distinguished from other husbands whose dependency is relatively brief and reactive to stress (for example, unemployment, medical illness, or the abandonment itself). This dependency is part of regression to an earlier developmental phase; once they feel well again, these men return to their normal level of autonomous functioning.

Passive–dependent men exhibit a pervasive pattern of dependent and submissive behavior that begins by early adulthood (American Psychiatric Association, 1987). They are chronically indecisive and need a lot of advice and reassurance from others. These men rarely initiate things or do things on their own, as they tend to feel very uncomfortable when alone. Abandonment is actually something they fear, and it is closely aligned with their extreme sensitivity to criticism and disapproval. They are poorly self-reliant, and typically their wives have made a lot of their decisions for them regarding their work and their interests. Their wives buy their clothes for them, make all of the decisions about running the household, and usually assume full responsibility for deciding what they do together socially and recreationally. These men have usually been unassertive and unambitious in their work so that they settle into low-level occupational functioning with no career progression. Some have long periods of unemployment with complete financial dependency on their wives or the state.

Regardless of the age that they married, most passive–dependent abandoned husbands have never lived on their own. They lived either at home with one or both parents before marriage or in some protected setting where they were taken care of by others. Consequently, they have never really learned anything about independent living both from the standpoint of knowing the mechanics or skills as well as from the standpoint of coping psychologically with it. I have found that it is not unusual for the wives of passive–dependent men to actually select and organize the new living quarters for their husbands once they have decided to separate. These men never want to separate anyway, so by their wives doing it all for them (as has been the pattern throughout the marriage), these women are then assured that their husbands will indeed leave. This action also alleviates some of the enormous guilt that these wives feel (and are made to feel) for "abandoning" their husbands. For this reason, these women feel much more emancipated and less guilty if they've gotten their husbands into treatment before, during, or after the separation. This is especially the case if their husbands have been depressed or have threatened suicide.

Mr. and Mrs. P came for marital therapy with the following complaint from Mrs. P: "I'm angry all the time now, and my husband and I have to decide whether to stay together or not." Mrs. P went on to explain her anger: "I'm fed up with running this whole show—I'm the only one making any money, I run the house, I organize our social schedule, and I do most of the housework. The only thing I don't do is take out the garbage and change the oil in our car." Mr. P agreed with his wife and said he didn't blame her for being angry. They were both 35 years old and had been married for 5 years. Mrs. P was a registered nurse, and Mr. P was a writer. "A writer-in-residence" quipped Mrs. P: "He never goes outdoors long enough to walk to the mailbox—how do you get anything published if you never mail anything away anywhere?" I learned in that visit and in subsequent individual visits that the two of them had met when Mr. P was hospitalized 7 years earlier with a fractured leg. Mrs. P had been his nurse on the orthopedics ward where he had been hospitalized for several weeks. They became friendly, and after Mr. P was discharged, she called him and volunteered to take him out for walks. Mrs. P said: "He was the handsomest guy I had ever met, and I loved his creative mind." Mr. P said: "She was the kindest woman I had ever met and a terrific nurse."

Mrs. P began their third visit with me by announcing that she had decided that therapy wasn't helping, and she wanted to separate. Because they had two dogs that were largely her responsibility and to which she was more attached, they agreed that she would remain in their rented home and Mr. P would move out. After several weeks of half-hearted attempts on Mr. P's part to find a small apartment, Mrs. P found a basement suite for him near their home, which he liked. They divided up a lot of their furnishings, and she went shopping with him to buy the other items he would need. She also sewed him some curtains. After they separated, he came by for quite a few meals at first until Mrs. P decided that they must have more distance from and independence of each other. This worked well for her; she made a few new friends at work, met other men, and began to develop more of a life of her own. Mr. P, however, on having only limited contact with Mrs. P, gave up his apartment and moved back home to live with his widowed mother.

Complicating Factors for Abandoned Husbands

When There's Another Man

Those men whose wives have become involved with another man either before they separate or shortly after they separate often suffer a more profound sense of abandonment and intensified anger. In fact, in anticipation of this, some wives who have actually begun the outside relationship long before the separation begins will try their best to keep the relationship totally secret and make it appear that they did not meet until after the separation began. Often there are other reasons for this as well, especially to protect their children and to spare them any additional hurt or embarrassment.

Although it is a rather dated term, some men describe an inner sense of being a "cuckold." There is a feeling of humiliation, of being deceived, of betrayal, or of being the brunt of a sick joke. These feelings may be magnified 10-fold if the abandoned husband knows the other man or, in some cases, has been a close friend of the other man. These feelings were encompassed in the words of one of my patients, a 34-year-old architect: "It's hard enough trying to accept that Laura doesn't love me anymore and wants a divorce . . . like right away . . . but to just find out that she and one of my best friends have been screwing their brains out together for the last 3 months is more than I can handle."

The occasional man is not fully conscious of the rage that he feels toward his wife and/or the other man. He assumes an accepting, understanding, and forgiving posture that is quite inappropriate to the reality of the marital crisis. A common manifestation of this stance is the development of a sexual problem, especially erective difficulties. This may occur with his wife in his attempts to compete with the other man or to woo his wife back to him. Indeed, these husbands are usually so hurt, confused, and unstable that they approach their wives with a mixture of sexual withdrawal and sexual redoubling. Impotence may also occur if the man has begun to date other women. One man who came to see me because of panic attacks after his separation had this to say when he learned that his estranged wife was dating another man: "Couldn't she have at least waited until the body was cold?"

When There's Another Woman

With the resurgence of the women's movement of the past 20 years and the upturn of the divorce rate, there have been a significant number of women forming love relationships with other women in their adult years. Many of the individuals in these couples are or have been married at one time, and many are mothers of young children. Whether this is a new form of lesbianism or an increase in lesbianism in our society or merely a heightened visibility of lesbian women is not really known, to my knowledge. It is not unusual for contemporary clinicians who do a lot of marital or divorce work to have individuals or couples in their practices where lesbianism or lesbian behavior in the married woman is one of the couple's concerns.

I have noted a particular constellation of symptoms in those men whose wives become involved with another woman either before they separate or shortly after they separate. In addition to anger and feelings of abandonment, these husbands also describe feelings of disbelief, belittlement, repugnance, abasement, and bewilderment. This subjective state in the man will be highly influenced by his pre-existing personality, especially his attitudes toward women, divorce, homosexuality, and sometimes feminism. Indeed, it is not unusual for married women who have fallen in love with another woman to describe husbands who are ideologically conservative, morally superior in attitude, and emotionally constricted. They decry a lack of intimacy and equality in their marriages, which they have found in their new relationship with another woman.

These abandoned husbands thus may be quite conservative and/or rigid in their beliefs, and in addition to rejection they feel a blow to their sense of masculine self-esteem. Sexist men feel outraged at the loss of their wives to a person of "subordinate status" (that is, another woman). Other husbands may have a lot of difficulty fully appreciating the complexity and the multiple determinants of these types of separations. They cannot appreciate their wife's own struggle with her lesbianism and homophobia and may tend to think and behave somewhat mechanistically and simplistically. They see the lesbian component as deliberate, willful, or silly, and in their desperation, make heroic efforts to satisfy their wives sexually or to convince them of their heterosexuality. They may assume much more than their share of responsibility for the marriage ending, blame themselves entirely one moment and their wives entirely the next, and struggle with guilt. Some will end up feeling very inadequate sexually; they may become quite depressed or rush very quickly into a new relationship or into a flurry of sexual activity with many women to reaffirm their sexual capabilities and shore up tarnished masculinity.

Here is an example of an abandoned husband who came for therapy when his wife became involved with another woman (Myers, 1988a):

When Dr. K, a university English professor, came to see me, he and his wife were about to separate. Mrs. K, a journalist, had fallen in love with another woman with whom she would be living immediately on leaving her husband. Their 14-year-old son, Mike, would remain at home with his father and see his mother on weekends. On the surface all was quite civil.

Dr. K was desperate. In his heart he was totally against the separation. He entreated me as a therapist to "try to talk some sense into her head—she doesn't know what she's doing—ruining Mike's life, my life, and ultimately her life." He went on: "Also, I don't believe she's really lesbian—I would call her a vulnerable neofeminist who's a sitting duck for an aging lonely lesbian to get her hands on. It's all my fault, or mostly my fault. I know I've let her down by being so picky, so perfectionistic, and so absorbed in my work." Dr. K's statements about his wife alternated between professing undying love for her and demeaning almost everything she had ever said or done.

I met with Mrs. K alone. She was happy her husband had come to see me. She saw him as "really falling apart—I worry whether he'll make it on his own—Mike will help a lot." She was afraid of him; he had struck her twice and had made very frightening threats toward her and her partner, Jane. She wondered about a restraining order but feared provoking him more for fear he would restrict visitation rights because of her lesbianism. She was quite clear about her own situation; indeed, she had been unhappy in her marriage for a long time. She said: "I'm not exactly certain about Jane and me over the long term—at the moment I love her dearly, and I'm experiencing something I've never ever felt before, any time in my life!"

Dr. K worked alone with me for several months. Being in therapy helped him to neutralize his rage and vindictiveness against Mrs. K. I am sure it prevented him from acting it out. He also worked on underlying issues—his intellectualism, his profound need for control, his sexist notions about women, and his guilt about his marriage failing. My support helped him to regain his self-esteem, which was quite shattered, and to begin to feel worthy again of someone's love and affection. I met with him and Mike together twice to address their adjustment to living together. I also met conjointly with him and Mrs. K to discuss changes in access, Dr. K's concerns about Mike's exposure to lesbianism, and Mrs. K's concerns about Dr. K having women sleep overnight and the impact of this on Mike.

Suspiciousness

There is a range of suspiciousness and mistrustfulness in abandoned husbands. Some is purely situational and arises *de novo* once the man learns that there is another person in his wife's life, and the marital trust has been broken. This is suspiciousness with an understandable, predictable, and rational basis. If the outside relationship has been going on for some time, and the husband has suspected something amiss but receives only denials when he confronts or questions his wife, then his suspiciousness will be even greater once he learns the truth. If he still loves his wife a lot and is hoping for a reconciliation, then he will remain quite jealous and suspicious long after they separate. This will usually continue until he fully accepts that the marriage is over and that his wife won't be coming back.

Then, there is longstanding suspiciousness that has been present throughout the length of the relationship and perhaps throughout the life span of the man. Some of these men are merely old-fashioned, personally insecure and domineering, and possessive of their wives. Their ideas about women and their roles and behavior in marriage are culture-bound and shared by many men of their reference group. They are not seen as unusual or atypical in their beliefs and attitudes by those around them.

There is another large group of men who have longstanding suspiciousness, and this is rooted in primary and individual psychopathology. I am referring here to men with personality disorders, especially paranoid, borderline, and antisocial types, as well as those with paranoid schizophrenia, delusional (paranoid) disorders of jealous type, psychoactive substance use disorders (especially alcohol, amphetamine, and cocaine), and organic mental disorders with delusions, especially dementia (American Psychiatric Association, 1987). In many of these marriages, the separation has become the final act in a lengthy and chaotic union punctuated by repeated episodes of wife battering, marital rape, and delusional jealousy where the husband is convinced that his wife is being unfaithful and deceiving him. He beats her because of this false reasoning (and for other reasons) and rapes her to punish her on the one hand and to prevent her "from fooling around" on the other. These husbands are highly suspicious, emotionally brittle, and dangerous—all aspects of which are accentuated when their wives leave them. Marital or reconciliation therapy is ineffective and usually inappropriate with these men unless their underlying psychopathology is treated with neuroleptic medication and individual therapy.

Conclusion

In this chapter I have described various types of abandoned husbands and delineated them as a specific group of men coping with divorce. They constitute a large group of men and, in my mind, an underserved group of men. Because their surface behaviors and actions are often provocative, unsavory, or frightening, many of these men alienate those around them, including clinicians. My plea is that we look beyond the "persona" to find the hurt and pain that lie within. If we can connect with the wounded being inside, then we can help.

CHAPTER 8

Men Who Have Been Divorced Before

Of all marriages registered in 1981, 11.8% involved a remarriage for the groom and a first marriage for the bride, 10.1% involved a remarriage for the bride and a first marriage for the groom, and 23.4% involved remarriages for both parties (Ahrons & Rodgers, 1987, p. 20). Compared to first marriages, the divorce rates are higher after remarriage: 54% of women and 61% of men who remarry will divorce (Glick, 1984). It has also been found that redivorces occur earlier in the marriage than first divorces: remarriages have a 50% greater probability of redivorce within the first 5 years than first marriages (Furstenberg & Spanier, 1984).

Hence, it is not unusual for clinicians to treat couples or families wherein the man or the woman or both have been married once or twice before. Nor is it unusual for clinicians to see a newly separated or divorced man who has had one or two previous marriages and divorces.

In noting these statistics about remarriage and redivorce, I want also to remind the reader of two other facts about men: they remarry sooner than women, and they remarry at a higher rate than women. Almost 85% of divorced men in North America remarry within 3 years of their divorces, as compared to 75% of divorced women. What are some of the clinical implications of this high level of "marital activity" on the part of men, given that many of them are spending significant periods of their adult lives forming relationships, maintaining relationships, dissolving relationships, and reestablishing new relationships?

One question that comes to mind when thinking about men who have been married and divorced once or twice before is: "Were they fully over one relationship before moving on to the next?" In other words, had they adequately or completely mourned that individual, thereby establishing a sense of psychological resolution, closure, or equilibrium for themselves? One would think not in the case of men who have already met their new partners extramaritally before leaving their marriages or men who become seriously involved with new partners shortly after separating. But time is not the only factor that determines whether a man has unresolved issues from an earlier marriage. Witness the number of long-divorced men, now remarried, whose present marital difficulties are partly, if not chiefly, the result of "unfinished business" from the earlier marriage and divorce.

Another question that comes to mind is: "Are men more dependent on 'being married' than women?" Again, it would appear so given the higher remarriage rates for men than women. And I think this holds even when one considers that large group of aging women who would consider remarriage but don't actually remarry because so many of their age-matched or older male peers are marrying much younger women. This fact plus the feminist and epidemiologic research that documents that marriage can be unhealthy for women and increases their psychiatric morbidity rates for depression help to account for the contentedness of many divorced women with not remarrying. These women may complain of loneliness and unmet sexual needs, but for the most part, these are sporadic complaints. Most divorced women are very self-sufficient, cherish their independence, and have a supportive network of friends and family.

My third and final question is: "Do men establish new relationships, including remarriage, in order to deal with or avoid the pain of the original marriage and divorce?" In other words, is the new relationship an unconscious attempt at problem solving? Put simplistically, does the man bargain with himself: "If I can be happy and successful in this new relationship, then I don't need to feel the unhappiness, anger, loneliness, sadness, guilt, and feelings of failure of the old relationship." This is a more dynamic, action-oriented, and instrumental model that is not uncharacteristic of men and how they lead their lives. It does help to account for the rapid entry into new marriages, a seeming dependency on the state of "being married," and the common phenomenon of unresolved issues from an earlier marriage being admixed with new issues in a remarriage.

Sam, a 36-year-old attorney, came for therapy with this complaint: "I need to sort out my life—although I'm living with a woman, I've met someone else, and I don't know what to do." Sam went on to describe his cohabiting relationship: "Marion and I met 4 years ago and began living together almost immediately. There was instant chemistry, and things were great for several months, maybe a year. Gradually things began to change. I became more and more restless, cranky, bored, and antisocial. I've been working really hard—I just became a partner in my law firm last year—and not paying a lot of attention to Marion. About a year and half ago, we each had a brief fling with someone else. I don't think either of us cared that much. We never really talked about the reasons why, but I know Marion's not very happy with our relationship either. I told her I was going to see a psychiatrist about all of this, which she thinks is great. I haven't told her about Cheryl, the woman I've just recently met." In the course of that first visit, Sam mentioned that he had been married before and that he was divorced from his wife. He queried: "I wonder sometimes how together I am about that" (that is, his divorce).

During further visits I learned that Sam and his ex-wife, Carol, had met as undergraduates at a university. They were both 20 years old then and dated for a couple of years before they began living together. At that juncture, Sam was beginning law school, and Carol was beginning medical school. They married 2 years later. Sam recalled his early years with Carol as immensely happy and exciting. They were both bright and ambitious, and they energized each other in their drive and wide range of interests. "We were dynamite together," were Sam's words. Also significant was Sam's attachment to Carol and her very secure and harmonious family. His own parents had divorced when he was in high school, and he was not very close to either of them or to his two brothers. As Sam stated: "Carol's family adopted me, and boy did I need it. I'm still closer to them than my own parents."

As Sam told it, he felt things were fine in their marriage as the years passed by. They both graduated the same year, followed by Carol's internship and Sam's articling year. Then they traveled around the world, stopping to live and work in Israel for a year. They returned home, and Carol began a residency in internal medicine and Sam began work with a large law firm. Their relationship became more distant and stilted as they got busier and busier with their careers. Sam felt this was normal and quickly attributed this to the usual strains of dual-career marriages. However, Carol met another man, another resident physician at work, and began a serious relationship with him. After 3 months she told Sam that she was leaving, moved out of their apartment the next day, and moved in with the man she had been see-ing. Sam described his reaction: "I was beside myself... I didn't know whether I was coming or going... I can't describe the feeling of devastation... and assault... that I felt inside my body... I'm not sure how I got through it... I just put one foot in front of the other and went through the motions of living." Two weeks later he met Mar-ion, another attorney, at a Christmas party. As I mentioned earlier, they began living together almost immediately.

Sam was unable to come to terms with the loss of a love relation-ship in a straightforward, progressive, and sequential manner. He moved rapidly from his marriage to Carol into a cohabiting relation-ship with Marion, someone whom he met at an extremely vulnerable time—when he was just in the early stages of bereavement.

Many of Sam's feelings—rage, abandonment, hurt, jealousy, guilt, and so forth—had been suppressed by the "instant chemistry" between Marion and him. I got the feeling that he was doing the same thing again, albeit in a less abrupt and more muted fashion, by beginning a relationship with Cheryl before knowing for certain the status of his relationship with Marion and whether it was still viable or not. This fact, plus the fact that he had had a "brief fling" a year and a half earlier, were significant and pointed to major problems in communica-tion, especially around the matter of unmet needs for affection and at-tention. This connected with his parents' divorce during his adolescence and possible unresolved issues of love and unhappiness there. It appeared that Sam could not be without a woman, that it was impossible for him to survive on his own, and that he felt he was noth-ing without a woman in his life. This lack of self-reliance and excessive dependence on women were crippling and cyclical.

Sam had a good capacity for insight, and he did very well with exploratory psychotherapy. He spent a lot of time talking about his family of origin and his boyhood years. He had long felt like a "misfit" in his family as the youngest of three boys. Neither of his brothers was very academically oriented: they were more athletically inclined and "into girls." Sam's relationship with his father was distant and cool, basically a "nonrelationship." His mother was the opposite: she was very emotional and somewhat intrusive into Sam's personal life. She tried to make him her confidant both before and after she and Sam's father divorced. Until he met Carol, Sam had never really talked about his family, especially his feelings of loneliness and unhappiness with them.

Sam also spent several sessions talking about Carol. He still loved her in many respects and indeed saw her as the most significant per-son in his life. He was very proud of her accomplishments as an aca-

demic internist, and he wished her well in her second marriage. Sam ended his relationship with Cheryl, and eventually his relationship with Marion improved. The two of them began couple treatment with another therapist when Sam's work with me ended. He mailed me a card a year later and told me how well things were for the two of them.

Undisclosed Earlier Marriage

Many individuals or couples who approach therapists with concerns about their marriages mention that they have been divorced before and do not want to go through that experience again. These are individuals who have insight (or a capacity for insight) into the connectedness of things and who have reflected a lot on how they relate to others in a committed relationship. Seeing the same or new concerns arise for them in a new relationship alerts them to the wisdom of reaching out for professional help.

Over the years I have seen a number of men who have had an earlier marriage that they have not disclosed to their present wife. Some have disclosed one previous marriage but not two. Often these are brief marriages that took place when they were quite young and didn't last very long. Some of these marriages have been annulled; others have ended in divorce. Usually there are no children from these undisclosed earlier marriages, but not always; some men have fairly lengthy previous marriages with wives they have deserted and one or more children whom they have abandoned. They move elsewhere to start a new life.

The above are men who voluntarily disclose in a private session with me this "secret" that they have never discussed with their current wife. There are other men who "forget" to tell me about an earlier marriage and divorce when I am in the process of taking a longitudinal history from them in the first or second session. They may "remember" this fact several weeks or months later, when they are well into therapy with me. This recall and disclosure is often in the form of a question: "Did I ever tell you that I was married before?" Some men who have disclosed an earlier marriage and divorce to their current wives also "forget" to mention this information in individual visits with their therapists. Anticipating this, their current wives are the ones who volunteer this information to the therapist, such as: "Did my husband tell you he's been married before? I'm not surprised if he didn't. He hates to talk about it, but he needs to, because that explains a lot of our problems today in our marriage."

What causes this "forgetting" and this secretiveness? It seems to me that there are both unconscious and conscious dynamics at work in some or most of these men. "Forgetting" suggests repression and the need to keep out of consciousness unpleasant ideas and emotions connected with the earlier marriage. And indeed some of the ideas and feelings, once relived and released, have been unpleasant. I have had men patients describe earlier marriages in which they felt betrayed (they caught their wife in bed with another man), belittled (they felt put down and humiliated by their wife for various reasons), and abandoned (their wife left the marriage for someone else). Other men have repressed feelings of being unable to successfully help a wife with a serious alcohol or drug problem. Sometimes there is a history of violence in an earlier marriage such as wife battering or child abuse. Some men describe profound feelings of failure that the earlier marriage didn't last, and they have never come to terms with these. Nor are they comforted with others' attempts to reassure them that they were young and immature then. They feel that "immaturity" is a copout and a rationalization.

Conscious reasons for not disclosing an earlier marriage suggest the notion of deliberate withholding of information from the current wife and/or the therapist. In these cases, the man anticipates disapproval and judgment of others. More specifically, because in his eyes he has failed once before in a relationship and now, faced with problems again, may "fail" again, he feels like "a loser." This points to a problem in his self-esteem and feelings of self-worth. These are difficult feelings to talk about and, in the intimidating early phases of the therapist–patient relationship, may be impossible to discuss. Once rapport is established and the man is certain that he can trust and count on the therapist, then he can disclose more information about himself.

Other men consciously withhold information from their wives or therapists because of unresolved transference dynamics from the earlier marriage not working out. And if they already have problems with trust, intimacy, and commitment that are rooted in unstable and deprived childhoods, they will have a very difficult time. One of my patients said to his wife in a conjoint session immediately after she upbraided him for not disclosing an earlier marriage when he met alone with me the previous week: "Why should I tell him, it's none of his fucking business whether I've been married before or not? She screwed me around and played tricks with my mind; how do I know he won't do the same thing?" Most men are not as angry and suspicious as this man, but his words do underscore my point that there are often significant and psychodynamically relevant reasons why some men deliberately do not discuss earlier marriages.

Some men intentionally withhold the fact that they were married and divorced before because they are dishonest and lie about many things. Omitting their having been married before is merely one of the many segments of their life stories that they neglect to mention. Men with antisocial behaviors or antisocial personality disorders are notorious for lying about, and then rationalizing, many things in life, especially their levels of education, their previous employment, any previous drug and alcohol abuse, a possible criminal record, and whether or not they have spent time in jail or prison. These men are at the more severe end of the spectrum. Their lying is often quite gross and quickly visible. There are many other men who are much more subtle and calculating in their deceitfulness. It may take some time, perhaps years, before their wives catch on to their caginess and stop bailing them out. These men eventually lose their credibility in their wives', and many others', eyes.

Finally, there are cases of simple ignorance and naiveté. Some men are not at all psychologically minded. They do not know that information about an earlier marriage, annulment, or divorce may be of interest or importance to their wife or therapist. They themselves have dismissed it as irrelevant and past, like many events in their lives. This is in keeping with the structure of their personalities and their philosophy of life. Knowing and accepting this, therapists can be more empathic and tailor their therapeutic approach along more structured and behavioral lines.

When the Former Wife Remarries

Some divorced men come for therapy at the point that their former wife decides to remarry or actually does remarry. This is because these men find themselves overwhelmed with feelings that come as a surprise to them. They may feel intensely jealous, very hurt, or very angry. Some are intensely sad and feel bereft. Many of these men fear that they are regressing to an earlier stage in the separation process, and this frightens them. Other men, especially those who originally initiated the separation and divorce, may find themselves experiencing these feelings for the first time. It doesn't always matter whether the separation was initiated by the man or the woman. Many husbands who wanted the separation from their wives find themselves with an intense reaction when their ex-wives remarry. This reaction can also occur if the man is settled into another relationship himself.

What accounts for this mixture of feelings in a man whose ex-wife is remarrying? Although the type of feelings, their intensity, and their duration will vary from one man to the next (based on his own personal dynamics as well as those that characterized his marriage), there are common themes. Most important, his wife's remarrying another man does symbolize the end of his marriage to her. Prior to this point, even if the man's former wife is living with another man, there may not be a final sense of completion. Her marriage to another man is a clear and powerful statement that the kind of relationship they once had is over now, and she is moving on. This is a feeling of further loss and hence explains many of the bereavement symptoms that the man might experience. They are like the feelings many people have at the time of their divorces, feelings that can catch them off guard, especially if they have been separated for a long time and thought their marriages were completely behind them.

In earlier chapters, I have talked about the separation distress syndrome as well as attachment. Attachment bonds are laid down early in the relationship and are intensified and reinforced at many nodal points throughout the marriage. These attachment bonds, in many respects, continue after separation and divorce, albeit in a modified and attenuated form. This concept helps to make sense of the reaction that individuals can have when an ex-spouse remarries. One of my male patients described his feelings in this way: "I know you'll think this is bizarre, but I still feel connected to Joan [his ex-wife] in many ways—not just as parents of our children but like we're still married. Even though I'm very happily married to Karen now and feel very secure about us, when Joan called me and said she was getting married again, I felt a real thud in my chest. I know I was speechless, because she actually asked if I was still there on the other end of the phone. I told her I was happy for her, but I don't think I was very convincing. We spent so many years together. I guess I'm not quite ready to let her get on with her life. And yet I've moved on. Haven't I?"

Many individuals who are separated and divorced harbor reconciliation fantasies with their ex-spouses, and these may be conscious or unconscious. I have heard many of my divorced patients describe these feelings on learning that a former spouse has remarried. Conscious thoughts are a variation of "I've secretly wondered if we might get back together (or remarry each other) some day," and unconscious thoughts a variation of "I've never considered reconciliation but in light of my intense reaction to all of this I've wondered if maybe I have hoped there was a possibility of us getting back together some day." Indeed, reconciliation hopes are so common in the early stages of a separation and divorce that I think therapists need to inquire directly about these so that they can be neutralized and normalized for their patients.

There may be other reasons why the man who has divorced his wife is upset when she remarries. He may still love her in many ways even though he has partly moved on in his own life and may be in a new relationship with no thoughts of reconciling. "I'm not ready to share her with anyone else yet" were the feelings of one divorced man I treated. Sometimes the man simply does not like or respect his ex-wife's new partner or husband. Indeed, it is very common for a divorced individual to make disparaging remarks about the ex-spouse's new relationship, often based on little or no direct involvement with that person. Often the man is making the comments because he himself is still hurting or still loves his ex-wife or simply cares about her welfare as a friend would and is assuming a protective stance. These, and other contributing dynamics, may be a challenge for the therapist to sort out with the patient, so that together they can determine what to make of his emotional reaction to the new person.

The ex-husband's feelings are also strongly affected by the children's feelings and attitude toward their mother's new partner. Not uncommonly, the ex-husband can feel a lot of hurt and jealousy if his children seem to really like, and talk a lot about, this man. Quite understandably, he may fear that his ex-wife's new partner is threatening his role as a father to his children, and, if he sees his own children much less often than this other man does, this may become an intense fear for him. By way of contrast, if his children don't seem to like their mother's new partner, then this may reinforce his own negative feelings for the man. It can become very confusing for the children if the ex-husband doesn't try to keep his own feelings to himself to enable the children to form their own relationship with their mother's new partner. Often children need time to get beyond their initial dislike of new partners for each of their parents.

Conclusion

In this chapter, I have talked about some of the issues for men in crisis who have been married and divorced before. I urge the clinician to "read between the lines" with these men because there are often so many unresolved and unexamined feelings from that earlier relationship, feelings that are coloring the present state of conflict. Many of these men are ripe for therapy when they are in crisis and thereby provide an opportunity for the clinician to work with them. Some need help with mourning. Some need help in learning to live alone. Most need help with their overdependence on women.

CHAPTER 9

Divorcing Men Who Are "Coming Out"

Research has found that approximately 25% of homosexual women and men have been previously married (Dank, 1972; Bell & Weinberg, 1978; Masters & Johnson, 1979). When one begins to consider that there are tremendous pressures in our society for people to marry, that homosexuality is defined as abnormal in many sectors of our society, and that not all people are aware of homosexual feelings at the time of marriage, then this figure is less striking. Because "coming out" is a developmental process that may take years to complete and that has several distinct stages (Coleman, 1982a), it is not unusual to expect that many young individuals will marry and divorce during this period of identity formation. These separations and divorces are often extremely complicated and psychologically painful for both of the partners, the children (when there are children), the extended families, and friends. They are a challenge to most therapists.

Homosexuality and Marriage

Complete unawareness of one's homosexual feelings or desires before marriage does occur (Wafelbakker, 1975), but it is not common. In Dank's (1972) study of 15 previously married men, all had been homosexually active before marriage. Coleman (1982b) studied 31 bisexual married men and found that all but one were aware of same-sex feelings before marriage, and all but four had acted on these feelings before marriage. Twenty-nine of the 31 men had been sexually active with other men since marriage.

In my clinical practice, I have found a wide range of same-sex erotic feelings and behaviors in married and divorcing men, and in this regard, the Kinsey (Kinsey, Pomeroy, Martin, & Gebhard, 1948) continuum scale is helpful (Kinsey 0—exclusive heterosexuality; Kinsey 3—equally homosexual and heterosexual; Kinsey 6—exclusive homosexuality). Not only are there some men who fluctuate backwards and forwards on this axis before and during their marriages, but the intensity of homosexual desire and activity before marriage does not always predict marital satisfaction or outcome. I have seen many men "come out" after marriage who had minimal homosexual ideation and no activity before they were married. However, I have also seen men who had a lot of homosexual activity before marriage, including one or more "lovers," who have completely satisfactory (by self-description) marriages with their wives.

Many unhappily married bisexual men and many formerly married gay men talk quite specifically about how unwanted and frightening their same-sex feelings have been for them. These feelings have made them feel different, guilty, lonely, and flawed. Years ago I treated a gay medical student for depression and an obsessional disorder. I recall trying to reassure him not to be so hard on himself in response to his extreme self-castigation at having missed the diagnosis in one of his clinical groups in internal medicine. He turned to me and said: "No offense, but you really don't understand, Dr. Myers. When you're a medical student, and you're gay, you can't afford any blemish, any carelessness; you have to put your best foot forward at all times." He went on to tell me that he felt he had a mission to prove that you can be a good doctor and still be gay. I also know that this is a feeling that many women have who work in male-dominated fields; they too feel they must be on their toes at all times and can afford no error of any sort.

There seems to be a complex mixture of factors that determine whether a bisexual man remains married or whether he goes on to separate and divorce. The biological and psychological urgency of his erotic feelings for men is one of these, and the strength and ascendancy of these feelings vary markedly from one bisexual man to another. How strong his heterosexual erotic feelings are is also important, but even if these are overshadowed by gay feelings, this does not necessarily cause marital distress if his wife is not that sexually interested. In many couples where the man is bisexual, what are more critical are the nonsexual components of marriage—the partners' level of communication, common purpose, mutual respectfulness, and the shared intimacy that they have created with each other. The relative ego strength and personal life satisfaction of each partner is a factor, and this includes how mature and autonomous each partner was before they met and married. Other factors that have a large bearing on whether the marriage continues are religious affiliation, past or present, the presence of children, whether there is a specific third party (the husband has met another man), whether or not the wife knows about this relationship or even knows anything about her husband's bisexuality, and their status or position in the community in which they live and work.

Therapists who treat divorcing couples where the man is coming out need to be cognizant of and respectful of the fact that there are many unconscious determinants that characterize marriage. This knowledge affords therapists a richer appreciation and understanding of why the two individuals have been attracted to each other and how they came to be married in the first place. Criticizing the man for "using" his wife to try to overcome his unacceptable homosexual feelings or condemning the woman for assuming she might "cure" him of his homosexuality by marrying him is not only inappropriate but naive and simplistic. In many of these couples, both individuals have had a host of unconscious needs satisfied by their relationship (Hatterer, 1974) despite the realization that other needs have been frustrated. It is not unusual for the marital crisis precipitated by the man's coming out to become the inciting and motivating force for both him and his wife to embark on constructive, and often long overdue, individual psychotherapy.

Marriages in which the husband is bisexual are far from monolithic, and when these couples come for help, therapists must guard against making stereotyped or premature conclusions about their viability. One must not underestimate the degree of complementarity in these marriages despite the surface manifestations of tension and unhappiness. The exquisite bonding of the two individuals plus their attachment behaviors with each other often account for the rather protracted process of emotional and physical separation if they conclude that their marriage cannot work and they must divorce. Those bisexual husbands who are very heterosocial and who have few if any gay friends will be quite isolated and may not separate that quickly or that comfortably because they have little support. On the other hand, those bisexual husbands who are more homosocial than heterosocial may leave their marriages fairly quickly. It is often their wives who are more isolated because not only are they the ones who are left behind and feel bereft, but they may not have a good support group of friends and family who can fully appreciate the unique features of this type of marital disruption.

For some bisexual married men, especially those men who married before the gay liberation movement of the late 1960s and 1970s, and for many bisexual men who are fathers, the coming-out process may take a number of years. Further, this process is not always a straightforward and linear one. These men may come out a bit, so to speak, then return to "the closet" for a period of years. Their evolution as a gay person within marriage is a progressive one, but it is highly affected by many of the variables I mentioned above (homosexual urgency, religion, having met another man, and so forth). How complicated this can be is illustrated in the following vignette from my practice:

Mr. B, a 40-year-old accountant, was referred to me in 1975 by his family physician. His complaint was: "I'm in love with another man; I think I'm finally coming out, and I'm scared stiff." Mr. B had been married for 14 years and had two daughters aged 12 and 9. His wife was also an accountant. Mr. B described his marriage as "pleasant and functional," but that it had become strained recently because of his involvement with Tom, the man he was in love with. They had met a year earlier through a service organization where each had volunteered his time and skills. Tom was a graduate student in political science at the local university. Mr. B had nothing but excitement for his relationship with Tom: "I've never been so happy in all my life. I've never experienced such sexual and emotional fulfillment. This is what I've been waiting for all my life. It's like a dream come true."

Mr. B's homosexual feelings dated back to before puberty. He had his first homosexual experience in high school and many more while at the university. He met his wife there and told her on their first date that he thought he was gay. However, because they enjoyed each other so much, and because their own sexual relationship was fairly frequent and mutually satisfying, neither of them worried much about Mr. B's homosexual desires. They got married a year later, and it was not until Mrs. B became pregnant in their second year of marriage that Mr. B had any further homosexual contact. From then, until meeting Tom many years later, he engaged in furtive and casual sexual encounters very rarely, usually in a gay bathhouse when out of town on business. The subject never came up at home until several months after Mr. B had met Tom. Mrs. B confronted him about being out so much and for withdrawing so much at home. He told her all about Tom. They had begun to discuss separation and divorce with a mutual decision that Mr. B would move out into his own apartment and pursue his relation-

ship with Tom. As the months went on, Mr. B made no effort to find an apartment, and he became more withdrawn and depressed; Mrs. B urged her husband to speak to their family doctor about a referral to a psychiatrist. It was at that point that Mr. B came to see me.

I actually found Mr. B quite depressed when I assessed him and wanted to prescribe an antidepressant as well as to begin psychotherapy. However, he declined, and we began a long course of psychotherapy of weekly visits for over a year. I also met Mrs. B alone on a couple of visits and together with Mr. B a couple of times. Mr. B's relationship with Tom continued intensively for about another year and then gradually evolved into a friendship when Tom moved to another city for his doctorate studies. Over the years, Mr. B has rented three different apartments for several months at a time, but he has never separated from his wife and daughters. He has stayed overnight once in a while in his apartment, mostly alone but occasionally with a sexual partner. He continues to have sporadic sex with men, but more rarely and more cautiously since AIDS. He and his wife continue to have a sexual relationship together. It is infrequent but satisfying to both of them. Mr. B continues to profess that he will eventually leave his marriage and live alone. He argues that he has too many responsibilities as a husband and father to do that yet. He feels that he deserves this and at the time of the anticipated separation will have earned his right to live out his remaining years as a "free gay man." I see him for a visit or two about every 12 to 18 months at his request. He attends a monthly support group for married bisexual men and formerly married gay men that he enjoys and finds helpful.

Pre-Divorce Decision Period

Earlier in this book I referred to the work of Kressel and Deutsch (1977) on the various stages of divorce and described the pre-divorce decision period. This is a critical stage in all divorces, but it is especially so when homosexuality is one of the contributing factors. This stage may take a very long time to negotiate as the man alternately accepts and rejects his homosexuality. While he does this over a period of months (or years, in some cases), he alternately accepts and rejects the "option" of divorce. I have found that many married men who are in the process of coming out tend to deny the magnitude of the changes occurring within them and how much they are pulling away from their wives and the marriage itself. After years of suppressing or repressing their homosexual feelings, or years of infrequent homosexual behavior, they now become much more absorbed and preoccupied with themselves as they come to a more comfortable level of self-acceptance. Most of these men have underestimated how egocentric they've become and how alienated and resentful their wives feel. At this juncture, the men may begin to bargain with themselves and their wives that separation is not necessary, that it is unhealthy and wrong, that it is not inevitable. They argue that it is possible to be actively gay and to remain married.

Couples are commonly referred for marital or separation therapy at this point, or each of them may seek individual treatment. This is usually because their marriage has become very tense and punctuated with arguing and fighting, or the marriage has become lifeless and depressing. Often both individuals are symptomatic and welcome the support and guidance of a therapist. Anxiety symptoms, panic attacks, alcohol and drug abuse, and depression are common findings in married men who are coming out but are not yet separated. They describe a subjective sense of "being stuck," "sitting on the fence," and "spinning my wheels." Their wives may also feel depressed but for different reasons. They feel rejected, hurt, abandoned, and bereaved. Their self-esteem has been dealt a severe blow as well as their inner sense of sexual attractiveness and desirability as women. Further, if they have come to accept that separation must occur, then they will be ready to get on with it. They will resent their husbands' ambivalence or resistance to it, or they will be angry at themselves for not being more assertive in "pushing" their husbands out or in moving out themselves.

For many married men who are coming out, the "gay world" or the "gay life style" is alternately appealing and frightening. It is especially intimidating for men who have been married a long time, who are quite heterosocially ensconced in their residential and occupational communities, and who have very few gay friends, acquaintances, or colleagues. They feel isolated and scared. Many fear that they have a great deal to lose, especially the structure, predictability, and social acceptance of heterosexual marriage. Embracing separation, divorce, and gayness feels risky, a gamble. One of my patients, known for his wry humor, put it this way: "Am I crazy or what? Who gives up marriage with all its social strokes for the gay life? And in the middle of the AIDS crisis, no less? I'd rather be sky-diving, thank you!"

Some men wax and wane with respect to their own degree of homophobia (their attitudes and feelings about homosexuality, gay people, and gay values, norms, and customs). Some will make scathing and prejudicial remarks and statements about gay people or certain types of gay people. Therapists should make careful note of these in order to fully understand. Do these statements reflect simple ignorance and naiveté about homosexuality in our society? Are they statements that reflect severe internal homophobia and self-hatred in the man himself? Is he actually quite depressed about himself and his situation? Could he be suicidal? Or psychotic? Finally, is he just testing the therapist to see if the therapist is homophobic or homophilic or gay himself/herself?

Like many married individuals who are confronting the possibility of separation, the bisexual man who is coming out may be extramaritally involved with someone else. Their relationship may be intense and powerful (as many new relationships are), and the married man may find this man kind, caring, and supportive. However, he may at the same time be quite anxious about this outside relationship in that he is forced to face some serious decision making. He may fear a loss of control and struggles with the man having a hold over him. He may also be intermittently mistrustful and feels or fears that he is being seduced. Some of the variables that color the nature and intensity of the outside relationship are: Is the other man unattached and available or already in another relationship? If he is in another relationship, is this with another man or another woman? If with another woman, is he married or a father? How much is he already "out" as a gay man? Is he exclusively homosexual or bisexual himself? How much heterosexual experience has he had? Has he ever been in a committed heterosexual relationship or marriage? As a general rule, if this man has himself been married at one time, he will have a greater ability to empathize with the apprehension and ambivalence that the other man feels about ending his marriage and coming out.

In the early stages of the married man's beginning an outside relationship with another man, he may have no intention whatsoever of telling his wife. This will be so especially if his wife has no foreknowledge of her husband's bisexuality. He may be taking a "wait-and-see" attitude toward the outside relationship to see if it intensifies and grows in commitment and depth or peters out as "just a sexual thing" or "infatuation." He may also be trying to deny the relationship's seriousness to himself. By not telling his wife, he can deny his bisexuality in part, and he can certainly deny having to face a marital crisis and possible marital disruption. Many men enter therapy at this point. They rehearse in their minds the scenario of their wives' finding out about the other man, or they try to imagine themselves sitting down with their wives and telling them openly and honestly about the other man. Some men conclude that they cannot and will not tell their wives, at least at this point in their coming-out process. They elect to leave their marriages for "no specific reason" or advance vague rationalizations about "finding themselves" or "doing their own thing." Although these types of separations are not common, I have treated a few men over the years who leave their marriages like this. I have also treated a few newly separated women whose husbands have abruptly left them under mysterious circumstances with no plausible explanation. These women are usually devastated and left with nothing concrete, only their fantasies, in their attempts to make sense of it all.

In addition to debating whether or how to tell his wife, the married man who is coming out also begins to contemplate how to tell his family members, especially his parents and siblings, as well as his friends and possibly some of his associates at work. It is not unusual for gay men and lesbian women to be selectively "out"; that is, they make a conscious and rational decision to self-disclose to certain individuals only. This varies from individual to individual and depends a lot on many factors—one's overall degree of openness with others, one's perception of how much relatives and friends want to know, one's ethnic and religious origins and affiliation, one's occupation and the degree of acceptance of homosexuality by its members, and so forth. What is most important is the degree of mutual respectfulness that individuals grant each other about self-disclosure of homosexuality. Here is an example of relationship distress that was in part the result of misunderstandings about "coming-out concerns" (Myers, 1988b, pp. 107–108).

Tim and Frank, physicians in their 30s, had been together for 6 years. Tim had been married before, and he defined himself as having come out toward the end of his marriage when he met Frank. He disclosed his homosexuality to his wife, and after several months of pain and unhappiness for both of them, they separated and divorced. By this time, he had told his parents, siblings, and many friends and work associates about his homosexuality.

Frank on the other hand was very closeted. He had never discussed his homosexuality with his parents, who lived in another city. He had no brothers or sisters. He was very private in his personal and social life, and he preferred to keep this totally separate from his work life. In fact, to insure this, he deliberately accepted a salaried position in an adjacent community to which he commuted daily. Before he met Tim, he was friendly with only three people, a gay man and a lesbian couple; the four of them formed a tight group and did many things socially.

One of the reasons Tim and Frank began to fight with each other was that they had become polarized on the coming-out issue. Neither could understand the other's position; each felt hurt, controlled, and stonewalled by the other. When Frank's parents came to stay with them, Tim hated playing the charade that they were roommates with separate bedrooms. When Tim's parents visited, Frank felt that Tim deliberately tried to "embarrass" him by calling him "sweetheart" or attempting to hold his hand in their presence. Although he knew that Tim's parents accepted and loved the two of them, Frank continued to feel self-conscious and formal when they were around.

I want to mention, and emphasize, how anxious the married man is when he seeks therapy at this point in his coming-out process. He often feels shame and embarrassment about his situation—perhaps because of the homosexuality, perhaps because he is married and "unfaithful," or both. Consequently, he will anticipate and fear being judged by his therapist. And there may be a therapist-gender factor here as well. He may feel that a male therapist will not accept his struggle with homosexuality but will "understand" his infidelity, whereas a woman therapist will understand and be sympathetic about his homosexuality but will disapprove of his infidelity.

Another fear that these men have when they enter therapy is that the therapist will conclude immediately that he is gay and that he just needs to come to terms with it. This fear is not altogether irrational. Some married men who are coming out are literally told this in the first visit. Their inner distress, which is often substantial, is grossly underestimated by the therapist, and they are made to feel that they are wasting the therapist's time. This only increases the profusion of guilt that they already feel and enhances the isolation and loneliness that has been there for so long. Married bisexual men already tend to feel like misfits ("I don't fit in in the straight world, and I don't feel I fit in in the gay world either"); they don't need this feeling reinforced by their therapists. When these married men reside in large urban centers with many openly acknowledged gay therapists, they may deliberately avoid a gay therapist. They fear that they will be told that they are gay, and this will only make them more anxious. Some are also afraid they will be made to feel guilty for not being more gay-affirmative and more politically oriented. "I'd rather take my chances with someone who's a complete unknown" were the words of one married bisexual man, a lawyer, whom I saw in consultation recently.

When the married bisexual man elects to tell his wife that he is involved with another man, or she finds out and confronts him, there is always a period of marital crisis that ensues. Despite the intense emotions (of anger, hurt, sorrow, and guilt) that accompany this time, there are usually two other phenomena that occur—relief and discussion. The husband feels relief that his secret is finally out in the open, and his wife feels some relief that her husband's mood or behavioral change in the previous few weeks or months now makes sense to her. A lot of discussion usually occurs over the next few days or weeks because both parties feel a strong need to talk and to reconnect with each other. Their ability to talk frankly and honestly with each other, and whether they are able to resolve some of the issues together through discussion, are important qualities that render them amenable to couple therapy, which they may request at this point. The outcome of this marital therapy is dependent on many factors, especially the seriousness and emotional investment in the extramarital relationship, the urgency of the man's need for homosexual expression (both sexually and psychologically), and his wife's tenacity and resolve to preserve the marriage regardless of its shortcomings for her. Both the husband and wife may go into a "holding pattern" mode and let some time pass as they busy themselves with their daily lives and responsibilities.

What are some of the other issues for couples when the husband is coming out and his wife is now aware of what's happening? Most important is that both individuals are mourning what once was in the marriage. They mourn the happy times of their courtship, and, depending on how long they have been together, they will mourn the early years of their marriage and the easier, carefree times together. If they have children, they will mourn their planning, the pregnancies, the births, and the early years of their being parents together. They will each begin to mourn the hopes and dreams they have had about their future lives together—watching their children grow up, working less hard, retiring, traveling, and growing old together. Commonly they are at different stages of mourning: he has already done a lot of grieving some months earlier as he began to change and feel disillusioned with or charadelike in his marriage; his wife, however, may not have mourned at all, in that she has had no reason to do so—she thought things were fine. I have heard many of these women describe their inner-feeling state with a statement like: "A part of me has died; I can't explain the tremendous loss I feel inside."

Another feeling that the man who is coming out may have is a feeling of exhilaration and emancipation. He may not feel sad at all the way his wife does. Nor does he feel angry or emotionally "ripped off" as she feels. Despite the guilt he feels about hurting his wife, he simultaneously may feel unfettered, not from his marriage bonds but from his own oppressive self-hate. By way of contrast, his wife now feels oppressed and isolated. She needs to talk and share her "secret" with others but feels handicapped in having to be restricted and selective regarding whom she tells.

Divorcing Period: Childless Gay Men

The decision to divorce is not always a mutual one despite the fact that many individuals approaching separation will say that it is a shared decision. Usually, one of them is the initiator who all along has wanted to separate more than the other. Because the initiator often feels guilty or responsible for upsetting whatever marital equilibrium has been in existence, that person tends to want the partner to come to accept the decision to divorce as well. He/she may try to argue the unhappiness of their lives together versus the possible merits of divorce. He/she may cajole or coerce the partner into agreeing to separate by making life so miserable together that being apart is welcomed, not feared. Whatever is the couple's style and way of doing things together, the decision to actually separate may take several weeks, months, or years. Both may go backwards and forwards on this axis of whether to separate or not because usually both are ambivalent about it. When one is clear and decisive, the other is uncertain, and vice versa.

Some couples, but I think these are in the minority, separate on a trial basis only, with the option of getting back together after a few months of living apart. (By trial separation I am referring to a *conscious* and mutual decision to experiment with living apart to see what happens. I am not talking about the many couples who separate where one or both partners has an *unconscious* hope or wish that they will reconcile after a period of living apart.) During the period of separation, it is expected that the man will pursue "the gay life" or his extramarital relationship with the other man, if he is in one at the time of separating. His wife's willingness to accept and to agree to this depends a lot on how much she still loves her husband, how much she's come to accept the seriousness of their marital problem (Is she in part denying the intensity of her husband's homosexual interest? Is he partly denying this as well, thereby inflating her hopes of reconciliation?), how much compromise she is able to live with in marriage, and how determined she is to preserve the marriage, no matter what the costs. One of the challenges for therapists who work with these women is to sort out with them how much of their commitment to their husbands is healthy and will be adaptive over time and how much is personally unhealthy, maladaptive, and ultimately self-defeating. Women in the latter category require an affirming and empowering form of therapy because of their underlying poor self-esteem and sense of unworthiness as women.

Once the decision to separate is made, or once the separation is underway, the individuals may or may not decide to tell their respective families of origin about the reason(s) for living apart. Some families already know or suspect that something has not been right for some time; the actual separation then merely confirms what they have been wondering about, or fearing, for a while. Some couples give no details in the early weeks or months, especially if they themselves are unsure as to whether they might get back together or not. In some marriages, only the wife's family is told about the reasons for the separation in the early weeks. This may be because she is overwhelmed and needs to talk, especially if she has enjoyed a close, open, and supportive relationship all along with her family. However, some women who are not ready to fully disclose the marital circumstances will say there is "another woman," not "another man," in the early weeks in response to parents' queries. Her husband may not have quite as close a relationship with his family, or he may not be ready to come out to them. By not telling them, he is able to avoid an extremely difficult conversation.

News of their son's gayness and his leaving the marriage because he is coming out is very difficult for parents (and parents-in-law). They mourn too (Myers, 1982). They must accept their son's divorce as well as the loss of many of the hopes and dreams they had anticipated for him and their daughter-in-law such as starting a family, continuing the family name by having a son, giving them joy and pride as "a decent and normal couple." The degree of the parents' initial homophobia and their ability to change over time will greatly color their ability to come to terms with their son's divorce, his homosexuality, and how he leads his life as a gay man. After an initial period of shock, outrage, and sorrow, many parents are able to come around to a healthy level of adapting, including an acceptance of their son's new male partner if, or when, he is involved with someone. The parents may blame themselves, especially the mothers, for their son's gayness. Counseling can be very helpful for those parents who request it.

A word about the parents-in-law. They can benefit from brief counseling too, for a very specific reason. Normally when couples divorce, a high percentage of the sons-in-law continue some sort of relationship after an initial period of adjustment on both sides. Both the ex-sons-in-law and ex-parents-in-law seem to enjoy and welcome this continued and mutually respectful relationship. Even when they rarely see each other or only exchange greeting cards at holiday times or birthdays, there is satisfaction in the affirmation and security that they have had a significant history together in the family. By way of contrast, I have heard many couples whose son-in-law has come out as a gay man and left their daughter describe a specific type of mourning because they will never, ever have any sort of relationship with their son-in-law again. Initially, they may not want anything to do with him—they are furious, angry at him for hurting their daughter, and angry at him for upsetting them. They may also be disgusted with him or worried about his mental health. Or they may feel sorry for his parents. As time passes, though, and they feel better, and their daughter moves on into new relationships, they will miss him, especially if they had quite a positive relationship with him from the onset, and if it had been fairly lengthy. In most cases, the gay man himself also misses his ex-parents-in-law, but because he knows he has hurt them or that they have been angry and disappointed in him, he is not likely to contact them. Nor they him.

Returning now to the couples themselves, what happens next when the man who is coming out and his wife actually separate? Although they each begin to make lives of their own (in actuality, many couples have begun to do this long before they physically separate), many remain, or certainly attempt to remain, good friends. They may arrange to get together on a fairly regular basis and attempt to be mutually supportive as they each adjust. This will depend a lot on how much hurt and anger one or both feel and the degree of synchronism in their feeling states. Their ongoing relationship may be easier if they're both sad or both happy.

Many divorcing wives of men who are coming out enter therapy, or remain in therapy, at the point of separation or shortly after. She may want professional help in dealing with the loss of her marriage, the insult to her femininity, or the insult to her sexual attractiveness or desirability as a woman. This will depend a lot on how she felt about herself prior to meeting her husband, that is, whether or not she had a fairly good level of self-worth that's been slowly eroded by her husband's lack of sexual interest in her or whether she was fairly unsure of herself before meeting him and never received adequate support and nurturance of this in the marriage. Other issues that she may want to work on in therapy include concerns that she has about her judgment in choosing men (especially

if there is a pattern here of her forming relationships that are ultimately self-defeating), fears of never meeting another man like her
husband, personality-wise (especially if she was initially drawn to
his sensitivity, kindness, and his not exploiting her sexually), and,
connected with this, fears of never having children, especially if
they had been planning to have children together, and she is concerned about her "biological clock."

As I mentioned earlier, the man who is leaving his marriage because he is coming out may or may not have met another man already. If he has, they may immediately begin living together, or the
man may take his own place and live on his own as he explores the
relationship further. They may or may not last as a couple once the
man has separated from his wife and has begun a period of adjustment to being on his own. Many newly separated gay men are anxious and eager to explore the gay life; they are not interested in a
serious, committed relationship coming on the heels of marriage.
Although his male friend may understand this, it is only partial acceptance. He may feel a lot of hurt, anger, and rejection if their relationship ends.

Many men who are separating from their wives and coming out
at the same time will either enter therapy at this point or remain in
therapy once the decision to separate has been made. Some marital
therapists do not continue individual therapy or do separation therapy with people once they decide to separate. I strongly urge those
therapists to encourage their patients to continue therapy by beginning to see someone else. In fact, it helps when the marital therapist can facilitate the transfer of his/her patients to other therapists
for ongoing work. This is especially indicated for couples such as
those I've been describing because both of them can usually benefit
from the support of a therapist in the early weeks and months of
being apart. Also, both have matters they may want to be working
at in therapy.

What are some of the issues for a newly separated man who is
coming out as a gay man in our society? He may miss the structure,
predictability, and the approval of his family and society. There
may be fantasied or real loss of people who have been important to
him over the years of his marriage: the friends and acquaintances
that he and his wife have made, the extended family on his wife's
side, and colleagues at work. No matter how much he has tried to
prepare himself for the disapproval and rejection by people whom
he has known, it will be difficult to face and to accept. At times, he
may have periods of self-hate and regret that he embarked on this
course in the first place (as if it were entirely a deliberate, con-

scious, and impulsive exercise!), and he will long to be back with his wife when things were better and happy. Like many separated and divorcing people, he will struggle with feelings of failure, guilt, and fears about the future. Many men will also begin to mourn their potential paternity, the fact that they will never be fathers. Regardless of how ambivalent this feeling or desire has been, they will need to talk about it, for it is a common life-stage issue for many gay and bisexual men, regardless of whether they have ever been married or been in a relationship with a woman. It may be less of an issue for those men who have found a compromise solution for their nurturant and paternal needs—if they have nieces and nephews that they are close to, if they are involved with a gay father, or if they work directly with children as teachers, child-care workers, and so forth as closeted gay men.

Another issue for those men involves their finding a comfortable position for themselves in relation to their family of origin. Some men who are not close with their families will not disclose the details of why their marriage ended, at least in the early stages. And they will ask their wives to respect this too. However, most men will be candid about their coming out and what happens after that will depend a lot on many factors: how their families react, how much they want to know, how much the man himself wants to say, how much they are used to communicating at an open and frank level in a particular family, and, most important, what transpires with the passage of time. Therapists can be extremely helpful in assisting the man as he explores his relationship with his family and their relationship with him. The therapist's objectivity, professional neutrality, and sensitivity to the family dynamics will be of great help to the man in the midst of this emotional minefield as he ponders about whom to tell, when to tell, when not to tell, and so forth.

Coming out is a process, and an evolution, of increasing self-definition and self-acceptance for the man in relation to the world around him. This is another area he may want to work on in therapy, and it is an area where he can derive benefit from the therapist's permission and guidance. The man may have reservations about coming out to certain individuals or in certain situations, as opposed to having no reservations about coming out completely or "going public" (Lee, 1977). It is important to remember that each man's journey in coming out is unique and idiosyncratic—the man must be comfortable within himself as to how much he reveals to others. Some men who remain fairly closeted because of personal, family, or professional concerns may feel guilty about this (that they are not advancing the cause of gay liberation or that they are disappointing their politically active gay brothers). Many men will feel better just ventilating these feelings in the neutral context of the therapist's office.

Another issue for men who have left their wives and are coming out centers around their exploration of a specific aspect of the "gay world," the bar or club scene. For most men, except those who were quite involved with a lot of gay people before or during marriage, this is quite a new experience. It is also an experience about which they may be quite ambivalent. There may be a mixture of feelings: excitement, fear, enthusiasm, disappointment, attraction, repulsion, comfort, discomfort, euphoria, and sadness. Like newly separated men in general, they may feel "over the hill" and "out of it" in the singles scene, but with an added twist: they aren't used to the rules of the game and the idea of men "coming on" to them. Some men will experience a series of brief, and largely sexual, relationships (although this has changed considerably in the last few years since AIDS) during the early months of separation, become disillusioned, and leave that life style behind them as unfulfilling. At this point, the desire to be in a serious, committed relationship is more prominent, or they wish just to be on their own with the company of their friends.

The separated man who is seriously involved with another man whom he met before separating or shortly after may have a different set of concerns that he brings to therapy. One concern is his need to come to terms with his marriage ending at the same time experiencing and working on his new relationship. A second concern may be a push–pull type of dynamic that is occurring between him and his new partner. This may be rooted in his mixed feelings about becoming intimately involved with someone so quickly after his marriage and his defenses against this. It may also be a result of his internal homophobia, especially his feelings of anxiety and self-loathing about loving, and being sexual with, another man. A third and not uncommon concern is communication difficulty in his relationship with this man. He may find that they, as two men, communicate very differently than he communicated with his wife in their marriage. His communication style has developed in a heterosexual context over the years; he may find that what worked before no longer is effective. Faulty and puzzling communication leads to frustration and misunderstandings that can lead to anger, despondency, distancing, and sexual dysfunction.

If these concerns become quite serious, I begin to discuss couple treatment with my patient at this point. I usually do this myself, but if my patient, or his partner, prefers to start afresh with a completely new therapist, then I do what I can to suggest a different therapist and try to facilitate the transfer. A couple approach, which is usually conjoint, enables each of them to talk about his personal and interpersonal frustrations with the relationship and helps to make their respective positions clearer to each other. Both need to know that their feelings are legitimate and perfectly understandable and that they are not deliberately trying to hurt or disappoint the other. They also both need to know that the timing of their relationship is responsible for a lot of their tension, that one of them may not really be ready for such an intense or serious relationship. They also need to be helped to respect their differences about their self-acceptance as gay men. Usually the newly separated man is still quite undecided or unsure of himself, regardless of how much his partner thinks he's gay and "just needs to get on with it." In fact, the partner needs to be helped to not push this and needs to realize that his forcefulness may be based in a feeling of anxiety and self-doubt that the relationship won't work out, that the man will leave him, that the man might even return to his wife.

Divorcing Period: Gay Fathers

When a married man who is coming out is also a father, the separation and divorcing period are generally more complicated. The pre-divorce decision period usually takes longer too, because these men, and their wives, often feel a lot of ambivalence about separating. It is not unusual for the man to actively fight the homosexual feelings and behavior that are happening to him, no matter how intense or compelling. Likewise, his wife will also fight against the painful reality of what is happening to her husband, to herself as his wife, and to their family. Neither wants to believe it.

When a man does reach the point that he has decided to leave his marriage, or must leave his marriage, statements like the following are not uncommon: "Despite the guilt that I feel for my marriage ending, I feel that I've finally come home." Or: "I can't explain the comfort, the joy, the ease I feel when I'm with a group of gay men. They know my struggle, my pain, that inner sense of loneliness and isolation for being different, that I've been fighting all my life. It's a feeling of recognition, of knowing, without having to say a word. And there's a nice sense of solidarity, that we're all in this together."

Although the ages of the man's children may be significant in shaping the process of how he and his wife may separate, age itself is highly fluid. Some bisexual men separate when their wives are pregnant or when their children are very young. The precipitating factors might include the man's anxiety about expectant or actual fatherhood and its attendant degree of responsibility clashing with an inner disequilibrium about his sexual orientation; the man may feel emotionally neglected by his wife because of her focused attention on the pregnancy or the children and becomes vulnerable to having his emotional and sexual needs met outside the marriage; the man may already be in the early stages of coming out, his marriage is beginning to deteriorate, and his wife becomes pregnant "accidentally" or in an unconscious attempt on both their parts to deny what is happening to them individually and as a couple.

There are many gay fathers of young children who make a conscious and deliberate attempt to suppress their homosexual feelings and behavior in order to keep the marriage going until the children are older and are leaving home or have left home. These men may do this entirely on their own if they have never talked about their gayness with their wives or if their wives have never suspected anything. However, in most couples that I see in my practice, the man's wife knows about her husband's homosexuality, and they embark on this plan together. Usually they have had some type of marital crisis sparked by his exploring his homosexuality or by his having an affair with another man. They may or may not have separated and reconciled over this crisis that has now brought the two of them to the point of trying to preserve the marriage and sense of family at all costs. This will work for some couples but not for all. One or both of the individuals cannot live with the marriage relationship as it is, and as the months or years pass by, they decide to separate.

What are some of the issues here that color the man's, and his wife's, attitudes and feelings about divorce? First, no unhappily married father wants to put his kids through a divorce. It is therefore natural and normal for him to deny his gayness or its urgency in his life or for him to avoid thinking about it or its ramifications for him and his family. Therefore, to "fence-sit" and do nothing is both adaptive and to be expected. Second, all men who are married parents and who are coming out are very sensitive to the stigma of homosexuality in our society. They have lived with this for many years; they don't want to put their kids through this additional stress if they can avoid it in any way. *Ergo*, their plan not to say anything until their kids are older and "may be better able to understand" or "not be traumatized" or "not hate me for it." Third, these men are very afraid of losing their kids, both formally and legally (that is, that they will be denied any form of custody, access, or paternal rights) as well as informally (that is, that their children will reject and disown them). Understandably, a gay father who is considering divorce may have a lot of fear that his wife's hurt and anger toward him may lead to bitterness and retaliation. If he would like joint custody, he fears she wouldn't even consider it but would automatically file for, and be granted, sole custody. He may fear that she will forbid access all together or grant only restricted access so that he can see the children but never at his own residence or in conjunction with his partner or gay friends. Finally, if he has a son or sons, he may also fear that she'll be wary about his ongoing father–son relationship and limit their contact. Worse yet, if their marital relationship has become extremely hostile, the man will fear that she'll manufacture an allegation of sexual abuse against him.

Regarding the issue of gay fathers openly discussing their homosexuality with their children, I have seen a range of situations from complete self-disclosure at one extreme to complete secretiveness at the other. Some fathers assume, perhaps correctly, that their children know they are gay, but their preference is not to discuss it openly with them. As a general rule, those fathers who are most closely involved in their children's lives, especially those in joint custody arrangements, have discussed their gayness, once again depending on the age of the children. The men who are the most secretive often have the most internalized homophobia or are in the very early stages of coming out. Some of these men open up to their children down the road a little.

There are some clinical situations in which I encourage my divorcing gay-father patients to tell their children about their sexual orientation. The most common is the situation in which the man's estranged wife cannot stand covering up for him or making excuses for him or frankly lying to the children anymore. Also common is the situation in which the man suspects that his estranged wife has told the children but because he is not speaking to her, he doesn't know for sure. Or he suspects that the children may have overheard her talking about his gayness to her friends or family. In some cases, the children begin to act out when around their father, or they refuse his affection, or they refuse to visit him at his home because they are living with a lot of ambiguity about their father. Telling the children therefore becomes essential.

I suggest to the man that he be frank and candid and gear his statements and language to a level that is appropriate to their ages and psychological sophistication. When he has more than one child he should also spend time speaking to each of them alone, because their psychological needs will vary. The children must be reassured of their father's continuing presence and involvement in their lives. He can also expect that his teenage children, especially his sons, may have more difficulty with his sexual orientation than younger siblings. They may be angrier and more confused about it. The door must be left open for continued dialogue as the weeks and months pass.

Good therapy is imperative here and throughout the entire divorcing process. Ideally, it is best if both the man and his estranged wife receive individual therapy, either with the same therapist (concurrent therapy) or with different therapists who keep in touch with each other (collaborative therapy). Conjoint visits to discuss coparenting matters may also be helpful as well as one or more family visits. The children may benefit from counseling, too, for them to be able to talk about and to ask questions about their having a gay father and living with a social, and sometimes family, secret. If they have concerns about becoming gay themselves, they need a place where they can talk about these concerns, especially because they may have misconceptions about the complex determinants of homosexuality.

It is especially critical for therapists to assess carefully the mood of the divorcing gay father because if he is quite depressed, he will be pathologically guilty, dysfunctional as a worker and parent, and perhaps suicidal. Even less severely depressed gay fathers may be so racked with guilt and self-loathing that they will forfeit their rights to their children and will not have the strength and inner resources to fight for what is fair and equitable as a contemporary and caring father. For the same reasons, they may avoid seeking legal counsel or be in no condition to properly and effectively advise their attorneys as to their wishes.

At the opposite end of the spectrum is the bisexual man who leaves his wife and children either quickly or in an impulsive manner. This man is neglectful of his wife and children and does not appear to have any sensitivity to their needs whether they be physical, emotional, or financial. His actions are highly egocentric and reflect his immaturity, if he is quite young or delayed in his psychosocial and psychosexual development, or they may reflect a character defect or disorder. In the latter case, there were usually signs of his self-centeredness and insensitivity to others long before he married, became a father, and began to come out. These men rarely request to see their children, or if they do, they may not always follow through or keep their word. Their coming out may take an explosive, intense, and all-consuming form as they plunge into the "gay life" totally and completely. In this process, at least in the early weeks and months, they may also reject and ignore their family of origin as well as the heterosexual friends they have established over the years and since marriage. Some of this neglect is because of their excitement and relief at coming out, finally, but some may be the result of their not yet being fully comfortable with being gay. They anticipate, sometimes correctly but also erroneously, that their family relations and heterosexual friends will not accept them and approve of their being gay. So they avoid them until more time passes.

When these men come for treatment, they can benefit not just from the therapist's empathy for the dilemmas of coming out but also from the therapist's inquiring about their fathering. For those men who are simply underestimating the importance of their continued and ongoing relationship with their children, both for the mental health of their children and their own mental health, the therapist's guidance and suggestions will be very beneficial. For those men who really don't seem to care, or who don't wish to continue a relationship with their children, the therapist's efforts will not be well received. These same men usually don't pay child support either, and they are best managed via family court and new legislation in some areas to prosecute fathers who are delinquent in their payments.

Divorce and AIDS

For some unfortunate men and their wives, AIDS is the precipitant of their marital crisis and their marital demise. Suddenly the bisexual man must face his homosexuality and its ramifications for his family at the same time that he must confront the severity of his illness and the inevitability of his death. If his wife knew nothing of her husband's bisexuality, then she must come to terms with that, his having led a "double life," his infidelity, and now the reality of losing him through divorce, death, or both. The children also have to come to terms with their dad's homosexuality and his impending death. Needless to say, the stresses for the immediate family alone, to say nothing about the extended families, are phenomenal, and the losses are too catastrophic to even begin to consider. I can think of no other type of marital or divorce situation where the individuals are as symptomatic, or are at risk of being symptomatic, as this one. The psychiatric imperative of having mental health services available and in place for early diagnosis and treatment is especially urgent at this time.

Apart from AIDS itself, bisexual married men who are healthy but fear they might be antibody-positive to the HIV virus may be in crisis whether to have the test or not. They may assume that they are antibody-positive and automatically begin to avoid having sex with their wives. Men who are in the process of coming out and separating from their wives at the same time, and who also test positive for antibodies, may become quite depressed. Some of these men have committed suicide without ever telling their wives the results of the test or that they even had it done. Estranged wives of bisexual men are not only fearful that they may have become infected with the virus themselves but are beginning to seek damages for "AIDS phobia" (Dullea, 1987). There are other legal ramifications of AIDS and divorce: some women are hiring private detectives to investigate their husband's behavior (whether bisexual or not) to see if they are possibly at risk for exposure; there is a return to fault finding in this era of "no-fault" divorce; some wives of men who have AIDS are being counseled against divorcing their husbands because their 50–50 settlement will be much less than their inheritance when he dies. The implications then for therapists who work with these men, or their wives, during the period of separation and divorce are self-evident. There is an enormous amount of work to be done.

Conclusion

My mission in this chapter has been to describe and discuss the unique and complex dynamics of divorce when the homosexual man is in the process of "coming out." These are a smattering only; I have not talked about situations where there are many other variables that are operative, such as the man's age and stage of life, his racial, ethnic, and cultural group, his religious affiliation, his occupation, and so forth. Many of these factors provide the rich and idiosyncratic context in which these couples separate and divorce. I have merely touched on the gay father's relationship with his children. Let me turn now to a more detailed and more general discussion about divorced fathers and their children.

CHAPTER 10

Divorced Fathers and Their Children

An Open Letter from a Father

"I am a father. I am likely going to be 'shafted' in the destructive process of adversarial divorce. The process should be outlawed because it pits parents against each other when they should be working together to protect the most important relationship in the marriage: the children's relationship with their parents. Usually in a contested divorce, the child–mother relationship emerges intact, and the child–father one is destroyed. Yes, I know there are irresponsible men out there, but the good men are being treated unfairly by a process designed to punish and hurt rather than heal.

"I made a mistake 5½ years ago. I married a woman I did not know for very long. I was young and not ready to marry. It was not all my fault. She knew me no better. She was as young and insecure as I was and not ready to marry.

"One of us had to grow up, and it would have been ideal if we had arrived at that point mutually, but I got there first. The biggest factor in my decision to leave was my children—our two sons. I left her in order to save our sons from the fate of growing up with a depressed father and a resentful mother: two good people trapped and miserable in a rotting marriage. I felt terrible knowing that my children regularly fell asleep to the sad lullaby of 'marital disputes.' And this was their Mummy and Daddy. I wondered what kind of lessons they were learning about love between a man and woman. Certainly not the lesson I learned as a child nurtured in a happy home.

"She is no more an evil person than I am. We chose to marry each other and build a family together, but our marriage was sick from the beginning because we were incompatible. I was naive enough to keep trying through 5 years and two children. We both admitted to each other a while back that had we chosen to live common-law we would have split up within months of our union. I began to question the vows I had made as I watched my sons getting bigger. 'For richer for poorer, in sickness and in health.' Where in that contract did we agree to destroy our children's mental health, to subject them to bitterness, perpetual conflict, silent, tense dinnertimes?

"I lost my faith. I realized there are greater goods than marriage for its own sake. I realized the children would be better off if their Mummy and Daddy were apart.

"I chose the lesser of the two evils: to add my children to the now majority that grow up in 'restructured' families rather than to condemn them to a sick upbringing in a 'castrated' family. I reassured my wife that I would carry my share of the financial burden if she chose to keep the children. I offered to take our sons to live with me if she resented the 'life style compromise' that they would afford. But she laughed in my face and engaged a lawyer. And so our family unit, already suffering, was plunged from the purgatory of our marriage into the hell of our divorce.

"Now I feel like a wrongfully prosecuted man, except for me, it's 'guilty until proven guilty.' I am persecuted by a total stranger who is employed to portray me in the most negative sense possible, to interrupt my work with such nuisances as registered letters and legal threats. My wife calls me worse names than she did when we were together. She is correct only when she calls me angry. I am angry because I am treated unfairly in this system. I am only a man who is trying to preserve some sanity in his sons' upbringing, and admittedly in his own life too, but I am being portrayed as some kind of monster. When in my wife's presence my anger comes to the surface, she undoubtedly goes to her diary and jots down my words. She keeps a log of how many minutes a week I spend with my sons. Whatever I do or say can be used against me. She tells me about all the divorce settlements that women have won over the years. She smugly lectures me on how I have abandoned my sons. Apparently lawyers call this a circus, but this is an awful circus that no child should ever experience.

"My wife knows she can take full custody of our sons now, and I say that's unfair because for the children, their father's role is reduced from one involving input into their education, their discipline, their destiny to that of a friendly babysitter, a kindly old eunuch, who participates in their upbringing as a passive observer. Contested divorce is not, as other legal proceedings are, a win/lose game. It is a situation where everyone (at least the children and the father) loses. Shouldn't it be win/win for all? So here the divorcing father lies, prostrate before society, awaiting what amounts to buggery by court order. To the woman I loved before she chose to become my adversary, I say:

"I give up. I let go. Take my sons. Since you are mentally competent, and you are a woman, you get them. Take my money. Since I am the 'wrongdoer' you'll surely get some of it. Please be decent and use it sensibly on our children. Take everything. I am sick of this hell. But I want you to know you can never take my fatherhood from me. Your sons will always be my sons too. One day they will seek me, and I will become their friend as well. All I ever intended was to be a good husband and father. You may claim I have failed as a husband, but I believe that as a father, the most responsible decision I could make under these circumstances was to let go. I know you will be a good mother to our sons. You, like me and our sons, are just another pawn in this stupid process of contested divorce. I wish you well. Now please take what you want and leave me in peace.

"To my sons I say in anguish:

"I regret deeply that I have deprived you of the physical presence of your father, but I am always with you in spirit and I must hope that 'one day you will understand.' I feel good that you will always have each other. It was in your interest that I let your mother 'win' rather than prolong this ridiculous conflict. She will now dominate your lives until you are men. When you reach manhood, should you chose to marry, do it more carefully than I did, or don't do it at all. Should you one day become fathers, my wish is that the system will treat you and your children better than it treats us now.

"So, my boys, be good, do what your mother says, and stay out of trouble. Know that wherever you are, wherever I am, I'll come when you need me as your grandfather, my father, always came when I needed him. I love you both dearly, now and always. I am your father."

The above letter was written by one of my patients, Alan, in August 1987, and it is quoted here verbatim with his permission.

Alan had first come to see me 3 years earlier for depression, something that he had been struggling with off and on for years. It was really his wife, Barb, who pushed the psychiatric consultation because she was finding Alan increasingly difficult around the house. He was irritable, withdrawn, and barely assisting her with the care of their 2-year-old son, Jason. Barb was also concerned at the way Alan became impatient and sharp with Jason. His temper would flare, he would make harsh statements to her and Jason, and, on a couple of occasions, Alan had struck her. Barb's other concern was that Alan's attention to his studies had slipped (he was a law student); he was missing classes and not doing much homework. Indeed, Alan admitted to all of the above, plus a lack of energy, trouble concentrating, and an increased need for sleep. Once I was able to convince Alan of his need for an antidepressant (there was a three-generational history of depression and suicide), he took one and responded dramatically. In a conjoint visit, Barb expressed happiness and relief about Alan's improved mood and behavior around the home. She found Alan more involved as a husband and father, their sex life had improved, and neither she nor Alan was worried about their marriage. He stopped his medication after 2 months.

I did not hear from Alan or Barb for about 6 months. Then Alan called to let me know that the two of them had "mutually" decided to separate. This was in response to marital tension, bickering, and fighting. They felt that they each needed a "cooling-off" period. I had individual visits with each of them during their separation. They began spending increasing amounts of time together, both as a couple and as a family. This resulted in their reconciling after 3 months, with agreement and enthusiasm on each of their parts. Alan did not have to resume taking his antidepressant.

Six months before the letter quoted above, Alan returned to see me. He was calm and controlled. He told me that he had left Barb a couple of weeks earlier and was living on his own. They now had a second child, another son, William, 4 months of age. Alan argued that he no longer loved Barb and mused whether he had ever loved her. He told me that he was separating to preserve his own sanity, that of his children, and ultimately Barb's. I was very concerned about his judgment and feared that he was mildly hypomanic. He refused medication but agreed to careful monitoring of his mood by me during those early weeks of separation. I interviewed Barb within a few days. She was very ambivalent about the separation and angry. Not only did she feel abandoned by Alan, but she felt overwhelmed bearing full responsibility—emotionally and physically—for their sons. Alan was calling infrequently and not seeing his sons on a regular basis. He very quickly met another woman and began spending a lot of time with her. Barb began bracing herself for divorce and unassisted single parenthood. It was with this sentiment that she sought legal counsel. By the time that Alan wrote the impassioned letter that I have quoted, he was much less disorganized in his behavior and thinking, he was less emotionally labile, he was more adjusted to being on his own, and he was more interested in becoming an involved father. Barb, however, remained very mistrustful of his statements and actions and she had grave reservations about his credibility. His support payments were erratic and less than Barb expected. Alan argued that he was doing his best.

This is some of the background to Alan's letter. He became quite depressed about 6 months into his separation and restarted his antidepressant; I also referred him to a hospital day care program. This meant that he had less income for about 4 months and had severe financial worries. This context dictated both Barb's and Alan's actions and feelings.

How men father, and what they expect of themselves as fathers, has changed enormously over the past 15 to 20 years. Many men have moved away from an exclusive and traditional role of breadwinner and authority figure (the instrumental role defined by Parsons, 1954) to a more nurturant and more actively engaged paternal role. The resurgence of feminism in the late 1960s and the revolutionary sex-role changes of the 1970s have resulted in a large body of scholarship on men in general and fathers in particular. Because so many men are actively involved in family planning, are more sophisticated about birth control, are attending prenatal classes and are present in the delivery room, and are participating in the actual care of and decision making about their children, it is not surprising that contemporary fathers are deeply affected when their marriages are threatened by divorce. Between 1970 and 1979, the numbers of single fathers increased by 65% because of separation and divorce (U.S. Bureau of the Census, 1980), but despite this enormous increase, single fathers remain subject to misunderstanding, discrimination, and stereotypes by the legal and helping professions (Robinson & Barret, 1986, p. 87).

Most contemporary fathers will describe themselves as functioning very differently than their own fathers. What they expect of themselves, and what is expected of them, are very different than a generation ago. Research has also shown that the father–child relationship is extremely important and emphasizes that for biological and social reasons, "most children have two parents—one of either sex" (Lamb, 1979, p. 938). As I have stated earlier in this book, when marital separation occurs, the mental health of the children and their father are interconnected. Their further personality growth and development are highly dependent on their continued relationship with their father, as his emotional adjustment to separation and divorce are dependent on this same relationship. It is essential, then, that we mental health professionals do as much as possible to preserve and protect the father–child relationship when divorce occurs and remain on guard for outdated, inappropriate, and prejudicial thinking and actions in our patients, other professionals, and ourselves.

I have also mentioned earlier that one cannot always predict the nature (both qualitatively and quantitatively) of the father–child relationship after divorce by the nature of the father–child relationship before the divorce. In other words, some actively involved and highly engaged fathers do not maintain this behavior after divorce. This is especially so in the early weeks or months of separation, when the father may be mourning (he is withdrawn, dysfunctional, and hardly seeing anyone) or, less charitably, when the father may be in a highly charged and egocentric state, going out a lot, and is totally preoccupied with satisfying his own emotional and sexual needs. Many of these men do come around, after several months, to resuming an active and involved fathering relationship with their children. There are also many men who, prior to divorce, were not particularly invested in a participatory or nurturing relationship with their children. However, after divorce, they evolve into model fathers. Sometimes this is simply the result of maturing and "growing into" their role as fathers; other times, it is because they are "reborn" or emancipated from a highly constricted, demoralized, or pathological marriage where neither partner was functioning at his/her best as a parent.

The father–child relationship before and after divorce is also sensitive to a couple of other variables—the ages of the children and their father at the point of separation and the respective life stages that they are all experiencing (Erikson, 1963; Levinson, 1978). For example, if the child is a baby and the father is in his early or mid-20s when the separation occurs, he may not have the maturity, knowledge, or experience to forge out a father–child relationship. This is especially so because the baby mainly needs caretaking—feeding, diaper changing, receptive stimulation, and protection. These activities and tasks are not as interesting for fathers as participatory activities that fathers can do with toddlers or school-aged children, such as reading stories to them, playing games and sports, or teaching some type of skill or lesson. Similarly, if the child is an adolescent and the father is in his 40s when the separation begins, there may be a lot of personal dynamics on each of their parts that affect and determine how they are together. The adolescent may be experiencing tremendous upheaval and turmoil (pushing for more independence, experimenting with drugs and sex, beginning to slip academically, and so forth) at the same time that his/her father is very busy career building, is having difficulty aging and accepting his limitations, or is in the midst of a new relationship with a younger woman. In situations like this, the father–child relationship is often severely threatened and strained: both parties are in a state of disequilibrium. They don't get enough time together, and when they do, it is tense and unpleasant. Thus, each of them has difficulty fully appreciating what the other is experiencing.

The Relationship between the Divorcing Partners

The father–child relationship is highly affected by the relationship between the man and the woman who are separating. This is particularly so in the weeks and months before separation and the early weeks, months, or years after they separate. How the husband and wife, or the divorcing husband and his wife, feel about each other and their relationship to each other highly affects their co-parenting relationship. After they do separate, this may be blurred, either positively or negatively, by how they felt about each other before they separated. Those individuals who can put their own relationship with each other aside, for better or for worse, and who can respect each other as parents are fortunate. They recognize and respect that they each have an important and unique role to play in the care and development of their children. They further acknowledge that they are people with equal rights as parents to their children, and they do their best to protect this tenet as they implement change and evolve into a divorced family.

However, separation and divorce when there are children is usually so calamitous that it is hard, if not impossible, for parents to be civil and fair, as much as they would like to be. Their ability to discuss the children and to negotiate with each other about them is largely emotionally determined. And these emotions are powerful and complex. They include anger and bitterness, hurt and fear, and almost always guilt, no matter how attenuated or camouflaged by the other more visible or pressing feelings. Thus, what is critical in framing how the parent–child relationship is defined is how their relationship as a married couple evolves into that of a divorced couple from the time of the pre-divorce decision period through the various stages of divorce. Through this process, both individuals may vary a lot, or a little, on how they parent and how they view and describe the other as a parent.

Because they are each grieving and struggling with loss, the man and the woman will miss whatever earlier ability they had to share the responsibility of the children and the opportunity to have a face-to-face, good faith, and cooperative talk about them. They will hate the frustration of having to accept their ex-spouse's right to a continued relationship with the children, or if they accept this in principle, they may resent the mechanics and inconvenience of its implementation. If they have separated in part because of very different values and expectations, they may have a lot of difficulty respecting each other's life style. In fact, they may feel and believe, somewhat self-righteously, that their own way of living is correct and that the other's is wrong, damaging, or confusing for the children. They wish the other parent would just go away, or, at times of peak dismay, they wish that he/she were dead.

Alice and Tim had been married for 12 years and had two children, Jason aged 5 and Jennifer aged 3 when they separated. One of the contributing factors to their separation was Tim's extramarital involvements with women at work and Alice's hurt and resentment about these. She partly blamed herself for Tim's behavior because she had had two serious post-partum depressions and "wasn't there for him" as well as the fact that she had gained a lot of weight and didn't feel very attractive or interested in sex. She partly blamed Tim for "having no morals." They came for separation therapy toward the end of their marriage, and I assisted them for several months in disengaging and in working out a comfortable and mutually respectful visitation schedule for the children. Alice wanted sole custody, and Tim had no objection to this. I also saw each of them individually for a time for support.

About 1 year after they had separated, there was a crisis, and I scheduled a conjoint visit for the two of them. Alice was threatening not to allow Tim to have the children for overnights at his apartment, overnights that until recently had been uneventful. However, he was now in a new relationship with another woman, Jane, who was beginning to sleep over at his place. The weekend before calling me, Alice had learned from Jason (partly volunteered, partly questioned, I think) that on Sunday morning the two children had crawled into bed with their father and Jane to watch cartoons. Alice said that Tim and Jane were naked. "It's typical of him—he's amoral—he'll bring home any

*trollop he meets and expose her, without batting an eye, to my chil-
dren." Tim's reply was that they were not naked, that he was wearing
underwear and that Jane was wearing a nightie, and that she was not
a trollop but "my girlfriend." He then counterattacked with: "Stop lay-
ing your uptight, Bible-thumping, and hypocritical religious trip on
me, and my children" (Alice had recently become a born-again Chris-
tian.) I was able to help them work out a compromise: Alice would
continue to allow the children to spend overnights at Tim's, provided
that he and Jane keep their bedroom door closed and that the TV be
moved into the living room. Tim also offered that he and Jane would
get fully dressed in the mornings before interacting with the children.*

By way of contrast, there are many divorcing or divorced couples who strive to work out as best as they possibly can a relationship with each other that enables them to get together as a group
from time to time. They have come to accept that they will not get
back together and that they are leading separate and independent
lives. They may rarely, if ever, even see each other as a couple, only
as a family. These may be informal and sporadic family outings
that are spontaneous, or they may be structured and formalized
around important holidays such as Christmas or Passover or family
events such as birthdays, graduations, or weddings of the children.
These are experiences that mean a lot to the children and to each of
the parents. As I said earlier, when the man and the woman can
organize and experience these events, they are fortunate and all the
more enriched by the occasion.

The Mental Health of the Mother
during and after Divorce

The dynamics of the father–child relationship will certainly be affected by the mental health of the children's mother throughout the
divorcing period. If their mother is symptomatic (for example, anxious, depressed, suicidal, drinking excessively, or irritable and verbally or physically abusive), the children may feel a lot of anger
toward their father. Regardless of their ages or their capacity to
comprehend all of the reasons for their parents' divorce, they may
totally blame their father for causing their mother's ill health. Or if
they don't exactly feel that he is the sole cause of their mother's
suffering or misfortune, they may still be angry at him for abandoning them to her. In other words, they find themselves subjected to
her wrath and violence, much of which may be displaced aggression

that their mother feels toward their father, and they have become the target of this aggression.

In some divorcing families, one or more of the children may identify with the mother, and they band together, consciously or unconsciously, in a pact. I am referring now to a situation where the husband has been the initiator of the divorce; his wife is against the divorce, and she feels rejected and abandoned. The mother and the child collude together in a mutually supportive way, which in the early stages of divorce is adaptive because they are both hurting and feeling aggrieved. However, if this persists, they can both become stuck in this dyadic position, and neither moves on. The child, especially a female child, does not want to see her father or visit with him because of her resentment toward him. Her mother, because of her own resentment and insecurity, may be unable to foster and promote her daughter's relationship with her father, and she accepts all of her daughter's misgivings and reservations at face value. If this female child is actually a teenager who has been rejected by her boyfriend at about the same time as her parents' divorce, this may complicate matters even more. She and her mother become mutually dependent in their grief and shared resentment toward men, and this may become a problem for months or years to come.

When Mr. S, a 58-year-old businessman, came to see me, he had been separated from his wife of 30 years for 6 months. Although he was having some difficulty in adjusting to being on his own, this was not his major worry. What he was most troubled about was his relationship with his youngest child, his 18-year-old daughter, Marilyn. Basically she was refusing to see him on a one-to-one basis, although she was often present if he went to visit his estranged wife or if they all got together as a family for a birthday or similar occasion. She was the only one living at home with her mother while she attended college. Mr. S's other three children lived on their own (one was married), and he saw them at regular intervals. Mr. S told me that he had made several overtures to Marilyn to get together for a meal, either at a restaurant or at his apartment, but that she often begged off. She made excuses that she was already committed to someone or too busy with studying. A couple of times she had agreed quite enthusiastically to meet him but then called and canceled closer to the date by leaving a message on his answering machine or with his secretary. She never spoke to him directly.

Mr. S told me that his leaving the marriage was "devastating" for his wife and that she was not doing well. He had heard from his 25-

*year-old son that Mrs. S had been quite depressed, was seeing a psychi-
atrist, and was taking an antidepressant. As much as he felt guilty
about this, he also felt relieved to be out of the marriage—he complained that Mrs. S had always been too dependent on him. I could
sense that he harbored a lot of resentment toward her, and he alleged
that she was now controlling Marilyn by being depressed and that she
was undermining his relationship with Marilyn by her actions. He
went on to tell me that he and Marilyn had always had a difficult relationship, often close but often distant. For a long time he had worried about her social skills and relationships with her peers. His words
were insightful: "She's always been a different sort of a kid, almost too
serious about life, never really a child. Of all my children, I think that
she sensed from a very early age that her parents were not happy together. I think she took on the role of family mediator and tried to make
us both happy. What a job for a kid! I'm sure she thinks she's failed
because I've left the family. What can I say to her? These are some of
the things I need to talk to her about. But I don't want to burden her
with our marriage troubles. I want her to start leading her own life."*

*Regarding Mr. S's relationship with Marilyn, I didn't really have a
lot to offer except a supportive ear. I did tell him that as more time
passed, and all parties had more opportunities to heal, Marilyn might
become more responsive to his overtures or, better yet, might initiate
contact herself. He declined my invitation, with his consent, to call his
wife and arrange an individual visit with her. He also did not want me
to contact his ex-wife's psychiatrist regarding any possible collaborative work. Mr. S's work with me ended with no change in his strained
relationship with Marilyn.*

Let me comment further on the mental health of the mother
being an important variable that affects the relationship that the
children have with their father after separation. Even when the
woman is not clinically ill as I've referred to above, there are
separations wherein the newly separated woman has attitudes or
feelings about her husband as a father that are not healthy, appropriate, or accurate. These attitudes may be misconceptions from the
marriage itself or about men in general and how they parent. Commonly they stem from her own background and how her own father
was or wasn't a father to her. These are then perceptions and ideas
that she has brought with her into the marriage, and they have contributed to how she looks on and interacts with her husband. When
a separation occurs, she pulls the children toward her and consciously or unconsciously excludes her estranged husband. This behavior may be partly out of her own anxiety and emptiness causing

her to feel that she needs the presence and comfort of the children, but it may be partly a matriarchal notion that only mothers can parent and that a mother's relationship with the children takes primacy over that of a father. This dynamic may be very confusing for the children because they may feel guilty for having their own positive or affectionate feelings for their father and would like to see him. If their father is passive about seeing them or backs away in response to their mother's attempt to control and dominate the parenting, they will feel rejected by the father and not quite trust their own feelings for him.

Recently, Gardner (1987, p. 67) has described a disturbance in which children are preoccupied with deprecation and criticism of a parent—denigration that is unjustified and/or exaggerated. He calls this disorder the parental alienation syndrome. Although it may be caused by brainwashing (conscious programming) of the child by the opposite parent, there may also be unconscious programming as well as situational factors and direct contributions from the child himself/herself. Gardner's observations are not only helpful in assessing and treating children involved in protracted custody litigation, they are also helpful in assessing and treating divorcing men who have one or more children who "hate" them and refuse to see them.

Some, but not many, divorced women become stuck at some stage of their bereavement. They become chronically despondent and sad about their situation, or they are bitter, resentful, and envious of others, or they develop an array of physical symptoms such as back pain, frequent headaches, "colitis," or frequent virus infections. These women come to be labeled as hypochondriacs or as long-suffering or as martyrs. Their dependency on others, even when they deny it, becomes palpable, and their children grow weary. Indeed, their children have ambivalent feelings—as much as they feel sorry for their mother, they also get angry at her for not moving on with her life. They resent her dependency on them. They may continue to harbor anger at their father for his part in her mental state. Or they may enjoy their relationship with their father, but they cannot share this with their mother because she feels so miserable. They get tired of feeling guilty and for feeling responsible for their mother, especially if they are late adolescents or young adults and still live at home. They want more joy and freedom in their lives, but they may feel very guilty moving out and "abandoning" their mother.

What about the situation in which the father is awarded custody of the children because of mental illness in the mother? Examples from my clinical practice include mothers who are severely and incorrigibly alcoholic or drug dependent, mothers who suffer from schizophrenia or severe mood disorders, and mothers with personality disorders who are unfit to provide adequate and competent care for their children. What is essential here is that the children's relationship with their mother be protected in some way and that the father–child relationship take this into account. In other words, it is important that the custodial fathers not lose sight of the fact that the children and their mother have a right to preserve and continue a relationship with each other, no matter how erratic or limited, provided it is not damaging to either party.

I emphasize this point because of the large numbers of patients I have treated who were not given a clear or satisfactory explanation at the time their parents divorced as to why they could not or would not be seeing their mother. They may resent their father for this, or child-care workers, or other court authorities. Many try to locate their mothers or try to form a belated relationship with their mothers in their adult years. I am not talking about mothers who desert their children here; I am talking about mothers who weren't encouraged to see their children because they might frighten them or upset them. The children's fathers have often taken a similar position; these fathers have tried to spare their sons or daughters from their mother's illness and potential upset. They remarry and strive to create a happy and "normal" family life. Unfortunately, many of these children just end up confused, with many unanswered questions and many unpleasant feelings. Having a healthy or satisfactory relationship with their stepmother isn't enough. It is better that they are given some type of visitation relationship with their mother and that this be monitored in some way over the long term. This grants the children a modicum of control, which is their right, in their relationship with their mother.

Finally, let me mention the situation in which the woman leaves the marriage in order to preserve her sanity. This type of separation includes many women who are battered—both physically battered and psychologically battered. They take their children with them, but it may be disorienting for the children, depending on their ages, to know why they are not seeing their father or why their mother left their father. Explanation helps, but even the most honest or accurate explanation does not always reassure the children that their mother has acted in their best interests. They may still be angry at her for leaving and taking them away from their father. And unfortunately, this anger and antagonism toward their mother will be reinforced if they are having some telephone or physical contact with their father who "works on them" from his perception of events and claims he has been abandoned "for no reason at all." He is sad, he is lonely, he will fight to get them back, and so forth. Although their mother is really mentally well, in fact much healthier than when she was in the marriage, they may not understand this. These children perceive their mother as "sick" or "bad" for breaking up the family, and if she is on pretty shaky ground without psychological support from others, she may be highly influenced by her children's statements, come to doubt her sanity, not trust her judgment, and begin to lose perspective. If she returns to the marriage, the whole cycle repeats itself.

The Mental Health of the Father during and after Divorce

As the dynamics of the father–child relationship are affected by the mental health of the mother throughout the divorcing period, they are also affected by the mental health of the father. If the father is depressed, his ability to parent will be altered, both qualitatively and quantitatively. More specifically, he may be quite withdrawn and self-absorbed, and it may seem, at least on the surface, that he is not interested in seeing the children or doing things with them. In fact, he may be visiting the children less and less often, cutting his visits short, coming late to pick them up, or canceling at the last minute. If there has been a struggle around access or visitation, something that he initially fought hard for, this may have changed; his attorney notes that he seems indifferent now, or apathetic, as to whether or not he obtains more contact with the children. After visits with their father, the children may complain to their mother that the visit was boring, that they didn't do anything with their father, or that they had to fend for themselves regarding meals, bedtime, and so forth. Or they may complain about the disarray of their dad's apartment or that there was no food there or that he seems sad all the time (or, alternatively, that he's angry and moody and yells all the time). Although much of what I have described here occurs in many father–child relationships, I urge the reader to consider a diagnosis of depression when these observations are severe and persistent or if they represent a change in the usual character and functioning of the man.

Another common mental health concern in fathers during the divorcing period is excessive drinking that has a profound impact on how the man relates to his children and how they relate to him.

It is a serious, yet touchy, subject because it is so often denied by the man himself. Of all the male patients whom I have treated during or after their separations who have problems with alcohol, I have seen very few who directly or subjectively complained that they were drinking too much, were worried about this, and wanted to do something about it. Almost always, I have had to ask about it specifically because of other clinical symptoms or signs that have suggested alcohol abuse (tremor, forgetfulness, flushed facies, irritability, and so forth), or I have been alerted to it by their wives or children who are concerned. Many of these men will then admit to excessive drinking and will cooperate with treatment, especially if the drinking is fairly new and clearly related to the stress of marital separation. This is not so, unfortunately, with many severe alcoholics whose alcohol addicition led to the divorce in the first place. Their afflication is so severe and so all-consuming that it matters less to them whether they see their children or not.

Abuse of alcohol by the divorcing man is a common symptom and a frequent complaint of their estranged wives. Mental health professionals are often asked to assist and advise because these women, quite understandably, are often very reluctant to entrust the care of the children to their ex-husband when he's been drinking or has a known drinking problem. We can offer assistance in many ways—by making simple suggestions, by scheduling a conjoint visit with the man and the woman and acting as a mediator for them, and by confronting the man in a gentle yet firm manner and implementing treatment for him alone.

What about men who overwork and do not seem very invested in fathering during the divorcing period? Or what about men who "overdate" during the early weeks or months of separation and are out all the time with many different women? I am reluctant to include these common trends in men in a section on "mental health concerns in fathers" because they are not "mental illnesses," but they are certainly habitual ways that men use to cope with separation and loss. What is most important is that the clinician try to sort out whether these are temporary behaviors, which are largely coping strategies and will recede in time. The man will then return to his former life style that is less egocentric and more engaged in fathering. As I have said earlier, how a man fathers in the long term cannot always be predicted by his conduct just prior to, or immediately after, separating.

In a more general sense, it is wise for the clinician not to jump to conclusions about either parent's ability to parent during the first few months or the first year after separation. There is often enough stress and turmoil in the man's life, the woman's life, and the children's lives to strain the coping ability of all members of the family. It is also wise to remember how much the parents' attachment to each other before separation affects their relationship to each other after separation and their individual relationships to the children. In many separations, the parents can't let go of each other and allow the other to have autonomy and freedom. Or they let go one moment and cling the next. This attachment behavior helps to explain the long period of indecisiveness and ambivalence about separating before people actually do begin to live apart despite being unhappy and tense with each other for some time. It also helps to explain the repetitive cycle of separation–reconciliation–separation that characterizes many couples before their final separation and divorce is underway.

Maureen and Morris were both professionals who came for marital help with what they called "your typical dual-career marriage mess." Maureen stated: "We never see each other, and when we do, all we do is bicker, or we do a dance around each other to avoid bickering." Morris agreed and added: "Like most professionals, we don't spend any time together as a couple on the weekends because we feel guilty that our kids are with the housekeeper all week and that we should be doing just family things on Saturday and Sunday." They had not been away together as a couple for 6 years, since before their children were born. They had not made love in over a year. Their social lives had become quite separate, and they now shared few friends and acquaintances. Each of them had come from homes where their parents had divorced when they were pre-adolescents, and both of them had been married before, briefly. Neither had children from these earlier marriages.

I'll summarize my work with Morris and Maureen, which was complex and memorable. They were much more than "your typical dual-career marriage mess"! After assessing each of them in individual visits and learning about their personal and family dynamics, I embarked on a course of conjoint marital therapy with them. During these visits, Maureen disclosed to Morris that she had been having an "affair" with another woman in her law firm for several months. She couldn't decide whether to remain in the marriage or not. I then began to meet each of them individually and occasionally together. As Maureen pulled further away from Morris, she also pulled away from the children—she began smoking a lot of marijuana, listening to rock music constantly, and spending most of her free time with this other woman, including many overnights. Morris became the primary parent—he cut down on his work hours and gave up virtually all of his

social and athletic activities to be both mother and father to his chil-
dren. After several weeks of this, Maureen moved out and began living
with her woman friend. Things began to stabilize a bit more for Mau-
reen: she gave up marijuana and began to see the children on a regular
and predictable basis, although Morris remained the primary parent. If
anything, he went overboard in a somewhat self-righteous and control-
ling manner, obliquely demeaning Maureen in the process.

Four months after the separation, Maureen began to express many
concerns about Morris's ability to parent. The children did not always
have the attention to grooming and diet he normally provided on week-
ends when his housekeeper was off duty. He was yelling at the children
a lot and had been violent on a couple of occasions. He seemed less
interested in their well-being and less protective of them than before.
Maureen found his speech slurred on a couple of occasions and won-
dered if he had been drinking. Morris denied all of these allegations
and deflected her concerns about him in his visits with me. A few days
later, on a holiday weekend, the police were called to the home by a
neighbor who found Morris standing out in his backyard, in the mid-
dle of the night, naked, shouting and screaming about a Fascist plot to
destroy him and his family. He was taken to a hospital and committed
for involuntary treatment. He was psychotically depressed. Maureen
moved back into the house and took over the care of the children for
several months while Morris was dysfunctional. She remained prima-
rily responsible for the children for about 2 years as Morris regained
his health and increased his visitation time. At that point, they began
a joint-custody arrangement with equal time in each household
(Morris was living alone, and Maureen had resumed living with her
friend), and that was the final decision when they divorced. After sev-
eral months and until my work with them ended, that arrangement
seemed to be working well for all of them.

Custody

Historically, the "tender years" doctrine, that young children
should not be separated from their mothers for fear of damage to
their personality development, dominated divorce and custody proceedings (Robinson & Barret, 1986, p. 87). Consequently, the mother
was favored as the parent most suited for custody. Nowadays, with
many mothers of young children working outside the home, plus
much more research on the significance of the father on child development, custody is not as often automatically awarded to the

mother. The rights of fathers are being emphasized more, and there are now increased numbers of joint-custody families and father-custody families.

When the Man Wants Sole Custody

Clinicians who do a lot of marital and divorce therapy become familiar with many different situations in which the man talks about wanting sole custody. I want to discuss these because there are often powerful and underlying dynamics that drive his wish for having custody of the children. Also, there is an enormous difference between the man who merely *threatens* sole custody when he is anxious or angry, at one end of the spectrum, and the man who is totally obsessed with sole custody, to the point of child-snatching or kidnapping, at the other end of the spectrum. In between somewhere is the man who wants sole custody because he truly believes that he is by far the better parent.

What are some of the underlying forces that shape a man's desire for sole custody? Angry husbands who aren't even separated yet, who don't want to separate but have wives who do, often threaten their wives that they will fight for sole custody. This is usually because they feel abandoned, hurt, and furious at their wives for leaving them. In order to begin to feel better about themselves and regain their self-worth, they have to do something. Threatening sole custody, or even fantasizing about it, helps because they are fighting for their rights as fathers and also getting back at their wives for hurting them at the same time. Some men deny the element of retaliation in their wish for sole custody, but it is very common, especially in sexist men, because they are so outraged at their wives' actions in wanting a divorce.

For some men, the whole idea of being rejected and evicted from one's home, from the family home, when one doesn't even feel unhappy in the marriage or has never even considered separation is beyond comprehension. Their wish for sole custody may be not so much driven by rage and retaliation as by a human wish or need to be with one's children on a regular or daily basis. These men are very aware that their children are extremely important to them and regulate a large measure of their self-functioning, purpose, and reason for living. They can't imagine living on their own, for the most part, and having only visitation rights to their children.

In both of these situations, I am describing men who aren't even separated yet and who clearly don't want the separation. These are men who are still in the very early stages of separation discussions and negotiations. Psychologically, they are just beginning the long process of divorce. Many of the men and their wives settle on some other type of mutually acceptable custody situation many months or years later when they have been able to put more emotional distance between themselves. Their talks are less charged, and they trust each other better.

What about the husband who wants sole custody after he and his wife have already separated, with or without a separation agreement or custody determination in place? Usually there has been something occurring that has upset the equilibrium between the two of them, or their arrangement has been more precariously balanced than they realized. Or, perhaps the husband has reflected further and doesn't like the arrangement. Again, the man's desire for sole custody is commonly driven by anger at his wife or at the situation. He may feel that his estranged wife has too much control over his access to the children. Her definition of "reasonable access" or "generous access" may be out of line with his. He may find the arrangement just too restrictive, both in the number of hours or days per week that he has the children and in the structure of the arrangement (that is, that visits are too rigid or predetermined). He may charge his estranged wife with controlling access in a punitive manner, depending on his behavior *vis-à-vis* the children and whether he's punctual to pick them up, on time with his support payments, whether he fathers "properly" in her eyes, and so forth. He may define himself as the model father and may allege that she is erratic in allowing him access depending on her moods and what is happening in her own personal life that in turn affects how she feels about his seeing the children. Behind this, of course, is the fact that these separated men feel angry and threatened as parents who should have equal rights to their children. This was poignantly expressed in the tearful words of one of my patients, an electrician: "Wouldn't you want sole custody too if someone you hate played malicious games with your heart and soul?"

There is another type of separated man who wants sole custody of his children because he is highly critical of his estranged wife's life style, and he wants to "protect" his children from her and it as much as he can. The intensity of this desire will also vary a great deal depending on the situation, the man's personality, and how far along the two of them are in the separation process. Indeed, in the early weeks and months of separation, when emotions are still quite intense and both parents are sensitive, anxious, and guilty, there is a natural tendency to want to protect the children as much as humanly possible from any more upset than what they have experienced already. This tendency, coupled with a sense of self-righteousness that one's way of parenting is the "only way," the "right way," or the "healthier way," will set the forces in motion to acquire sole custody. For many men, the fantasy of sole custody is also one way of simplifying things, of not having to "deal with" the children's mother, and of getting on with things. Most important, it is also one way of regaining control over one's life, control that has been lost over the weeks and months of preparing for and coming to terms with the separation itself. In general, the more rigid, ordered, perfectionistic, and controlled the man is, the more he fantasizes that sole custody is the only way to raise the children. This need for closure is sometimes related to the common fantasy that many separated people have and that makes some of them feel guilty—the wish that the other parent were dead. "Raising the children would be so much easier" epitomizes the sentiment.

There are common "life-style" complaints that men have about their estranged or ex-wives, some of which are rooted in the man's need for control, as described above, some of which are related to his still loving her and feeling jealous and resentful, and some of which are related to his personal ethics and moral conservatism. He may be upset that his estranged wife has a boyfriend and that this man monopolizes a lot of her time, time that (he feels) she should spend exclusively with the children. He may also have concerns about whether this other man sleeps overnight with his former wife and the impact of this on the children. Indeed, if the boyfriend is there a lot and spends a lot of time with the children, the father may feel quite upset because he fears that his role of father is being usurped, especially if he doesn't see his children nearly as often himself. The father may also feel quite threatened, and jealous, if or when his children describe the many one-on-one activities, events, or trips that they share with their "other dad"—experiences that he is not granted the contact time for or experiences that he cannot afford financially anyway.

Some separated men complain that their estranged wives do not spend enough time with the children. They do not like the fact that their wives are working outside the home, even if it is a financial necessity, or complain that their wives are working too many days or hours per week. A separated man may begrudge his wife any leisure time to go out with her friends for recreation. He may feel the children are with babysitters too much. He may complain that she parties too much or that she's seeing too many different men.

Some separated men want sole custody if, or when, they learn that their estranged wife is now in a relationship with another woman—that she is "coming out" or has already "come out" as a lesbian mother. They are threatened by this and fear the children will be damaged psychologically. More specifically, they fear that the children will be confused about their own sexual orientation, or that they will become preferentially gay or lesbian by modeling and identification, or worse yet, that the estranged wife and her partner may deliberately and consciously "mold" them into gay individuals. Although research on lesbian mothers has demonstrated that their children are not at greater risk for psychiatric disorder or for homosexuality than the general population (Green, 1978; Kirkpatrick, Smith, & Roy, 1981), this is not always reassuring to men and fathers who are in this situation. And even when these men are themselves quite liberal and psychologically enlightened, they are still subject to prevailing homophobic attitudes of the extended family, friends, acquaintances, judges, and society at large.

These are only a few of the "life-style" concerns that separated men may have about their former wives that contribute to their wanting sole custody. These concerns border on and merge with concerns that some men have that their wives are mentally unfit and are unable to provide healthy, adequate, and safe care for the children. If there has been a history of psychiatric illness in the woman, especially one of the more handicapping illnesses such as schizophrenia, bipolar affective disorder, or major affective disorder, her husband, fearing a recurrence of the disorder, may be more apt to want sole custody. If the woman abuses alcohol or drugs and her husband does not, he may also want sole custody on the grounds that she is unfit to look after the children. If his former wife has been violent or abusive in other ways to the children, the man may want sole custody; or he may want split custody, if the conflict just lies with one or some of the children. He will take them, and his wife will have custody of the remaining child or children. There are also, of course, some divorces in which the mother does not want custody; she is happy and relieved for her husband to have sole custody.

To conclude, there are many situations in which a man wants sole custody of his children and talks about this in therapy. Sometimes this is a mature, carefully considered, and pure desire to have sole responsibility for his children, but many times the man's desire for sole custody is ephemeral and contaminated by residual emotions from the separation proper. It behooves the clinician to try to sort out the reasons for this wish with his patient so that the man can proceed with legal deliberations when indicated or simply make alterations in the present arrangement when that is the best course to take.

When the Man Wants Joint Custody

Joint or shared custody has become increasingly common in divorce over the past 10 to 15 years, and there is now a significant body of research on this subject (Abarbanel, 1979; Greif, 1979; Steinman, 1981). One of the benefits of joint custody is that the father's right to decision making and equity of control over the lives of his children is protected. His rights are protected even if the children do not spend an equal amount of time in his home but spend more than 50% of their time with their mother. Fathers who have joint custody have more involvement with their children, and this is of benefit for both them and their children. They feel and express a greater measure of self-satisfaction as a parent and a greater degree of attachment and bonding to their children.

The man who wants joint custody, then, is usually a man who has been quite actively involved as a father long before the separation began. Even if he has not been that actively involved in day-to-day activities and child care, he may still want joint custody if he defines himself as a man with equal rights to his children and a man whose responsibility to his children equals that of his wife. The ages of the children are important here too; if the separation occurs during the pregnancy or when the children are babies or toddlers, the man may still want joint custody because he has envisioned himself as spending equal, or almost equal, amounts of time with the children.

Joint custody is most commonly a middle- or upper-class phenomenon. It is costly to have two separate homes for children as well as duplicates of many items of clothing, toys, games, and sports equipment. It also requires a fair amount of job flexibility for the period of time that one has primary responsibility for the children. This is easiest for parents who are self-employed or who have understanding employers or who only need to work on a part-time basis. Joint custody also requires a certain amount of mutual respectfulness of the former spouse's ability and right to be a parent and a good ability to communicate with each other about the children. Judges expect this when the two parents request joint custody. Those women who are working outside the home, whether this is largely out of economic necessity or because they have careers, are generally more interested in joint custody. Their marriages are already established along more egalitarian lines, with shared child-care duties and activities, and they wish to preserve this. They do not want, nor do they feel it is fair to have, complete and full responsibility for the children.

Having said all of this, there are other men who want joint custody despite the fact that they have only been peripherally involved in the lives of their children. In general, these are men who do not trust their former wives' agreement or ability to grant them reasonable access to the children; they fear or sense too much control on their wives' part, and they therefore begin to want joint custody to protect their rights as fathers. They do not want their wives dictating to them after the divorce, and in some cases, this perceived dynamic has contributed to their leaving their marriages in the first place. Unlike men who want sole custody, these men highly respect their wives as mothers of their children, and in many cases, they do describe their wives as the primary parent. Therefore, they do not want to disrupt the relationship that their wives have with the children in any way.

In this type of deteriorating marriage and beginning separation, the woman may find it a joke, or an outrage, that her husband would like joint custody with her. She may describe him in quite unflattering terms—as hopeless, inadequate, and unrealistic in thinking that he can manage the children 50% of the time. She may also feel that he'll burn himself out, that he's too busy and work-oriented, if not self-centered, to put some of this aside to assume primary responsibility for the children half the time. These concerns and sharp comments by the man's wife, which smack of sexism and female chauvinism, are not always a result of her bitterness or feelings of intimidation about the impending separation. They may in part stem from what has happened to the family dynamics in the last several months or years of the marriage. More specifically, as the marital communication and intimacy has eroded and waned, she has turned more inward *into* the family to bond more tightly to the children at the same time that her husband has turned more *away* from the family, into his work, outside interests, new friends, or other women.

Mr. A, an accountant, was referred to me by his family physician for depression. He was already taking an antidepressant by the time we had our first appointment, and he remarked that he felt a lot better. He attributed his depression to being very unhappy in his marriage and to the pressure of having a serious and surreptitious relationship with an-

other woman. He felt that he needed to come to a decision about his marriage and queried whether marital therapy might help. He was reluctant to leave his wife because he didn't want to hurt her. He also didn't want to put their three children through a divorce. Because he and his wife had been virtually leading separate lives for about 5 years, and because he was so seriously in love with the other woman, I told him that I didn't think marital therapy would help. Further, he was unable to really make a commitment to work at his marriage at that point. Mr. A preferred not to make further appointments but to leave the door open.

Months passed and Mr. A returned. He and his wife had attempted marital counseling with their pastor, but Mr. A refused to continue after three visits. He had told his wife about the other woman, and he had attempted to end the relationship with her before starting marital counseling. Mr. A began seeing this woman again after 1 week. By the time Mr. A came back to see me, he had found an apartment and was moving out of his home in a week. He had tried to discuss joint custody with his wife, and she was adamantly against it. She told him that she thought joint custody was a form of exploitation of children and that the children would remain with her and not be dislodged. She told him that they were upset enough already with his "shenanigans" and that she would decide when and if they wanted to see him. Needless to say, Mr. A was tremendously upset about his wife's attitude to custody and statements about him. When I asked him further about joint custody, it emerged that what he really wanted was protection of his relationship with his children. He had not really thought the matter through from the standpoint of his three children living with him half the time. Indeed, he thought that would be impossible anyway given the number of hours he worked and the amount of unexpected travel in his job.

I suggested that I meet with Mrs. A, and Mr. A was quite happy about that. She was quite interested in coming in to meet with me. She acknowledged that she was very hurt and very angry at her husband. She knew that her feelings were affecting her judgment of him and that they were getting in the way of his relationship to the children. She knew that she had no right to deprive the children of their father, and him of them. What she was more alarmed about was how neglectful he had been during the past year or so toward the children. She was aware that the children had been pulling away from him because of their hurt and angry feelings toward him. She hoped that with the separation his fathering would improve, and she stated that she would do her best not to undermine his efforts by providing structure and predictability from her end. Despite her own sadness and anger about the divorce, she was

*able to smile at one point and say: "I hate to admit it, but he really
is . . . or was . . . an excellent father."*

Kolata (1988), citing the results of a new study by Wallerstein
at the Center for the Family in Transition, in California, has noted
that joint custody may not always be beneficial for the children
and, in some cases, may be detrimental. In amicable divorces, there
was no difference in the child's development between joint or
single-parent custody. In bitter divorces, joint custody appeared to
be worse for the child than single-parent custody. What was more
important than the actual custody arrangements were (1) the quality of contact with caring adults, (2) the age and sex of the child,
with boys and younger children having more psychological difficulty, (3) parental psychological functioning, with anxiety or depression on either parent's part contributing to problems with the
child, and (4) ongoing conflict between the parents, whatever the
custody arrangement. Wallerstein warns that the conclusions of this
study reflect only the first 2 years after divorce; they cannot predict
how a child might fare beyond that at this point.

When the Man Wants His Ex-Wife
to Have Sole Custody

When a man wants his wife to have sole custody of their children,
this may mean that he simply trusts and respects her regarding
their care, well-being, and authority. If their marriage has functioned along very traditional lines with his role being that of financial provider and her role being that of caretaker, he may be quite
happy being the noncustodial parent. He may quite willingly and
dutifully pay alimony to her, when indicated, and child support to
her in amounts that they collectively, or the courts, determine as
adequate. He sees the children regularly, and both he and his ex-
wife are happy with the frequency of the visits and the quality of
the relationship that he maintains with the children. In short, their
post-divorce relationship is a cooperative one, and they respect each
other's ongoing parental roles and behavior.

Unfortunately, there are many other men who want their wives
to have sole custody for less noble reasons. These are men who do
not assume or accept equal responsibility for their children, either
by contributing financially to their care or by getting involved psychologically in their upbringing. At the risk of sounding moralistic
and judgmental about some fathers and defensive and apologetic

about others, I must comment that these men really are a mixed bag. Some are clearly irresponsible, self-centered, and guilt-free. They father children with no regard for their welfare or their future. They expect the state or their ex-wives to bear the responsibility for the children after separation and often before separation. In fact, as this is occurring, they have often moved on in their personal lives; they may be already in a new relationship and have started another family.

Other men define themselves as involved financially and emotionally with their children, but their self-definition of being a responsible father by no means meets societal contemporary standards. In other words, despite their means, they really do not pay much in the way of child support, or they pay the bare minimum, and they do not give much of their time to their children. Often they have moved on too, into a new marriage and a new family, which appears happy and economically comfortable. Their ex-wives, and children from the first marriage, have a much more difficult time financially and psychologically, and they may harbor a lot of resentment about that. These men in turn are often very defensive and self-righteous about how well they have provided for their ex-wives and children, and they resent the bitterness that characterizes the attitude of their ex-wives and children.

Another group of men underestimates the importance of their continued involvement as fathers after divorce. That is, these men are uninvolved not because they don't care but because they don't realize how important they are to their children. If they grew up with a distant father or with no father, they may not have much understanding or experience with what fathers can and should do with their children. These men may be able to step up their contact time with their children by both education (about fathering) and supportive encouragement. Because remaining involved with their children and paying child support often go hand in hand, these men may also respond to external pressure to keep up their child support payments by legal enforcement from one jurisdiction to the next or one state to the next.

Recent research by Isaacs (1988) of 103 separated mother-custody families has shown that stability in the visiting arrangement is more important than the frequency of the father's visits. Children who had a visitation schedule in the first year and still have one in the third year after separation have fewer behavioral problems. The more hostile the parents were toward each other in the first year, the less likely they were to have a predictable visitation schedule, and therefore intervention by clinicians early in the divorcing process is particularly critical. By working with each of the parents, the therapist can assist them in setting up and maintaining a regular visitation schedule.

Finally, there is another group of men who want their wives to have sole custody because they cannot bear equal responsibility, either financially or emotionally, for their children. Many of these men are simply inadequate. They have never been able to be very independent in their functioning or very self-supporting. They may be chronically and intermittently dependent on others. Some have a long history of medical or social problems. Some have a long history of psychiatric illness, which may have been in remission when they married but has recurred during the marriage or during the divorce. They may have enormous difficulty just remaining well themselves; they rely on their ex-wives to be strong and to raise the children as best as they can—a very tall order indeed, especially when their ex-wives also have some type of handicap, perhaps less severe and manifest but all the while significant.

When His Ex-Wife Cohabits or Remarries

The relationship that a separated or divorced man has with his children may be affected when his estranged or ex-wife begins living with another man or remarries. His self-image and sense of inner security as a father to his children may become threatened by this kind of development. He may feel pushed aside, usurped, or thwarted in his ongoing relationship with his children. For some men, their attitude of antagonism and hostility toward the other man may be merely the surface manifestation of underlying feelings of inferiority and inadequacy compared to him. I am referring now to situations in which this new man is "superior" in the divorced father's mind: he may have more money, a better job, more education, more status, or be younger, better looking, and so forth.

These feelings of anxiety or dejection or inadequacy may be even greater if the man still loves his wife and has retained hopes of a reconciliation at some point in the future. Even when the man has accepted that the marriage is over and that he and his wife will never reconcile, the boundaries between the relationship that he has with his children and the relationship that he has with his former wife are blurred. He may still love his wife in many ways, and he has carved out with her a comfortable level of friendship, a friendship that is inevitably threatened by her involvement with her new partner. If the man and his former wife were accustomed to doing things with the children "as a family" from time to time, these activities or events may also be altered or may end completely. This will be upsetting for him, and he may become competitive with the other man, either to preserve what he has had or to vie for more time; he may request or fight to see his children more often now. This is in contrast to the less assertive father who goes into a state of mourning over what he has had with his former wife and children. He may become despondent, withdrawn, and not see his children until he begins to feel better again.

This changing dynamic when the man's former wife becomes seriously involved with or marries another man is usually hardest for those men who are quite isolated and who have not moved on to establish either a new committed relationship themselves or a support group of friends. It becomes depressing for him to hear about the flurry of activity and sense of family in the "new home" as his perception of what he continues to offer the children pales in comparison. In the early weeks or months, the divorced man's coldness or hostility toward the other man, no matter how much he tries to conceal it, may be easily sensed by the children. Generally they will feel protective and defensive of their father and unwavering in their loyalty. They may take a long time to "warm up" to their stepfather and to get beyond their distrust of and antagonism toward him. And again, if the children had hoped their parents would reconcile, this period will take longer. Eventually, in the best situations, everyone adjusts to the various nuances of their respective relationships with each other.

Finally, some fathers are more specifically alarmed about the possible threat to their established relationship with their son(s), as opposed to their daughter(s), when a stepfather appears on the scene. The reasons vary. Some fathers, although they may deny it, prefer the relationship they have with a son to that which they have with a daughter. In terms of common interests and as a role model for identification, this is gender based. They share activities, outings, and sports together. A "man's man" type of father does not want a stepfather encroaching on the relationship he has with his son. Some fathers, during their own childhoods, have lost the love and guidance from their own fathers, either because they died or they "disappeared" after divorce; therefore, they do not want their own son to experience that loss that they so painfully recall many years later. They may have had a stepfather themselves, whom they hated; this experience has remained with them and now affects their attitude and behavior toward their son's new stepfather. Some fathers, whose own homes were not disrupted by divorce when growing up, may remember a great deal of male sibling rivalry between them and their brothers. Indeed, there may have been a lot of competition between and among the brothers for their father's love. This dynamic has now been sparked and set in motion by another man entering the family system and potentially "taking something away"—his son's love and respect for him as a father.

When the Father Is Overinvolved with His Children

I hesitate to use the word "overinvolved" because it implies judgment. Some people might argue that a father can never by "overinvolved" with his children. What I am referring to is the divorce situation in which the father is very attached to his children and his personal functioning is not possible without them. This may take several forms: he may cling to them and have trouble being physically apart from them; he worries about them constantly and fears harm will befall them; ego boundaries are blurred, and he needs to control them as if they were parts of himself with no autonomy whatsoever; he overindulges them and gratifies their every need so that they develop an omnipotent sense of themselves.

The basis for this kind of fathering may be simply bereavement. The man feels abandoned by his wife and feels alone and lonely. Quite naturally he reaches out to his children for sustenance and companionship. This is common in many wife-initiated divorces and therefore is a normal stage of adjustment and adaptation to the separation. With time, the father begins to reach out more to age-appropriate peers, friends, and other family members. However, there are situations that are not so normal or transitory. In these cases, the father may be psychotic. He binds the children to him because he is psychotically depressed and cannot exist without them. If he perceives a threat to this relationship, he may murder them and then commit suicide. If he becomes paranoid, he may incorporate his children into an elaborate delusional system and come to believe the children are plotting against him, spying on him, and may be harming him. He may believe that his ex-wife is masterminding this and using the children as her agents. Thus, he doesn't want the children to be out of his sight.

There are other divorces in which fathers are overinvolved with their children, and this is a deliberate, conscious, and self-serving maneuver on their parts to compete with their ex-wife for the children's love and loyalty. In a more sinister manner, some fathers systematically attempt to destroy the mother–child relationship by saying things about their ex-wives that are not true. Men with severe personality disorders lie to the children about their mothers. Men who are psychotic taint the children's perceptions of their mothers with their delusions. Tragically, the children grow up with an extremely distorted and confused picture of each parent, and in the process, they become highly anxious and mistrustful themselves.

At the milder end of the spectrum are those fathers who are overinvolved with their children, not so much with the pathological intensity I have described above, but they are overinvolved in duration. In other words, they "hang on" to their children beyond the first few months of separation when they are hurting the most and are the most needy. They appear to be stuck somewhere in the separation process and haven't moved on to meet other people or to make more of a life for themselves. What happens is that the man's daughter, especially if she is an early adolescent (or his son, in some cases), becomes his "wife"—they do a lot of things together, she runs the house, he confides a lot in her, and so forth. Their relationship becomes too close, and it is unhealthy for the child who doesn't progress through the normal developmental stages of life. The daughter takes on too much responsibility for the mental health of her father, and in some homes, there is intergenerational blurring of boundaries and frank role reversal where she comes to parent her father. She may also turn against her mother, whom she blames for rejecting her father. When children are younger, and their fathers are intensely involved with them, this may become quite frightening for the children's mothers. They fear or suspect incest, especially when they have daughters, and allegations of sexual abuse are now becoming more common in divorce proceedings (Hopkins, 1988; Dullea, 1988).

There are another group of fathers who overinvest in parenting because they are angry at their ex-wives, and they disapprove of their mothering or their behavior in general. Examples might include the following situations: the former wife is working full time at a career and has a nanny at home or places the children in day care; the former wife's life style is more liberal or politically left of the man's more conservative and conventional values; the former wife is socializing a lot or is in a new relationship—she is not with the children as much as the man feels she should be; the former wife is in a relationship with another woman, and this is causing the man a lot of anxiety. What ensues is that the man attempts to become the ideal or model father because he has assumed now that he is the better parent. He may do this in a competitive manner with his ex-wife, or he may do it in a self-sacrificing and martyr-like fashion. This endears him to his friends, acquaintances, co-workers, and extended family, who perceive him as the perfect "new age" father. Needless to say, this infuriates his former wife, who not only feels misrepresented as the "neglectful mother" but also feels outraged at his arrogant manipulation of their separation dynamics. His motives may be largely unconscious—he is so shattered and wounded by the separation that he needs all of the love and attention he can get from others in order to feel psychologically replenished, or he is so raging at his former wife for leaving him that this is the only way he can retaliate and destroy her.

The "Guilty Father Syndrome"

In earlier chapters, I have talked about men who struggle with a lot of guilt, especially men who initiate their separations. In the pre-divorce decision period, men who are prone to guilt remain ambivalent about separating for weeks or months, maybe a few years. They feel guilty for no longer loving their wives, and they feel guilty for wanting to leave them. They associate separation and divorce with selfishness and self-indulgence and shirking of one's responsibilities as a man and father. The unhappily married man's guilt, or propensity for guilt, is worsened if his wife will not, or cannot, accept the separation, and one or more of the children are aligned with her. Were it not for therapy, many of these husbands and fathers would remain feeling trapped and miserable in their marriages indefinitely.

One of the most common groups of men who suffer from the guilty father syndrome are professional men in their late 40s or early 50s whose children are now in their late teens or early 20s, and whose marriages have been quite traditional. Their wives have devoted most of their adult years to being a wife, to having and raising the children, and to running the home. These women love their husbands and look forward to having more time with them for leisure, shared activities, and travel. Unfortunately, their husbands do not feel the same way; in fact, they may be growing weary and find their wives and adult children an increasing financial worry or strain as their capacity for work and their ambition for work begin to wane. If the man is considering separation and has met another woman, especially a younger woman, he will vacillate enormously about whether to leave his marriage or not. Should he make the decision to separate after much deliberation and reflection, he will delay all of the various stages of the separation. This is usually because he becomes overwhelmed with waves of anxiety and guilt as the separation progresses. He may feel powerless in the face of his children's demands for his support, either emotionally or financially, because he feels so torn up and guilty inside.

In my therapeutic work with these men, I have been struck with how bottled up they are. Many talk with no one about their feelings; a few do talk with a trusted friend or colleague, especially if that person has also been divorced. I find that very few of them actually talk with their adolescent or adult children about what they're going through, especially how much they have struggled before deciding to separate and how much they are still struggling. These men talk as if any self-disclosure to their children would be burdening them or embroiling them in their parents' conflict; they feel this would be damaging and inappropriate. I am not suggesting that fathers use their children as sounding boards or confidants, but I am suggesting that fathers give their children more information and explanation. This helps the children to make sense of why the separation is occurring and to understand better their father's actions and behavior, which they have often misunderstood and misinterpreted. This lack of information or misinformation often accounts for the way that the children treat their father that he finds so upsetting or confusing when they withdraw and sulk around him, when they are openly angry or defiant toward him, when they refuse to visit him, and so forth. In response to this, he may feel even more guilty, and a vicious cycle is set in motion.

The guilt that a father feels is an extremely powerful determinant of his actions throughout the entire process of divorce. His judgment and decision-making ability are profoundly affected in many instances: when he engages an attorney, and the type of attorney he selects; how he works with and advises his counsel; what type of separation he wants, the actual settlement itself, how much access, and the type of custody arrangement; how comfortable he is living apart and whether he should reconcile or not; whether he should continue to see the other woman (if there is one) or not. Therapists need to monitor the man's guilt carefully to see if it waxes and wanes and to see if it is indeed within the range of normal for most men of his reference group who are going through a divorce. When or if the man's guilt is very severe, unrelenting, or paralyzing, and if there are other changes such as despondency, agitation, a sleep or appetite disturbance, diminished ability to concentrate and to do his work, then he has become clinically depressed and possibly suicidal. He will need more aggressive and specific medical treatment.

Mr. X, a 52-year-old bank manager, came to see me 3 months after he had separated from his wife. He told me that he had a lot of mixed feelings about being separated and wondered: "Is this normal?" He and his wife had been married for 28 years, having met as college students, and they had five children ranging in age from 25 to 15 years old. He said that he had been unhappy in his marriage for many years but that he never considered separation because he was Catholic and because he had always felt that divorce was a selfish act, "great for the parents, cruel for the children." Two years before he left his wife, he met another woman, Mary, and they became "just friends" for many months. They didn't see each other often because she lived and worked in a nearby city. However, they gradually became more intimately, and sexually, involved. Quite naturally, Mr. X was then forced to make a decision; after several months of soul searching, contemplation, and consultation with his parish priest, he decided to leave his marriage.

When I asked Mr. X how his wife and the children were handling the separation, he told me that his wife was a "brick." "She's been very understanding and brave; I know she feels humiliated inside. I'd feel better if she'd get angry at me, or if she hated me, but she doesn't." His children were divided, along age lines, about the separation—the three older children were somewhat detached about it and felt that their parents just had to do what was best for each of them. His oldest son told Mr. X that he was surprised that his father hadn't left 10 years earlier. The 15-year-old and 17-year-old, both girls, were very upset about the separation and were both angry at him. They made frequent excuses not to see him and often canceled scheduled plans they had made to do something with their father. They both admitted to their father that they might have been more "forgiving" if there weren't another woman, "especially someone 15 years younger than Mom."

Mr. X, initially relieved and excited to have made the decision to separate, began to feel increasingly guilty as the weeks and months went by. He was no longer enjoying his relationship with Mary and now felt guilty about that. Ideas of reconciling became increasingly urgent, and he began discussing this with his wife. They went out a couple of times: "the first time it was wonderful; the second time it was horrible." Mary became threatened and worried about this, and she decided to pull back from the relationship. About this time, Mr. X also found it hard to do his work as efficiently and conscientiously as he normally did. He was preoccupied and forgetful; he developed early morning dread and wakefulness. He lost his appetite. He agreed to take an antidepressant, which helped him to begin to cope again. His guilt lessened, and he was able to feel more confident in his decision making. He abandoned his notions of reconciling. After a few weeks, he had a frank and open talk with his teen-age daughters, and they began to warm up to him a bit. Eventually he and his wife divorced.

The Weekend or Sunday Father

The father who sees his children every other weekend, one day on the weekend, or some variation of these has a restricted or limited relationship with his children. The mother has sole custody so that the ultimate authority over the children plus most of the decision making and the actual rearing of the children rest with her. Some fathers prefer their relationship with the children to be this way. They are satisfied with the amount of time they have with their children and with the degree of control and responsibility. Yet many fathers resent this type of arrangement, and in the early weeks and months of separation, they will miss the regular and daily contact that they were accustomed to having with their children. They may ask their former wives for increased visitation privileges, and if thwarted, they may fight for increased time with their children through the courts.

The nature of the father–child relationship is highly affected by how long the man and the woman have been separated; whether the man is dating other women, is involved with someone else, is cohabiting, or is remarried; how resourceful the father is in how he actually spends time with his children; whether he has parents or other extended family in the community wherein he resides; the ages of the children; and so forth. Some men who are weekend fathers describe themselves disparagingly as "good-time Charlies" or "year-round Santa Clauses." They always feel driven to be entertaining the children, to keep them busy, "to always be doing something" as opposed "to doing nothing." They are often aware that they overgratify their children with material things and resent it when the children behave in a "spoiled" manner or talk with an air of entitlement. These men also describe feeling worn out or exhausted at the end of a day, or a weekend, with the children. Sometimes it is because they are not used to it, and sometimes it is because they are so busy running around doing things and trying to cram so many "father–child" activities into such a limited space of time. What in most homes is only *part* of family life becomes the *entire* form of family life when the children are with their father. In general, most mothers of children who have weekend fathers hate this type of arrangement or have mixed feelings. They want the children to have a relationship with their father, and they like the break from the children, but they detest the way their ex-husbands father. They find the children wound up, bratty, or aggressive after a visit with their father, or they worry about how this overindulgence will affect the children over the long term. They may also resent their ex-husband being seen by the children as "the nice guy" and their being seen as "the heavy" who does the mundane day-to-day living with them and all of the disciplining.

Weekend fathers give other reasons for trying so hard with their children. Some feel guilty for leaving the marriage and putting their kids through a divorce; they therefore feel the need to make up for this in some way by either spending high-quality or high-intensity time with them or by indulging them materially. Some fathers feel abandoned, insecure, and unloved; they therefore want their kids to like them and to not be angry or rejecting toward them. Some fathers feel lonely; they create a flurry of activity and events to offset this painful feeling. Some fathers admit that they don't know any other way of parenting, nor do they have male friends who are divorced fathers, or if they do, these men father in the same manner. This applies especially to newly separated fathers of young children who are still finding their way and learning how to parent. Also, many of these men live in small apartments with spare furnishings and few possessions to keep children busy. Thus, they feel obliged to get out with their children because of confined and close quarters, which then leads to eating many of their meals in restaurants and paying for entertainment. When they can afford it, I always urge men patients in situations like this to spend money on furniture and accessories to get their place looking like a home. Doing this with their children is best because then the kids have a say in "their new home." The children can also rest assured that their father has a comfortable place to live in.

When the situation is the polar opposite, children complain and feel unhappy. I am referring to the situation in which the father picks up the children, takes them to his place, but then doesn't do much with them. These kids are bored. They don't want to go to their father's place because there's nothing to do there; they miss their toys, their own rooms, and their friends. They may complain to their mother then about their father, about his apartment, about his cooking. Some of these fathers are in touch with their children's feelings of unhappiness and do not feel defensive about their com-

plaints. These men admit that they do feel isolated and inexperienced as fathers or that they don't feel very creative or energetic in
planning their scheduled time with the children. I like to make concrete suggestions to these men of things they can do *in the home*
with their children like small projects, baking cookies or a cake, or
playing board games. I also suggest they visit their local library
with their children. Some community centers and schools offer
courses on parenting that may interest some separated fathers.

If their father has a new woman friend or wife, the children
may feel pushed aside on their visits with him. They may find that
seeing their father becomes an unpleasant routine or a ritual, and
they are merely "visitors" in their father's new home or new life.
This feeling may be enhanced if their father starts a family with his
new wife or if children from his wife's earlier marriage are living in
the home on a full-time basis. The father–child relationship may
deteriorate quite severely such that they are barely engaged with
each other. The children continue their visits, but they do little
more than sit around watching video after video and eat a lot of
junk food, sometimes in the forced company of stepsiblings whom
they barely know or even like.

Weekend visits with their father are usually better in those divorce situations where the children have grandparents living in the
area. In this way, the man can take his children to his parents'
home, which not only provides some variety in the weekend routine
but more importantly fosters three-generational interaction from
which all parties derive psychological benefit. The added love and
attention are also beneficial for those children whose parents' marriage and divorce has been especially unstable and chaotic. These
vulnerable children need as much unconditional nurturance and
care as they can get, and usually grandparents, being one generation removed, are in the best position to provide this. When there
are no grandparents nearby, there may be an older friend or a
neighbor who functions as a "surrogate" grandparent. Many cities
have "volunteer grandparents," older individuals who love children
and enjoy being visited by them.

The Newly Separated Father Who Is Negligent

What do I mean by negligent? I am referring here to those men who
visit their children only sporadically or barely at all. Commonly
they do not pay their child support payments either. Or they are
delinquent or in arrears. These are the men that so many therapists

hear about through their wives who become patients. When and if these men become patients themselves, they do not tend to talk about their children. They may be spending a lot of time at their jobs and socializing when they are not at work. Their parenting leaves a lot to be desired, and many therapists cannot help but form a negative feeling about these men with regard to their fathering.

As I have mentioned at several points before, this negligence may be only temporary and may end after the man has adjusted somewhat to the separation. His parenting then returns to the level it was earlier, before the separation, or if his parenting had suffered much earlier, then it may reach a level, both qualitatively and quantitatively, where it has never been before. Some of these men become model fathers. Unfortunately, some do not change at all, and the father–child relationship remains a problem and a struggle for years to come.

I have seen many fathers in my practice, especially young fathers, who seem to have what could be best described as a delayed grief reaction. They carry on for several weeks or months after the separation in what appears to be a normal or slightly facilitated state. They are busy and active in their working and personal lives. They have minimal to no contact with their children, to their wives' chagrin. She begins to write her husband off as a selfish and totally hedonistic man who cares for no one other than himself. Then suddenly he begins to call and desperately wants to see the children more often. In fact, he may begin to cling to the children in a somewhat frightening way. It appears to his ex-wife that he can't function without them. He may also begin to talk about reconciliation. He may have a mixture of emotions inside—intense grief, remorse, and guilt—that seem to come over him in waves, waves that are pathognomonic of grief. Often these men can benefit from a psychiatric assessment to sort out what is going on for them. Indirectly, their wives and children can benefit too, since they do not know whether to trust him or not. A few of these men may be quite depressed and may need specific treatment for depression.

Having said all of this about men who are depressed or who are having a delayed grief reaction, there is another group of negligent fathers whose dynamics are quite different. These men have been truly unhappily married for years and have felt very constrained in their marriages. Their pursuit of the "good life" and their egocentricity in its pursuit seem to be a reaction against a feeling of inner deprivation. They feel deserving of their freedom and their independence, and they doggedly go after it. When these men come back and want to step up their involvement with their children, their ex-wives and the children are jarred. They have all felt neglected, sad, and angry. Now they are expected to welcome him with open arms! They may be cold, wary, and offensive toward him, especially if they have bonded together into a tight family structure for survival and self-preservation.

The Victimized Father

These men present a real challenge to therapists. They come for help with sad and extremely upsetting stories of how poorly they've been treated by many people around them—their wives, their friends, their in-laws, their children, the courts, and sometimes previous therapists. As a therapist, one cannot help but feel some degree of empathy for a man who is in a situation like this, no matter how much one reads between the lines or views him with a jaundiced eye. One can feel his sorrow, his loneliness, and his sense of isolation. One usually feels anger as well: anger at the present state of marriage in our society, anger at the high index of marital breakdown, anger at the judicial system, and anger at specific individuals who have been involved in the particular man's life. Therapists who themselves are parents, especially men who are fathers, have a host of feelings when assessing and treating fathers who feel victimized.

What is a given, and a bottom-line given, is that our present family courts and the judges within these courts vary enormously in their fairness to fathers in terms of custody determination and visitation rights. There is a lot of variation within each jurisdiction as well as between jurisdictions. Many fathers do not get a completely impartial hearing, and the mothers' rights are favored. This engenders enormous rage in fathers and contributes a lot to their sense of victimization. While our society remains in this transitional period of revolutionary change in the relationship between the sexes, and until there is greater dissemination and acceptance of the new research on parenting into the legal field, I think that this state of affairs will continue.

Moving beyond this more macroscopic level of evaluation, these men still must be assessed more carefully for psychopathology. What is this man's character structure like? Does he have a character disorder? How much does he need to present himself in a good light, both unconsciously and consciously, in order to win the therapist's approval? Is victimization a style with him, or is this new behavior, implying that he might be symptomatic and regressed, that is, clinically depressed? Is the man attempting to manipulate the therapist in any way; for example, does the patient need a report for his attorney in a forthcoming court appearance? If the patient is manipulating the therapist, what are the underlying dynamics of this? There may be valid and fully justifiable reasons why the man needs to use this particular way in order to get his message across to his therapist.

Some of the more common reasons why former wives, friends, family, and the courts appear so hostile to this type of father are the following: the man may have been violent to his wife, children, or both; if not overtly violent, he may have threatened violence to her or the children; the man may have behaved in an impulsive or unpredictable fashion in the past that has seriously jeopardized his credibility in the mind of his wife (examples might include his disappearing from time to time with no warning or explanation, excessive drinking, drug abuse, attempting or threatening suicide, severe and frightening temper outbursts, etc.); the man may not have functioned very competently as a caretaker of his children (examples might include leaving them unattended, not attending to their grooming, not feeding them properly, and in the case of handicapped children, not attending to their special needs); the man has not been paying child support when he can well afford to pay it or part of it depending on his means.

Many victimized fathers who come to see therapists do not begin to talk about the above matters easily and openly. Many do not have a lot of insight into their behavior and therefore do feel at a loss to understand why people are being so rejecting of them. Confronting the man about the possible factors that I have mentioned above may actually be countertherapeutic. He reacts with rationalizations or with denial. A more gentle approach is usually more productive, and once rapport and a therapeutic alliance are established, he can begin to look at some of these issues.

The matter of child support and its prompt and steady payment is one that I wish to highlight. It is well known that the majority of fathers do not pay any or all of the support that they are expected to pay. There are articles in the popular press about this appalling state of affairs almost daily, and there are increasing efforts both nationally and internationally to legislate payment and to go after these errant fathers. Not only is this a national disgrace, but it is also an urgent "men's issues" matter. It is a serious embarrassment to those men who are attempting to redefine men in terms of their respectfulness toward women and children. Even in

the safety and privacy of the therapist's office, many newly separated fathers do not talk easily about their financial obligation to
their children. Indeed, many men avoid the subject altogether and
cleverly evade its exposition if the therapist brings it up directly or
alludes to it. Other men are defensive and angry about it (some of
which is displaced anger about being separated at all) and don't
feel that they should be paying anything. And many men who are
already paying their support on a regular and punctual basis seem
to feel that they are doing their wives a favor by being "so good." I
look forward to the day when all divorced men of means will approach their financial obligations to their children with the same
attitude that they take toward their work, that it is all part of being
a fully functional and mature adult.

As therapists, I feel that we have an obligation to discuss the
issue of paying child support (and spousal support too, when indicated) openly and frankly with our separated and divorced male patients. With most men this can be done in a supportive yet firm
manner. Openly confronting the man just invites defensiveness and
alienation. I routinely ask my patients who are fathers to tell me
how much they pay and whether they pay regularly or are in arrears. I ask them also how they feel about the amount that they pay.
If the man is vague or evasive in his answers, I interpret this to him.
I try to assess the degree of moral conscience he has about his financial obligations as a father. I don't want to make him feel guilt-
ier than he might be already, but I also don't want to collude with
him if he is shirking a responsibility that he can and should be
meeting. And I don't want to "excuse" him on mental health
grounds when there are none, and he can indeed afford to make
payments. In a psychoeducative sense, I explain to him that his
credibility as a father in his former wife's eyes and her cooperative-
ness with access and visitation are intimately related to his honor-
ing his financial obligations to his children. It is especially
important to emphasize to the man the transactional dynamics involved here—that his "withholding" of money precipitates his
former wife's "withholding" of the children. Many fathers know
this.

I do not verify or check whether my male patients are being
truthful about paying child support payments. Like many therapists, I pay attention to my instincts and intuitions. I support in
principle legislation that is being advanced and enacted to force
fathers to pay child support. I also know from treating many
separated and divorced women that their former husbands are delinquent. With their permission, I discuss this with their ex-

husbands when those men are my patients as well. Frequently I hear rationalizations and counterarguments from the men. I try my best to deflect these statements and get them to focus on the needs of their children. I do *not* refer all of these contentions to their lawyers because this is often a delaying tactic on the part of the man. I urge him to pay up and to try to keep his anger toward his former wife as a separate issue. I also watch for those situations in which the man's "girlfriend" or new wife (because she has a financial stake in the system as well) is reinforcing and supporting his rationalizations not to pay child support. She may or may not have all of the facts, depending on how truthful and self-disclosing the man is.

I want to conclude this chapter on divorced fathers and their children on a more upbeat note than the last few pages convey. We are living in very exciting times for fathers, whether they are in marriages or are divorcing. Increasing numbers of men are striving for balance in their lives. They are trying to put work in its proper perspective, and they are realizing that they have many other needs that are not met in the workplace. They are much more conscious of their needs to be with their children, to play with their children, to be there to listen to their children, to touch their children, and to be touched in return. When their lives are turned upside down by divorce, we therapists have a huge mandate not just to help them get through the crisis but to be on guard for those social forces that work against the preservation and continuation of their relationship with their children. Both groups, the men and the children, are the benefactors.

Let me turn now to treatment of men who are divorcing.

III

Therapy

CHAPTER 11

Therapeutic Approaches

As a physician and psychiatrist, my approach to men who are divorced or divorcing is a biopsychosocial one. The biopsychosocial model was first described by Engel (1977), who had become frustrated with the limits of the biomedical model. The biomedical model has been the dominant scientific model in medicine, and its origins date back to Newton's mechanistic physics in the 17th century (Engel, 1984). Historically, Western medicine has been based on reductionism and mind–body dualism; the biomedical model is disease-oriented rather than patient-oriented. Engel felt that it was essential to begin to pay scientific attention to the psychosocial dimensions of medicine. He defined psychosocial as the range of psychological and social issues that are germane to health and illness and that are involved in the physician's everyday understanding and care of the patient as an individual and a social being. This is the so-called "art" of medicine.

Some years ago, I was asked to see a patient on the gastroenterology service of the teaching hospital where I work. The patient was a 32-year-old man with Crohn's disease, a serious inflammatory disease of the small intestine. When the resident physician called me, he told me over the phone that the patient was a genuine behavior problem on the ward. He described him as very uncooperative with the nurses, said he called out for attention a lot, that he argued constantly with the nursing staff, and that he was also insulting toward them in their efforts to assist him. The doctor also said that the man questioned his medical judgment a lot and didn't really seem to trust him. He wondered if the man might be depressed but could see "no valid reason" why he should be. I went to see the man with one of my medical students.

Paul was the patient's name. Tension was written all over his face, and he was very upset about having to see a psychiatrist. I got called away to another patient in the emergency room, so to Paul's relief (I thought), I left the medical student with him to complete the assessment. When I came back about an hour later, Paul was in tears when I walked into the room. He attempted to regain some control, but the student reassured him that it was fine to cry and that it was good to get out the feelings. At this point, the medical student asked Paul if it would be O.K. if he summarized for me what they had talked about while I was gone. Paul gave his permission, and the student gave the following account of his interview:

Paul was first diagnosed with Crohn's disease when he was 19 years old and attending college. Although he missed a lot of classes that year, he passed all of his courses, and the illness went into remission. He graduated 2 years later and began work as a marine biologist for the government. He also got married that year to a nurse whom he had been dating for about 3 years. Their marriage had gone well as far as Paul was concerned, and they now had a 5-year-old son. Six weeks before Paul came into the hospital, his wife told him that she had met another man and was no longer certain that she wanted to stay in the marriage. He admitted to the medical student that he was completely overcome about his wife's "announcement." He had had no idea that she was so unhappy or frustrated in the marriage. He began to have diarrhea, abdominal cramps, fevers, and then he noticed that he was passing blood in his stools. He went to his doctor and was promptly admitted to the hospital. Although his wife had come in to see him once, she was very distant and cool. She told Paul that she had been to see a therapist who had told her that the marriage looked and sounded "pretty grim." The visit ended with the two of them discussing separation.

What was most disconcerting was that the ward staff had not been terribly responsive to Paul's distress. He had told them that his marriage was in serious trouble and that he and his wife might be separating. Unfortunately, they had difficulty connecting his "uncooperative" behavior on the ward with his impending separation and the fact that he was heartbroken. By their actions toward him, they grossly underestimated him and the normal reactions that people have to separation, especially separations that they do not initiate. One of the nurses had written on the chart that he had been observed lying on his bed "feeling sorry for himself again." The resident looking after him had *queried if he might be depressed but couldn't understand why, as if 32-year-old men and fathers facing separation shouldn't feel depressed.*

The medical student and I followed this man for the next 2 weeks until he was ready for discharge. He responded very quickly to the student's belief in him and his caring manner toward him. The doctors and the nurses also responded to the situation by attending a brief in-service teaching seminar that I conducted on divorce. Their attitude and manner toward Paul changed overnight, as did his attitude and manner toward them. He began to feel both physically and psychologically better.

This case example of Paul is a good illustration of the inadequacy of the biomedical model in medicine. I don't think Paul would have gotten better had the psychosocial determinants of his disease and its management not been uncovered and respected. He might have developed worsening of his illness, despite the correct drugs and electrolyte replacement, with life-threatening consequences. The disease might have progressed to involve more of his bowel and the possibility of surgery. Even worse, his desperation about his wife leaving him plus the growing sense of no one on the ward understanding his plight could have led to his leaping from his sixth-story hospital room.

Biopsychosocial Assessment

Biopsychosocial treatment begins with a thorough biopsychosocial assessment, and this can be broken down into its three components, depending on the patient and his particular needs.

Biological

Any clinician who is treating a divorcing man will want to make certain that the man is not physically ill, either as a concomitant to the separation process or with something that is completely unrelated. Psychiatrists may want to do some of this screening themselves by doing a thorough medical assessment and physical examination, especially if the patient is being admitted to the hospital. Other psychiatrists and nonmedical therapists will want to make sure that their patient has been thoroughly assessed and examined by his family physician or specialist physician. Separated men with symptoms of a panic disorder or a depression need to have illnesses such as thyroid disease, diabetes, and viral infections ruled out. Men who have had memory complaints, any loss of consciousness, or any periods of confusion need to be evaluated for possible head injury, drug toxicity, or other type of endocrine problem. This is extremely important to note in those individuals whose separation distress has aggravated their abuse of drugs or has led to physical fights and possible body trauma.

One of the most commonly abused drugs, especially in the newly separated, is alcohol. Because so many people deny the fact that they have an alcohol problem, the clinician may have to search very carefully for this or read between the lines with the patient. It is really critical to do this because it is difficult to engage the man in psychotherapy if he is abusing alcohol. It will be impossible to improve his mood if he continues to use a substance that depresses his central nervous system. Indeed, he may just get more depressed with psychotherapy, and with the disinhibiting effects of alcohol, he may make attempts at suicide. Irritability, missing appointments, memory lapses, tremorousness, and lack of progression from visit to visit are all signs that are suggestive, but not confirmatory, of an undisclosed alcohol problem.

Other biological factors to consider are whether or not there is a family history of psychiatric illness, alcoholism, drug abuse, or suicide. It is increasingly evident that many psychiatric disorders are genetically inherited, in part, although the precise means of inheritance are yet to be pinned down. This information is extremely important for the clinician to have because it allows a more accurate diagnosis to be made, which leads to more accurate and expeditious treatment. It also enables the clinician to have a better idea of the patient's prognosis regarding how he might feel as the separation proceeds.

John was a 28-year-old graduate student who was referred to our hospital outpatient clinic for "anxiety attacks." He was referred by one of the doctors at the student health service at the university where he was working. John's opening words were: "I'm not sure if I need to be here or not—I feel a whole lot better now than I did 2 weeks ago when my doctor referred me." The psychiatry resident that I was supervising had just begun his residency, and he proceeded to conduct a very good interview and psychiatric assessment of the man. We learned that John was separated from his wife and had been for about 3 months. Although he described the separation as "mutual," he struck us as having a lot of mixed feelings about being apart from his wife, Karen. John also told us that Karen was now seeing someone else and that he felt "fine" about that. One month after the two of them separated, John awakened in the middle of the night in a cold sweat and with his heart pounding. Although he felt a bit better after getting up and breathing some fresh night air at the bedroom window, he had a similar episode 2 days later in his lab in the middle of an experiment. This time he also felt very short of breath and thought he might pass out. He was fine again for several weeks until he had another "attack" in a movie theater. The next day he went to the doctor at the student health service.

The psychiatric resident explained to John the connection between his panic disorder and the marital separation. John agreed to return for at least another visit to explore more deeply his feelings about the separation. However, what the resident neglected to inquire into was that there was a strong family history of anxiety symptoms in John's family: his mother, a sister, and two maternal aunts had all seen psychiatrists for various kinds of anxiety syndromes. Further, his father was a severe alcoholic, and John himself was beginning to worry about his own use of alcohol, especially since he and Karen had separated. We also learned that John was drinking up to a dozen cups of coffee a day, as well, since the separation, and we wondered about caffeinism. This additional information greatly assisted us in our treatment planning for John because it wasn't enough in the long run for him to just return and talk about his feelings; he did have to take medication briefly when the panic disorder returned in full force.

When a man comes to a therapist complaining of difficulty adjusting to separation or divorce, it is imperative to attempt to establish how distressed the man is. Are the man's concerns well within the range of expected concerns for a similar individual going through a separation, or are they more severe and incapacitating? This is no easy task for the clinician, and one's training, diagnostic acumen, and experience with a range of people will be extremely helpful. When we err, we are more apt to err on the side of underdiagnosing. This is not always because of the clinician's lack of understanding or lack of experience. It is sometimes a result of the therapist's attempts to reassure the man that he is "normal," which in itself is not such a bad thing. However, one does have to be careful not to inadvertently make the patient feel worse when he doesn't improve as quickly as he thinks he should. And patients who have a biological vulnerability to develop a clinical illness (such as a depression, an obsessional disorder, a brief reactive psychosis, and so forth) when going through a separation are at greater risk. One must always learn if the patient has had a psychiatric illness in the past, no matter how mild, and whether he received professional help or not.

Tony was a 33-year-old emergency room physician who came to see me 8 months after he and his wife separated. He began the visit with the following statement: "I feel rather foolish being here . . . I can't seem to get it together about being separated, . . . I can't seem to get on with my life, . . . I'm the one who left the marriage, and I'm relieved to be on my own, . . . I just can't figure out why I'm not happier." Tony went on to tell me that he felt physically very well, that he was doing his work with no difficulty, and that he exercised on a regular basis. He was going out with a woman whom he described in very positive terms and whom he planned to continue to see. He denied feeling depressed, and indeed he certainly didn't look or sound very depressed. He had spoken to one of his male friends about the way he was feeling, but that was not very helpful—he came away feeling he had just made a fool of himself.

On more careful examination, there were two findings that concerned me about Tony. First, he was awakening very early in the morning, about 4 a.m., and he was unable to return to sleep. Being quite driven, he didn't think too much of this; he decided to use the extra hours of wakefulness to work on a sailboat that he was building. Second, when I asked him if he had ever had any psychiatric troubles in the past, he said no. However, a bit later in the interview he told me that he had had two periods of complete emotional and social withdrawal as a medical student. The first was in his second year of medical school, and it lasted 2 weeks. He took the phone off the hook, didn't go outdoors, and lost about 10 pounds because he wasn't eating. He suddenly felt better and returned to classes. The second episode was similar except this time he felt severely depressed; he had a well-organized plan to hang himself from a rafter in his basement apartment if he did not feel better by a certain date. Fortunately, he spontaneously began to feel well again!

I made a provisional diagnosis of clinical depression and kept a close eye on Tony's mood throughout the course of our work together. He responded very well to supportive psychotherapy and did not require medication.

One final note of caution, and this is with regard to divorce in the later years, which I described in some detail in Chapter 5. Biological factors that may contribute to, and complicate, the symptom picture are very common in men who are undergoing divorce at this time of life. These men are at risk for a severe clinical depression that may mimic dementia, or a depression may be superimposed on a dementia. Suicide risk also goes up for men who are divorcing and are getting older. The clinician must always do a very thorough biological assessment, or insure that one is done, when treating men of advancing age who are in the process of divorce. And this applies no matter how long the man has been unhappily married or if he initiated the separation or even if he appears quite relieved to be apart. Some men who leave their wives at this stage of life do have impaired judgment because of undiagnosed depression or an early dementia; thus, the clinician must be certain that the man is using sound and rational thought in his decision making.

Psychological

By taking a complete history from the divorcing male patient, the clinician will be able to derive a good psychological understanding of the man's symptoms and concerns. This also includes a thorough mental status examination, especially the man's appearance, his ability to cooperate with the interview, his ability to form a working alliance with the therapist, his verbal ability, his mood, his thinking, his judgment, and his capacity for insight into his situation. Any man who does not seem in full reality contact or who might possibly be psychotic will also require a careful evaluation of his orientation, his memory, and his intellectual functioning.

Because divorce is a type of mourning, one must assess the degree and the extent of the man's sense of loss. How much is he grieving? When taking the man's history, it will be important to note if he is also dealing with other losses concurrently. It is not uncommon to see male patients who, in addition to going through a separation, are also adjusting to recent unemployment or recovering from surgery or a parent's death. Sometimes the losses are connected, as when the stress of the divorce renders the man more vulnerable to ill health, which then leads to a risk of job loss. One must always remember too that the number of losses associated with divorce, and the personal meaning of each of the losses, will vary enormously from one man to the next. It may not matter much at all to Patient A that he will be leaving his home, comforts, and neighbors when he separates from his wife, whereas Patient B will feel terribly bereft when he leaves his marriage. On the other hand, Patient A may be very saddened about the potential threat to his relationship with his father-in-law on separation, but a similar threatened loss is not upsetting for Patient B at all.

Knowledge about previous losses and how the patient coped with these losses will be very helpful for the clinician. This says something about the man's overall ego strength and problem-solving ability. Did the man lose a parent by divorce or death during his childhood? If this is so, he may be at risk for adult depression in the face of loss. If his parents did divorce, did he have a continued relationship with his father, and if so what was it like? If the man had a parent die while he was a child, how was that for him? Was there a stepparent at any time, and how was the relationship with that person? Were there geographical moves when he was growing up and an associated loss of friendships with peers? Have there been any previous serious relationships, or marriages, that ended in separation or divorce? What were they like for the man?

One's earlier ability to cope quite well with separation does not always grant an immunity to the pain of separation a bit later in life.

This was the case for Fred, a 39-year-old teacher, who had a terrible time when his live-in "girlfriend" of 4 years left him for another man. He developed an enormous amount of anxiety and a severe sleep disturbance that required a tranquilizer in addition to weekly supportive psychotherapy and the support of his friends. Several weeks later, when he felt no better, and he began to lose his appetite and his ability to concentrate on work as well as to develop thoughts of suicide, he required an antidepressant medication. Fred was dumbfounded by the extent and duration of his distress (which went on quite severely for well over a year) because he had had several quite serious relationships before that he had gotten over fairly quickly. In two others, he was "left" as well, once for another man. Fred stated that he hadn't been happy in this most recent relationship for a long time and was just waiting for it to die a natural death, to use his words. He stated: "I had no idea I'd take it this hard, . . . the only explanation that I can come up with is that I'm older now, and I don't like being on my own and starting all over again at this age." There was no family history of psychiatric illness, nor had Fred ever felt anything like this before.

Sociocultural

A major factor to keep in mind when assessing a divorcing man is the sociocultural matrix in which his divorce is occurring. How isolated is the man from a supportive network of friends and family? Is he new to the community in which he resides, or has he lived in the area for some time? If he has children, is he quite separate from them; that is, does he live near them or does he see them very often? What are the cultural values, norms, expectancies, and attitudes that shape how he feels about being separated and how others around him feel about him? Is he a part of the dominant culture in which he resides or a member of a racial or ethnic minority? Does the man have a religious affiliation, and, if so, what are the religion's beliefs or laws about marital separation and divorce? How does the man's sociocultural context ease or impede his reaching out for professional help? What are his socioeconomic circumstances like? Can he afford to live reasonably comfortably as a separated man or to provide fair and just support to his children and to his estranged wife when that is indicated? Can he afford decent health care and legal counsel?

Wayne was a 32-year-old architect whom I began to see with his wife, Miriam, while they were in a marital crisis. Miriam was newly pregnant and ecstatic about this; Wayne was not as happy about the pregnancy because they were only recently married, and he wanted more time to adjust. The tension and the fighting between the two of them became more and more severe with a lot of very damaging verbal put-downs and emotional withdrawal from each other. When Miriam couldn't stand it any longer and feared for her health and the pregnancy, she suddenly moved out. Wayne was shattered but could see the necessity of what he thought would be only a cooling-off period. He had now come to accept the pregnancy and hoped that they would be able to reconcile at some point before the baby was born or shortly afterward. From this point on, I began to see each of them separately rather than conjointly.

Within a week of separating, Miriam decided that her marriage was over and that she could not envision ever getting back together with Wayne. Although they had only been married for about 9 months, they had been living together for close to 6 years. They had had two other separations before they were married. Initially, Miriam entertained the idea of becoming a single parent but decided against this. She decided to have an abortion and told Wayne. He was very upset about this but did not stand in her way. That was the last contact that they had. Immediately after the therapeutic abortion, Miriam filed for divorce.

With this information as background, let me now mention the sociocultural factors that colored Wayne's reaction to the separation. First, as an architect, he was not able to find much work in his field and could not make enough money to afford an apartment that he felt was appropriate to his socioeconomic level. He therefore lived in a downtown apartment hotel for a few months until he could save enough money from his free-lancing assignments and driving taxicabs in the evenings. He found this humiliating and feared that he would be

*called at some point to pick up someone he knew and didn't know how
he would explain his situation. Second, as a Chinese man, he felt
ashamed and resentful that his wife had left the marriage; he could not
think of a rational explanation for the divorce, nor did he know how to
explain it to his parents and siblings. Third, he had a lot of ambivalence about seeing a psychiatrist; he saw himself as weak and a disappointment to himself and to his family. He considered the fact that I
am Caucasian an advantage; he said that he could not imagine talking
to a Chinese psychiatrist about his situation. He also feared that a
Chinese psychiatrist might recognize him as a member of the local
Chinese community, and he feared his privacy might be invaded. And
fourth, as a fallen-away Roman Catholic, Wayne had tremendous ambivalence about Miriam's abortion. He felt like an accomplice and
thought that if he were a stronger man he would have overruled
through the courts Miriam's decision to have the abortion. Similarly,
until they were fully divorced, Wayne felt paralyzed regarding seeing
other women because he said that he would feel like an adulterer.*

Treatment

Biological

The first step in the management of a divorcing man is the treatment of any underlying or associated medical problems. I need not
belabor this point because I have already alluded to it. If a man's
diabetes has worsened because of the trauma of separation, then his
internist will need to make the necessary changes in the man's regular treatment. If a man has developed headaches while going
through the divorcing process, he may require a thorough medical
and neurological work-up to determine whether he is merely mani-
festing his distress via this symptom or whether he has the findings
of someone with a brain tumor or other disorder. If the man suffers
from alcoholism and his disease worsens during the separation, he
may need to be hospitalized for detoxification or for the treatment
of alcohol-related illnesses such as pancreatitis, peptic ulcers, or
pneumonia.

From a psychiatric standpoint, there are several issues to keep
in mind when treating a divorcing man biologically. If he is highly
and diffusely anxious, or if he has become phobic, or if he has developed a panic disorder, then he may require an anxiolytic medication, a tranquilizer. Because these medications are habit-forming,
and people can become tolerant to them, they should be prescribed

carefully and only for brief periods, if that is possible. If a man has quite a few symptoms of depression and does not seem to respond well to psychotherapy alone, then he may need an antidepressant drug. If he does not respond to conventional doses of one or more of the many antidepressants, or if he worsens rapidly or becomes acutely suicidal, then he will need to be admitted to a psychiatric unit for more intensive treatment. In a hospital setting, he will be safer: he can be observed on a 24-hour basis, and the doctors can try higher doses of medication. Some patients will require, and can be treated successfully with, electroconvulsive therapy (ECT).

Psychological

Let me focus now on the most common form of treatment for men who are going through a separation or a divorce, psychological treatment. There are a range of psychological therapies that fall roughly into three broad categories: supportive, behavioral–cognitive, and insight-oriented.

SUPPORTIVE

Supportive psychotherapy is indicated in almost all men who come to therapists with symptoms associated with their separation or divorce. They need to be listened to, and listened to objectively. With supportive therapy, the clinician also helps the man focus on the most painful issues and feelings because these may not be immediately obvious to the patient, or they may be defended against. Most newly separated men appreciate, and need, the reassurance from the therapist that they will get better and that time is a great healer.

One of the most central aims of supportive psychotherapy is to provide an opportunity for ventilation of feelings or emotional catharsis. This cannot be emphasized enough when one is treating men who are divorcing. It is essential that they have somewhere to do this, not only because it is therapeutic for them to release their feelings but also because they are often not doing it anywhere else. Many men come to their therapists so heavily defended that they don't even realize how bottled up they are until they begin to explore with their therapists the normal feelings that accompany a marital separation. Other men who are more in touch with these feelings welcome the chance to begin to disclose and discharge them in the safety of the therapist's office. I use the word "safety" because of the fact that so many men are frightened of their feelings and fear that they are the forerunners of a "nervous breakdown." Other men find the therapist's office safe because they can trust the therapist as someone who won't laugh at them, mock them, or judge them for feeling as vulnerable as they do. Because they may be afraid of alienating their friends, they also are happy to be able to vent a lot of their feelings with a professional person whom they don't need to worry about.

BEHAVIORAL—COGNITIVE

This form of treatment includes the longer-standing behavioral therapies based on classical conditioning and operant conditioning as well as the newer cognitive therapy. It is a treatment that is used a lot in marital therapy, but it can be used in individual one-to-one therapy with divorcing men. Several symptom states come to mind: generalized anxiety state, panic disorder, depression, eating disorders, alcohol abuse, and various sexual dysfunctions. It is also indicated for problems that are gender-specific with men such as inexpressiveness, unassertiveness in relationships, male instrumental behavior patterns, and Type A behavior (Goldfried & Friedman, 1982).

I have found that a behavioral—cognitive approach can be quite useful with those divorcing men who are quite symptomatic, who are highly motivated to make changes in themselves, and who are in a hurry. I don't mean to imply that this form of therapy works any faster than others, but I do think that it appeals to certain men who are more action-oriented than others. With obsessional and phobic men, it has been found to be far superior to insight-oriented psychotherapy, with or without medication. Relaxation principles are very beneficial not only with felt anxiety but also with tensional states. Cognitive restructuring is useful again with obsessional men and men who are depressed. With regard to the latter, a cognitive approach to depression can be extremely beneficial with those divorcing men who have longstanding problems with poor self-esteem and negative thinking. Often these problems antedated the marital separation, and they may have actually contributed to the marital demise. Cognitive therapy also appeals to those men who are moderately depressed, who might benefit from an antidepressant, but who are totally against taking any form of medication.

Men who have been separated for a while and who are beginning to explore new relationships can also benefit from a behavioral—cognitive form of treatment. They may be interested in doing communication work of some sort with their new partner and the therapist. This may be especially so with those men who have been left feeling that their communication skills were deficient in their marriage, and therefore they want to improve them in the context of the new relationship. This can be done with individuals who are merely dating but are becoming serious about each other or with couples who are cohabiting and considering marriage. I also find that separated men who are having a lot of conflict with their estranged or divorced wives over the children can also benefit a lot from various forms of negotiation training. The occasional conjoint visit can be helpful, especially for those couples who are not doing any form of mediation work with a mediation counselor or arbitrator *vis-à-vis* their divorce.

INSIGHT-ORIENTED

Insight-oriented psychotherapy is also indicated for men who are coming to terms with divorce, but its timing is important. It is contraindicated in the early stages of separation when men are the most symptomatic. They need a lot of support then, and they are really in no condition to look at their underlying conflicts. In fact, so many men are feeling guilty and vulnerable in the early weeks or months of being apart that they cannot take any added pressure of intrapsychic examination. Indeed, therapists must be careful not to embark on insight-oriented psychotherapy prematurely with these men when they are really not ready. Often this group of separated men request deeper and uncovering psychotherapy with the stated intention of wanting to know themselves better so that they "will not make the same mistakes again." This is a legitimate request, but therapists must be cautious because this request is made by a lot of men who are feeling depressed, and to stir up too much unconscious material can be dangerous. Such men may become more depressed and/or suicidal.

When one begins to consider all of the men who consult psychotherapists at the time of their divorces, there are very few who go on to do insight-oriented psychotherapy once they begin to feel better again. This is not unlike patients in general. Many cannot afford it. For many men it is not even indicated or necessary, nor is it something that they are interested in pursuing. What I try to use as my standard is whether or not a particular man would be a candidate for this kind of psychotherapy regardless of the divorce, because for him the divorce is only one of the surface manifestations of deep-seated, underlying conflicts that work against him and cause him repeated loss or failure in his life. This will be even more evident in those men who have had one or more failed marriages (or long-term relationships) in the past, or where there is a clear trend or pattern of problems with intimacy, mature love, and commitment to another person.

There indeed seems to be a bit of a paradox here when one begins to think about which separated men make use of psychotherapy and which men don't. I am sure that most therapists have had the experience of men bolting from treatment just at the time that they need it the most or could benefit the most from it. It is true that for most men, once their symptoms begin to recede, they are ready to go it on their own, whether the therapist feels that they could benefit from continued treatment or not. This is part of the male persona, to be independent and autonomous, in many cases. What I also find tends to happen a lot in my work with newly separated men who are unhappy and lonely is that they meet another woman very quickly and rapidly begin to feel better again. They are no longer interested in therapy because they feel so much happier, and "there is nothing to work on," so to speak. Although many men leave treatment at this point, some do return at a later time if the new relationship or subsequent ones do not seem to be working. They may realize at that point that they have some underlying issues that are getting in the way of their moving on, often unfinished business from the marriage that they haven't been able to look at until now.

Social

The most common form of social treatment for men who are newly separated or who are going through a divorce is group therapy. There are several types of groups that might be indicated, depending on the individual and his specific needs. Alcoholics Anonymous meetings can be very helpful for the man who has decided to stop drinking before or during the separation period. Even if the man is already involved in A.A. at the time of his separation, he will find the fellowship and the support of the group members helpful. Some men who have been hospitalized with a depression during the separation will find the groups on the inpatient psychiatric unit beneficial. After they are discharged, they may attend some type of weekly after-care group that will make the transition from the hospital to living on their own a bit easier. Other men who are not ill enough to be hospitalized but yet are too ill to work may improve by attending a hospital day program of some sort that will have various types of groups (for example, activity group, work skills group, exercise group, or communication skills group).

With divorce being such a common phenomenon in our society, many communities now have various kinds of groups available that are open to the public. There are uncoupling groups for people who are newly separated, about to separate, or merely considering separation. There are divorce groups for people who have been separated at least a little while and who can benefit from the experiences of others who have been separated longer or who are divorced. Most of these groups are community sponsored and secular, but in some communities there are groups offered by churches or synagogues for their divorcing congregants. Some of these groups are time-limited, say for 8 to 12 months; others are completely open-ended. Most are open to both sexes.

Among the groups that are restricted to men, two different kinds are worth noting. Groups for battering husbands are especially indicated for those separated men who want to come to a clearer understanding of why they are violent and what they can do to overcome it. Men who attend these groups are a mixture of men who are there completely voluntarily and those men who have been sent by the courts as part of their rehabilitation. Some are still with their wives, some are separated and hope to get back together with their wives, and the remainder are completely on their own. These groups are largely educational in focus in that these men need to learn appropriate ways of recognizing their anger and channeling it accordingly. They beat their wives to regain control or mastery or to get the last word in an argument or to gain compliant behavior (Adams, 1986). They are extremely controlling in their marriages, and their public image may be very different from their private image. Classically, they do not take a lot of responsibility for their violent acts, they minimize their propensity for violence, and they blame their wives, whom they see as controlling and verbally abusive. Their perceptions are self-serving, and frequently they argue that they have a right to be violent. These highly structured groups, with a strong leader and peer pressure as a motivating factor (plus a court order in many cases), are the treatment of choice for this segment of separated men.

The second type of group that I want to mention is the all-men's groups. Originally called men's consciousness-raising groups, these groups have been in existence since about the mid-1970s. Men who are in the pre-divorce decision period or who have already separated can benefit enormously from the sense of belonging and supportive fellowship of an all-men's group.

Stein (1982) has written extensively about men's groups, and he offers the following rationale for this type of group: membership in a men's group represents in itself a statement of nontraditional masculine values; men's groups provide an opportunity for men to relate to other men in an interpersonal setting without women; men's groups serve as a means for demonstrating to men how they behave when they are with other men; a men's group represents a nontraditional male activity for its members; the relationships in men's groups can serve to highlight the ways in which members have related to other significant men in their lives; a men's group can provide a setting in which to explore special topics that are frequently difficult for men to talk about, such as dependency and homosexuality; men's groups may lead to the greater understanding of problems for men, such as male diseases, an excessive need to achieve, reactions to divorce, and difficulties in parenting; men's groups can serve to alter the nature of adult male–male relationships by promoting caring and friendship between men; men may learn new patterns of relating to women in men's groups; and men's groups can serve to increase the social and political awareness of men as a basis for eliminating individual and institutional sexism.

Format of Treatment

Although most men who are divorcing will be treated with individual therapy, there are some men who will require, and who will respond to, a combination of therapies. A man may do some one-to-one work with a therapist, especially before and during the separation, and once he is more settled, he may wish to join others in group therapy. Alternatively, a man might begin treatment with others in group therapy, and as a result of becoming conscious of certain conflicts from his past that are too complicated, or too private, to work on in a group therapy setting, he might wish to begin individual psychotherapy with someone.

I have treated many divorcing men who initially came to see me with their wives for couple therapy. A few have come specifically requesting separation therapy, but most have come expecting marital therapy or with no specific expectations whatsoever. Their marriages have all been severely troubled. Some of these men and their wives come only for a few visits and then drop out, only to call again at a later date; others come for a few visits, realize that their marriage is no better or is worse, and begin at that point to engage in separation therapy with me. Depending on the particular dynamics of the couple and what each of them would like to do, I may then begin to see each of them separately for concurrent individual therapy. Some couples, after they have begun to live apart, may require and respond to an occasional conjoint visit, especially if there are items or issues that require ventilation and discussion before they can continue to disengage from each other.

When there are children, one or more family interviews may be helpful. Often I see the children alone as a group, depending on their ages. Usually they welcome the opportunity to express their thoughts and feelings about what is happening to them and what might happen in the future. They have an opportunity to ask questions and to receive responses to their questions, suggestions, and guidance from a professional. As the weeks and months pass, and I am seeing the man in individual treatment, it can be therapeutic to see him with his child or children if there are adjustment difficulties. If he has started a new relationship that is becoming serious, especially if they are discussing living together or marrying, a conjoint visit with the man and his new partner may be beneficial. Men who are fathers frequently complain of, and may require assistance with, the inevitable and ubiquitous conflicts that occur between their new partners and their children.

What I am alluding to, and suggesting to others, is that many divorcing men can benefit from a combined or integrated approach. If one looks at marriage and divorce as very dynamic processes that involve a number of people besides the two individuals, then one can avoid therapeutic rigidity and embrace a more flexible, and I think more appropriate, style of care. We are living and working in an era of phenomenally high marital activity with so many people marrying, divorcing, and remarrying, especially men, that I think we can best serve our patients by accepting this. Many men have no interest in psychotherapy (even if it were always available and they could all afford it) once they get to feel a bit better. They move quickly into new relationships, and if they are still mourning the first marriage while forming the second, then we must realize this and help as best we can when we are consulted.

Alternate Treatment Forms

Thus far I have largely discussed issues in the *individual* treatment of the newly separated or divorcing man. I would like now to mention other treatment approaches that I have merely alluded to earlier. These treatment forms are systems-based and emphasize attention being paid toward the various subsystems of the divorcing family. More specifically, this might include my interviewing and working with a range of groups: the man and his estranged or ex-wife to-gether; the children as a group; the man and his children; the man and only a particular child with whom there are conflicts; the es-tranged or ex-wife, alone or with the children; the entire family; the man and his new partner or wife; the blended family; and so forth. These are approaches that not only address the mental health needs of the man and how he fathers his children but also address the mental health needs of others in the family system—the children, the former wife, the new wife, and so forth.

In their book *The Difficult Divorce*, Isaacs, Montalvo, and Abel-sohn (1986) describe their approach to the divorcing family, which is a structural, family-systems one. Their work is predicated on four principles: first, therapy must focus on both of the parents' efforts to reorganize their relationship with each other and with the chil-dren; second, the well-being of the children must be a priority; third, therapy must deal with the realities of the divorce, and thus work must be conducted with the subsystems within the family; and fourth, hostile parents can be brought together for therapeutic work if the encounter is controlled (p. 4). They are on the lookout in their work for common stresses that arise in the divorcing family, such as lapses in parental responsibility, uncontrolled disputes, and recruitment of the children into taking sides. They try to prevent and soften protracted conflict in the parents with this approach.

Isaacs and her associates acknowledge that their priority in working with divorcing families is the children. They have a signif-icant—and sage—basis for this priority. It is true that in individual therapy with the divorcing parent the children's needs may be ig-nored or underemphasized. Therapists also may become so focused on the problems of the adult patient that they do not sufficiently inquire into how the children are coping. Many parents are so over-whelmed, at times, with their own distress that they cannot give an accurate appraisal of their children's mental health. In the family hierarchy, children indeed are more vulnerable. Consequently, their treatment goal is for each parent to continue to be responsible for the children despite the turmoil in their lives. They help the two individuals to work together as coparents and emphasize to them that their eventual adjustment to the separation will be enhanced when they are successful with their children.

Employing what they term the "controlled encounter" (Isaacs et al., 1986, p. 7), Isaacs and associates attempt to tame the volatil-ity that can arise in conjoint sessions with warring couples. They try reason and structure in their sessions, with problem solving as a goal. They watch for misperceptions and miscalculations that the spouses have for each other and set limits when necessary. They also avoid hasty resolutions and premature dismissal of difficult subjects. Their approach to the divorcing family is sound and courageous. It is not only balanced and fair but also more far-reaching than the more conventional, and fragmented, individual approaches.

Not all therapists are systems-oriented, however. And even when they are, they may not feel proficient or confident in working with a range of family subsystems. Those therapists with specialist training in child psychiatry generally feel more comfortable with the children's subsystem, especially when one or more of the children are symptomatic with the separation. They may be generally comfortable with the parents in the system as well, but if one of the parents becomes quite ill, necessitating medication or hospitalization, the therapist may prefer to refer that parent to someone else. Likewise, therapists who primarily treat adults may feel a bit out of their depth with the children. In those cases, collaborative work with a child psychiatrist may be very helpful and better in the long run for the divorcing family.

I have found it particularly therapeutic to work with both the man and his wife who are separating or who have separated. This may be a continuation of the treatment if they originally came for marital therapy and, in the midst of this, decide to separate. Or one of them may have originally come on his/her own. In the latter case, I often contact the estranged spouse to determine whether she/he will come in and consider engaging in separation therapy. This is usually a combination of conjoint visits and concurrent individual treatment. If the spouse is already in treatment with another therapist, it may still be therapeutic to have sporadic and structured conjoint visits to discuss visitation conflicts that are arising. My aim is to decrease as much as possible the hostility that exists between the parents and, through clarification of misperceptions, try to promote increased mutual respectfulness. The more harmony can be restored, the better it will be for the children. This has been supported by recent research of Isaacs, Leon, and Kline (1987), who studied 200 children from mother-, father-, and joint-custody arrangements. They found that hostilities between the parents were likely to alienate the child from the nonresident parent. They also suggest that this in turn may jeopardize the relationship with the resident or custodial parent as well: that relationship will not be as close. They conclude, and as a clinician I agree, that it is not only the individual relationship with each parent that is important to the child's sense of family but also the child's relationship with the parents collectively, and the parents' relationship with each other.

Divorce Mediation

Mediation is considered another model of divorce therapy (Glaser & Borduin, 1986), and this form of treatment is now about 10 years old. It was designed to remove divorce negotiations and settlements from the traditional or adversarial legal arena, which pits one spouse against the other. With the help of a trained mediator, the divorcing couple is expected to settle issues of child support, visitation, custody, and division of property (Coogler, 1978). Ideally, divorce mediation should enable the individuals to negotiate their way clear with less anguish, less hostility, and more dignity. And it should cost less than the combined fees of a lawyer acting for each of them. Mediators are multidisciplinary—some are social workers or psychologists or lawyers; others may not have formal training, degrees, or be licensed.

Because divorce mediation is usually highly structured, goal-oriented, and collaborative, I routinely discuss its merits with the divorcing individuals and couples that I see in my practice. Many couples have heard about or read about mediation as helpful and less costly than the adversarial system. They therefore appreciate the therapist's endorsement. However, not all couples will be able to complete mediation because of the overwhelming tension, mistrust, and hostility that exist between the two of them. No matter how skilled or how experienced the mediator, they cannot do it. They may be able to, several months down the road, and I always tell them that if they have tried a visit or two with a mediator and didn't return. Some of these individuals will engage a lawyer to act for them, or they may already have one in addition to attempting mediation. Many lawyers who practice only adversarial divorce law recommend respected and experienced mediators in their community to the clients that they see when they sense that a mediator can help. Some individuals oscillate back and forth from traditional lawyer to mediator over a period of months during the worst phases of their divorce, often frustrated with both types of intervention.

The main point that I am trying to make is that divorce mediation is an important and exciting alternative to the adversarial legal system. It works best for those couples who at least can speak to each other and who can be in the same room together. It also works for those individuals who, despite their rage and dislike for each other, realize that they still have to be able to forge some sort of continued relationship as coparents to their children. They have each accepted that the other parent is not going to disappear or die, no matter how much they might wish that would happen. It is still too early to compare the effectiveness of mediation with the older and more traditional approach to divorce settlement, but at the moment its impact seems promising.

This chapter has discussed modalities of treatment. The following chapter addresses some of the specific themes and issues that have to be resolved in the course of treatment.

CHAPTER 12

Common Themes in Treatment

In the course of treating divorcing men, I have encountered certain areas of concern so frequently that I have come to consider them common themes of the divorcing process. This chapter discusses a number of these common themes and outlines therapeutic approaches to them.

Anger

In Chapter 7, I described anger as a common finding in men who are left by their wives. These men have a subjective sense of abandonment. Some are overtly aggressive in their display and release of anger, whereas others are more passive and resistant as a way of dealing with their anger. When these unhappy men come for treatment, it is incumbent on the therapist to assist them with both the acknowledgment and the discharge of their angry feelings. As I have noted earlier and repeatedly in this volume, when a man can come in touch with, talk about, and vent his anger in the safety and security of the therapist's office, he will feel better, and he will be much less likely to harm someone else or himself. When his anger is within the range of normal, he needs to hear that said to him, for the information is reassuring and calming. When his anger is out of the range of normal and dangerous to himself and others, he needs to hear this as well. He may be relieved to know that his therapist is concerned and is taking action to help him, such as prescribing medication, restraint, or brief hospitalization.

However, anger is also expressed by those men who are the initiators of their separations and who have no ambivalence whatsoever about being apart from their wives. Oftentimes, these men are upset to find that they still feel so angry several months after the separation began. There are a lot of reasons for this: they resent having to start all over and may blame their wives for being the cause of the marriage breakdown; they may be having financial struggles, not having anticipated that the process of divorce is as costly as it is; they might have expected to be "free" of their wives once separation began, but they find that it takes a while to disengage fully; they may be having quite a time adjusting to being on their own, and this makes them angry. There are clearly some divorcing men who have been angry so long in their marriages that they hardly know any other emotion. Indeed, when therapists encounter men like this, it is wise to consider that the man may have longstanding personality problems that pre-existed the marriage and its unhappy ending.

Men who are passive–aggressive and have no insight into their anger as a felt emotion can benefit a lot from therapy that is tailored to this as a task. The therapist must look for those occasions that the man has reacted in a passive–aggressive manner, especially in the therapist–patient relationship, and make the appropriate interpretations over and over again as necessary. When the therapist has good rapport with the man, and the man is committed to do the work, the interpretation should be successful.

One word of caution. Therapists must be careful not to reinforce inappropriate and extreme forms of anger in those men who feel unjustly entitled to their anger. I am referring here to those men who are violent and who feel that they have a right as men to be violent. Connected with this, the therapist must also be cautious not to intellectualize with the man about his anger. This is not therapy. I will return to this theme when I discuss men's use of intellectualization as a control mechanism.

Dependency

Dependency is a common theme in the work that divorcing men do with their psychotherapists. However, because dependency needs are so often denied by men in our culture, it is the rare man who brings this theme as a conscious and troublesome problem directly to his therapist. Not only is dependency, and the defenses that men erect to hide it, a frequent part of a man's everyday life, it is also a common transference manifestation in the therapy. Because men are in a regressed state at various phases of separation, especially when they are the noninitiators, they will have a lot of dependency feelings at this time of their lives. When they can recognize and accept these feelings, they are on their way to having some insight into how they behave in relationships.

The psychoanalytical and sociological underpinnings of men's development emphasize rejection of the mothering figure and the pursuit of autonomy and separateness. This implies independence of others and a repudiation of the need for nurturance and connection with others. When men marry, they are always more dependent on their wives than they could ever begin to admit to their conscious minds. Bernard (1972) noted that marriage serves a protective function for men, and their indices of mental health and happiness, especially in traditionally defined marriages, are much better than those of single men and married women. This helps to explain the higher morbidity and mortality rates in separated and divorced men and serves to underscore the difficulty that adult men have being on their own. Lerner (1974) has taken this observation one step further, and she has noted how the envy that is common in some men when they feel threatened seems to be rooted in their overdependence on women. This is especially common in men who are sexist and disparaging of women. These men cope by attacking and devaluing women, in particular women who are quite independent and capable.

In her work with a college-age population, Dickstein (1986) has described the *white knight complex* in young men who were born in the late 1950s and early 1960s. These men have been raised in traditional homes to become heads of their own households, to desire power, to be competitive, and to eschew their personal vulnerability to life stresses. They deny the need for basic human supports and cannot recognize and express their dependent feelings. When their relationships collapse, they are overwhelmed by the panic that they feel and seek therapy at that time. Dickstein emphasizes the importance of helping these young men to recognize that being in charge or in control at all times is no longer acceptable, given the revolutionary sex-role changes that have occurred in our society over the past 20 years. She urges therapists to support these men as they learn to recognize, understand, and work through their unresolved and immature dependency needs. In this way, they will develop better self-esteem and new and more constructive coping mechanisms.

Until this point, I have really been talking about dependency and dependency problems that are in large measure merely a part of the male sex role. What about those divorcing male patients who have pathological dependency either in the form of traits or a personality disorder (American Psychiatric Association, 1987)? These men may tax the patience of their therapists because of their extreme difficulty in making decisions for themselves on what to do about their plight. Some of these men attempt to transfer the dependency that they had on their wives completely onto their therapists, especially women therapists. These men may be really stuck and completely incapable of making progress in coming to terms with being separate. They may be quite unable to do anything on their own regardless of how much they are pushed by their therapists. Often they feel very insecure with their therapists—they fear that their therapists will want to stop seeing them, are growing weary of them, and so forth. Sometimes these pathologically dependent men are hypersensitive to confrontation or to any form of criticism no matter how therapeutically intended.

When approaching the problem of dependency with a man who is divorcing, it is critical for the therapist to ascertain that the man is not depressed. To make interpretations to men who are only temporarily dependent because they are depressed and frightened is a mistake and may make the man feel even more depressed, worthless, and a burden on others. This is a common error that is made by inexperienced therapists and therapists who have only a brief and cross-sectional view of the patient. In other words, they do not have a longitudinal perspective on the man and a clear appraisal of his premorbid functioning before the separation began and he became ill.

Intimacy

Many men who are in the midst of separation from their wives, or who have been divorced from their wives for a while, will come to therapists with a voiced concern about intimacy and their difficulties with it. Some men will say that it was their inability to be intimate in their marriages that crystallized their wife's decision to leave them. Other men, especially men who are leaving their wives, will mention diminished or lost intimacy in the marriage as one of the reasons why the marriage is no longer functioning. When a man has become involved with someone else before ending his marriage, he may also state that the intimacy with his wife had ended months or years earlier and that this emptiness has contributed to his meeting another person. Other men who have been on their own for some months or longer might complain to their therapists that they are having tremendous difficulty becoming intimate with women.

Therapists must always ask the man what he means by intimacy. Not only is his definition of intimacy important to know, the therapist must also know what constitutes a problem of intimacy to him. One must learn what the man's expectations of himself are regarding his capacity for intimacy and/or his expectations of others in relationships. What does intimacy mean to him? Closeness? Commitment? Warmth? Trust? Friendship? Ability to communicate well? Does intimacy mean a bit of all of these things? In what way(s) does he associate intimacy with sexuality, or does he associate them at all? This is important to clarify in that some men will describe having no problem whatsoever with sex but that they don't feel intimate. Others will describe having no problem being intimate verbally or emotionally but that they don't feel like being or becoming sexual at all with the other person.

In order to explore a man's problem with intimacy, it is necessary to have a full understanding of his personal and family background. Only by reviewing his parents' ability to be intimate with each other and their children is it possible to begin to construct a framework for the man's object relations with others as he grew up. The sociocultural milieu in which the man was raised is also important in shaping his ideas, feelings, and comfort with intimacy throughout his developmental years. The next phase to be examined is the man's adolescence and how that was for him, especially with regard to dating and beginning to experiment with, and become less awkward with, physical touching and sexuality. A lot of men then move on into an early marriage, and it is this relationship that they may want to talk a lot about in relation to their problems with intimacy. For other men who are divorcing, their concerns about intimacy are much more confined to the most recent relationship or marriage. In fact, they may feel that they had no problems whatsoever with intimacy until things began to go awry in their marriage.

There are a number of fears that men have about intimacy, and I would like to elaborate briefly on some of these. Men who have been deeply hurt as a result of their marriages ending may have a specific type of intimacy anxiety, a fear of merger, in new relationships (Feldman, 1979). They have insulated themselves in order to heal emotionally and to cope with the realities of everyday life. Casual dating may be no problem for them, but should they meet someone whom they are especially attracted to, and who is seriously attracted to them, they may develop a fear of merging with her. For some men this fear is completely conscious, and they can talk about it in therapy. This enables the therapist to normalize the fear and to point out to the man that his fear is perfectly rational and understandable given how difficult and painful the separation was from his earlier, and trusted, relationship with his wife. This intervention, coupled with reassurance from the therapist that his fears of merger will decrease with more passage of time and more knowledge about his new partner, can be very helpful.

For some men, fears of merger are unconscious, and they may have a series of relationships that they can take only so far before they flee. This pattern may be one of the issues that they bring to therapy. Other divorcing men may come to treatment with a sexual dysfunction that is the surface manifestation of their unconscious conflict. The most common of these are impotence and retarded ejaculation. In the former, the erectile difficulty symbolizes their ambivalence about the relationship and its seriousness; in the latter, the inability to have an orgasm, to ejaculate, and to give up one's semen represents the withholding of one's self and the fear of surrender.

Other types of intimacy anxiety in divorcing men (Feldman, 1979) include a fear of exposure, wherein the man is reluctant to disclose much about himself, perhaps because of a high need for privacy or because of embarrassment or because he was betrayed in his marriage; a fear of attack, wherein the man fears that what he discloses about himself may be ridiculed or judged or be deemed unworthy or unacceptable (especially common in divorcing men who are depressed); a fear of abandonment, wherein he fears being rejected, especially when most vulnerable, in a new intimate relationship, much as he has been abandoned in the past; and a fear of one's own destructive impulses, wherein the man is concerned that if he becomes intimate with someone, he may do something to ruin it. This might be present in those men who have had one or more previous relationships or marriages that have ended because they became violent or alcoholic or irrationally possessive, and so forth.

Control

Control and the loss of control are common issues for men who are divorcing. Many men whose separations have been initiated by their wives complain about being "out of control" or no longer having "control" over their lives. Men who have a high need for control in their lives, in particular men with compulsive personalities or a lot of compulsive traits, will be highly anxious until they regain the control they are accustomed to having. Supportive psychotherapy that acknowledges the man's anxiety about being out of control will help him to feel a bit better.

What about control as a central dynamic that has played a part in the man's marriage ending? This is a problem that may have existed throughout the man's life but was never as serious until he got married. After marriage, he finds that he cannot control his environment as much as he thought. He learns that his wife has her own ideas, fantasies, and plans that are not always in concert with his. His attempts to control her cause tension, disagreements, and fights. This may lead to unhappiness and resentment. In time, his wife concludes that their marriage is in serious trouble unless they get marital therapy. If the man dismisses this as silly or unnecessary or simply refuses to go for marital help, she may have no alternative but to leave him. For many men, it is only after their wives have left that they begin to accept into consciousness the gravity of their wives' complaints about them. And it is at this point that they may decide to get some therapy. Other divorced men do nothing about their excessive need for control until they encounter the same complaint in a subsequent and new relationship with someone else. Or they find that they can't form new relationships because they are so controlling.

Insight-oriented therapy is the treatment of choice for these men, but they will find it difficult, simply because being in treatment means giving up some, if not a lot, of this control. Because their way of relating is so cognitive and so highly intellectualized, the therapist also has to be persistent in getting these men in touch with their feelings. The man may loathe having to relinquish this kind of control to the therapist. This takes time, and so does the treatment itself, which will also be frustrating for the man.

Sexuality

Many divorcing men have a lot to talk about in therapy about how they feel about themselves sexually. Because healthy and mutually enjoyable sex is one of the earliest and most common things to go in a troubled marriage, most divorcing men have had many months, and usually years, of not feeling good about themselves sexually. Young divorcing men may never have felt completely comfortable sexually if they were not very experienced before marriage and if their sexual relationship with their wives did not evolve and mature during their years together. If the divorcing man or his wife or both struggled with some type of sexual dysfunction in the marriage, this will be something that he will want to talk about in therapy. He will lack sexual confidence, he may feel inadequate sexually, and he may feel guilty and blame himself entirely (rather than in part) for the marriage not succeeding. Divorcing men who were sexually unhappy in their marriages for years and who had repeated sexual affairs with other women may also want to discuss this in therapy. They may have fears of this happening again in future long-term relationships or marriages, may feel guilty about "cheating" on their wives, may have concerns about their ability to be sexually intimate or to commit to one person, and may feel totally unable to communicate verbally about sexual problems in marriage.

Divorcing men who are sexually confident and in no conflict about their sexual ability may want to talk about being in transition and having to adjust to being single and dating again. Most of them will have been away from the "singles scene" for at least a few years and find it awkward, frustrating, and demoralizing. For most, the social norms and customs regarding dating practices and sexual activity will have changed from when they were single before. Many divorcing men have mixed feelings about being single again anyway, and so they approach meeting others with some cynicism and reluctance in the first place. They also have mixed feelings about being older—they are happy to be wiser and more seasoned but not happy to be less youthful looking and less sexually charged.

Men who are already involved with another woman when they leave their wives rarely have sexual concerns that they bring to therapy. Because the relationship is usually fairly new, and they are in love and excited to be in love, their sexual pleasure is in accordance with their overall feeling state. However, those men who are involved with women who are much younger, and there are many of these men, may express concerns about being able to remain sexually fit and functional as the years go by. They will feel better just airing these concerns. They will also respond to reassurance that the waning of sexual frequency over enduring marriage is not so much the result of physiological aging as it is of the lack of attention being paid to communication and to each other's best interests.

Some men who are divorcing their wives have fears of being or becoming gay. These men are to be distinguished from the men I described in Chapter 9 whose marriages are ending because they are "coming out" as gay men. I am referring here to heterosexual men who have had no gay thoughts or feelings of erotic attraction to men throughout their lives. Nor have they had any sexual experience with other men in their lives, or if they have, it was completely experimental and isolated. They fear being gay only because they were not very sexually active with women before marriage and therefore lack a solid sense of themselves heterosexually. Also, if a man withdrew sexually from his wife for long periods of his marriage, she may have begun to wonder if he might be gay and asked him this or perhaps taunted him with it to get him to become more sexually involved and to perform. This may have damaged an already weak sexual ego, which then has led him to doubt his heterosexuality. These men generally respond well to support, and once they begin to do some dating, their heterosexuality will be affirmed and validated.

Another group of men who are divorcing and who have fears of being gay are those heterosexual men who have been sexually abused as boys or sexually assaulted as young men. This type of psychological trauma has a serious impact on the individual's sense of himself as a man—his sense of masculinity or gender identity and his sense of himself as a heterosexual man (Myers, 1989). Hence, although the man may have been quite successful at repressing and suppressing the injury and has functioned very successfully with women, including his wife, he may find that the trauma of his marriage ending has put him in such a regressed or depressed state that he finds these unpleasant memories or worries returning. In this case, the therapist must help the man talk about this painful experience in order to work it through, to get in touch with his anger, his sorrow, his feelings of guilt and self-blame, and his feelings of loss. The formerly sexually victimized man will feel a lot better with this type of treatment.

Grief

The most common theme, and the most topical, for the divorcing man who comes for treatment is grief work. Very often these men do not know what to call that state of unpleasantness, of emptiness, of sheer terror that they experience. In some cases, they are bewildered by the intensity and steadfastness of their rage or by their remorse. They are puzzled by the waves of sadness that wash over them like breakers at the beach. They cannot fathom why they pine for someone whom they felt miserable with and whom they were relieved to escape from months earlier. Their guilt at leaving their wives, coupled with a regretful sense of wishing they had tried harder to make the marriage work, may also plague them.

"You're grieving" or "Does it feel like mourning?" are common statements that I make to these men, to give them the language, a name to describe their feeling state. It is interesting to note the flash of recognition in their eyes, or the "Yeh, that's what it is!" in their voices. This is tremendously therapeutic for divorcing men because it is calming, and it helps them to circumscribe their psychological state and not to be made so anxious by it. Knowing that they are mourning their marriages also makes men think of other questions to ask regarding their feeling state; this enables the therapist to answer questions that he/she may not have thought to address. With this dialogue, then, the man comes to realize that what he is experiencing is time-limited and reactive and that he will feel better again in time.

Having labeled the problem, the man can begin to do the grief work within therapy. He needs to vent his feelings, his anger, his sadness, his longing, and so forth. As I've mentioned at several junctures in this book, many divorcing men do not do much of their grief work outside the therapist's office, for many personal and political (in the sense of sex-role politics) reasons. Hence, the therapist becomes a pivotal figure in the patient's life during this period, and it is important that the therapist not underestimate the patient's distress and need for continuing treatment. Many male patients who are seeing therapists during their divorces directly state that they have nowhere else to go to talk about what they are experiencing. Some men do state that they have tried to talk to their male friends, but to no avail. They find that these men do not listen, are not available, give advice that is inappropriate and silly, or accuse the man of simply feeling sorry for himself. Some of this is inherent in the male–male dyad in that there is a de-emphasis on discussing deeply personal and emotional matters; some may be the result of societal norms and expectancies that divorcing individuals, not just men, should not mourn very long.

The grief work will be different for men who are the initiators of their separations and for men whose wives have initiated the separation. Nevertheless, both types of divorcing men will have to mourn. Some will do it more gradually and intermittently, long before they even separate; others will do it only after separating, and perhaps many months down the road after separating. This latter group of men have put their grief "on hold"—some have been preoccupied with a new relationship, some have kept themselves busy with their work, and some have simply denied that their marriage is over. All of these men can be helped by therapists who listen attentively and who meet them at the psychological place where they are. They can then explore their grief as they are ready to and accept as much feeling as they can tolerate.

Sexism

What about sexism as an issue for divorcing men who come for treatment? Those men who are able to identify this as a problem in their marriage that contributed to its failure, or those men who identify this as a problem in their meeting new women, are already on their way to changing because they accept it, no matter how begrudgingly, and are ready to work on it. Their sexism may be more than a product of their social conditioning as men growing up in our society (and many others); it may be directly related to the biopsychosocial matrix of their home and family of origin. Some fiercely sexist men who come for therapy at the time of their divorces defensively state how much more enlightened they are about women and the equality of women than their fathers ever were. In therapy, it may be revealing with some of these men to learn about childhood events and other happenings that shaped their inner sense of male superiority and lack of respectfulness for women. Understanding, insight building, and sensitivity may emerge from this uncovering and reworking with the aid of the therapist's more egalitarian vision.

Other men will not define, or even recognize, themselves as sexist. In this case, the therapist picks it up in the man's history, behavior, and what he says about women while in treatment. Gentle and tentative interpretation will be necessary. I say gentle because confrontation, especially early in treatment, will not work. The man will simply deny it and become defensive. If one has taken a thorough history from the sexist male patient, then it is easier to appreciate its defensive function in warding off his feelings of insecurity, or it is easier to understand his sexism in its racial, ethnic, or class context (when those factors are contributory). Treating sexist divorcing men can be extremely difficult, especially for women therapists. I will say more about this in Chapter 13 when I discuss countertransference issues in therapy.

Loneliness and Isolation from Other Men

I have mentioned the loneliness that men have regarding a lack of intimacy in their relationships with other men before. What can the therapist do about this? For those divorcing men who are not aware of the importance of close male friendship or who play it down, the therapist can help in an educative sense. This may stimulate the man to push himself a bit harder to make male friends or to challenge his existing friendships for more depth, communication, and sharing. The divorcing man may need to hear that he is overdependent on women, both as lovers and as friends, to meet all of his emotional needs. The therapist may be able to interest the man in attending an all-men's group that is specifically formed to address these very matters.

The male therapist, by cultivating a trusting and accepting relationship with his divorcing male patient, might be seen as a role model of someone who is interested in men and who is not afraid of men's vulnerabilities, secrets, and fears. Albeit this is a professional relationship, but merely because the two individuals have come together as therapist and as patient does not completely negate the primal and humanistic level of two men carving out a relationship with each other. There is a spin-off effect that occurs when there is a good fit between male therapist and male patient, and this effect may be corrective for the man as he lets go of old conflicts in relating to men and begins to approach new situations in his everyday life.

One word of warning to male therapists who treat isolated divorcing men. It is essential that the therapist realize, and accept, that therapy has a beginning, middle, and termination phase. I have seen many situations in which a divorcing man was engaged in productive and exciting psychotherapy with a male therapist, only to be abruptly terminated by the therapist or terminated too early or quickly without adequate explanation and support. These men not only feel angry and confused by this situation, but they also have many of their earlier concerns about men reinforced (that men are not really there for you, or they cut you off, especially if you become too dependent, or they can't be counted on and trusted). The termination phase of treatment is extremely important. It must be conducted carefully and in an interactive way with the male patient so that all his fears can be verbalized and so that he can be supported as he prepares to move on his way alone.

Male Inexpressiveness

This is a common and well-documented complaint that women in relationships or marriages have about their men. Many divorcing

men mention this at some point in their treatment: "My wife complained constantly that I never talked enough to her"; "I don't talk
about my feelings much—that always bothered by wife"; "I'm not
much for words—why talk unless it's important?"; "I hated talking
about my work with my wife—she always wanted me to—I just
wanted to put the day behind me and relax in the evening." Therapists should pick up on these comments to alert the male patient to
begin to look at this trait and to try to work at becoming more open
and self-disclosing. This simple and very superficial intervention
can be very helpful.

Other men will become more expressive as a result of having
been in psychotherapy. Not only does the patient come to feel the
value of revealing himself through the process of ventilation, but he
also becomes less fearful or reluctant to talk about himself, period.
The man who is inexpressive because of a longstanding sense of unworthiness and poor self-esteem should also become more expressive as his self-worth improves and as he realizes that he has
something interesting and meaningful to say. Some of the men who
join a men's group or enter group therapy also improve their verbal
skills.

Gender Identity

Many men in therapy while divorcing their wives express concerns
about their gender identity, their inner sense of masculinity or
maleness. Earlier I referred to one type of man with a gender identity problem—men who have been sexually abused or sexually assaulted earlier in their lives. There are other types of situations that
divorcing men describe. Some men have never really had a secure
or comfortable sense of themselves as men. Most commonly, this is
a result of the biological and psychological forces that have been a
major part of their boyhood, adolescence, and early adult years.
Marriage may have helped a bit to prop up the man's gender identity, but sometimes the problem is so severe or pervasive that marriage isn't very helpful. When the marriage doesn't work out, then
the man feels poorly about himself again. And not uncommonly, the
man blames his wife entirely for his weakened state when really she
was not responsible at all. In fact, she may argue that she had literally bent over backwards to make him feel like a man.

Frank, a 28-year-old graphic artist, was referred to me by his family
physician after attempting suicide. He had gotten drunk and taken an
overdose of tranquilizers a few days after his wife moved out of the

family home with the children. His brother had unexpectedly gone over to his home, found him unconscious, and called an ambulance. He was treated overnight at his local hospital and released the next morning. I assessed Frank and treated him with supportive psychotherapy for several weeks until the sting of his separation was less severe, and he was less depressed.

In the course of his work with me, Frank began to talk about the fact that he never felt very good about himself as a man. "Look at me—I'm 5' 1" tall, I weigh 125 pounds, and I'm hardly what you'd call good-looking—Tom Selleck I'm not." Frank described himself as being a bit of a loner as a child and felt that he never fit in easily with other boys. He was always artistic, and he especially liked to draw and paint with water colors. He loved animals and always had several pets. He hated team sports but enjoyed individual sports like swimming and cycling. He never competed in anything athletically. During puberty, which came late compared to his peers, he suffered from severe acne and terrible self-consciousness. He was also shorter than the other boys his age, a continual worry for him. He remembered going to one school dance, which he hated. He did ask one girl in his class to dance, but she said no. This was the extent of his high school socializing with the opposite sex.

While studying at art college in his community, Frank met Janice, the woman who was to become his wife. She actually took the initiative in being friendly toward him and trying to draw him out a little. Although Janice was 2 inches taller than he was, he did eventually ask her out on a date. Frank recalled discussing his sensitivity about his height on that very first date. Janice's being "easy-going" about his being shorter than she was endeared her to him.

Janice was his first and only girlfriend, and, after dating for 5 years, they got married. Their two children were born during the first 3 years of the marriage, and by the end of their fourth year together, things were very strained at home. Janice was at home full time with the children, and Frank worked at two jobs to make ends meet financially. Frequent arguments broke out, and on a couple of occasions, Frank was violent and struck Janice. Frank told me that he had become increasingly mistrustful of Janice and that he felt jealous and "uptight" every time that she went out with her women friends. He said that all along he was afraid that she would tire of him and leave him for another man. She did eventually leave, not for another man but for some peace and a respite from Frank's continual putdowns of her and from his badgering about her loyalty to him.

In Frank's therapy with me, he was eventually able to look at his poor sense of self, especially his sense of himself as a man in our society. He came to recognize that his controlling, dominating, and attacking behaviors were defensive and compensatory for an inner sense of inferiority and lack of self-importance. He also began to talk about homosexuality and his intense fear of possibly being gay himself. This was connected with his shaky gender identity as well as the fact that there had been two or three occasions during his late adolescence when gay men had made passes at him. Although he had quickly dismissed these, he did worry if he "gave off some sort of gay vibe" that had sparked these overtures. Just talking about these incidents and receiving some clarifying information from me (that is, he had never felt any erotic attraction to men, either in his everyday life or in his dreams) were tremendously anxiety-relieving for him. I eventually referred Frank to a mixed-gender weekly psychotherapy group, and he derived a lot of benefit from this form of support.

Any discussion of psychotherapy is incomplete without an analysis of transference and countertransference, and that is the subject of the next chapter.

CHAPTER 13

Transference and Countertransference

Transference and countertransference are important factors in the functioning of the psychotherapeutic dyad. This chapter addresses these issues in some detail.

Transference Issues

I want to discuss now some of the many transference issues that arise in the treatment of divorcing men. Transference is defined as "the unconscious assignment to others of feelings and attitudes that were originally associated with important figures (parents, siblings, etc.) in one's early life" (American Psychiatric Association, 1975, p. 147). Strong feelings of dependency on the therapist are not unusual in men who are in the midst of divorce (Myers, 1988a). There are several variables that affect the degree of dependency that the patient manifests in the therapist–patient relationship: the amount of premorbid and underlying dependency that is characterologic in nature; the degree of regression (and depression) that has occurred in the man associated with the divorce; the amount of rapport that exists in the therapist–patient relationship that "allows" the divorcing man to come to depend on the therapist; the age of the patient (some patients may be more dependent at various ages); the age of the therapist (the therapist should be mature or seasoned enough to understand and accept a dependent transference); and the sex of the therapist (some divorcing men may become more dependent on women therapists than they would on men therapists). As a general rule, the more symptomatic difficulty the man is having, the more needy he will feel of the therapist's strength, availability, and comfort. Also, this need will be greater for the divorcing man who is very much on his own and does not have the support of friends and family.

What about the male patient who defends against his dependency while going through his divorce and who resists the regression that is attendant on this process? These men may need therapy, and indeed do enter therapy, but they have tremendous difficulty being or becoming a patient or assuming a patient role. This is not uncommon in those men who themselves are accustomed to being the one in control or in authority. Any therapist who has treated other men in the caregiving professions—doctors, nurses, psychologists, social workers, and so forth—when they are in the midst of divorce will know what I mean. Accepting that they are not feeling well and that they must become *temporarily* dependent on the therapist until they feel better is hard for many of these men.

Male therapists must never forget the profound and pervasive societal dictates in North America that militate against men depending emotionally on other men (Pleck & Sawyer, 1974). These forces, which have been a part of a man's social conditioning since boyhood, are often at work in those divorcing men who must defend very strongly against their feelings toward the therapist. For these men, recognizing and acknowledging strong and perhaps tender feelings for the therapist would make them feel very vulnerable, frightened, and "less a man." If one has taken a good history and has a working knowledge of the patient's object relations with other men, this type of transference can be anticipated and used therapeutically. It is also important to recognize and anticipate this kind of transference reaction in order to be able to help the man who panics in the course of his therapy (because of his fears of dependency) and bolts.

I want to say a few words about trust and problems with trust in the transference reaction of divorcing men in treatment. All therapists know that they must earn the patient's trust and that the man does not automatically entrust the therapist with his concerns and fears. Again, conducting a careful and thorough personal and family history is absolutely fundamental if one hopes to be able to understand and empathize with the man's difficulties with trust. By reviewing those years with the divorcing man in a sensitive and interactive manner, the therapist not only gathers essential psychodynamic "data" but also establishes rapport and a mutually respectful working alliance with the patient.

Many patients, not just male patients who are going through a divorce, have a poor or shaky ability to trust. Their basic trust in others, as conceptualized in Eriksonian terms (Erikson, 1963), has never been established because of a chaotic or disruptive relationship with their parents or parent surrogates. Some people have had backgrounds where there was little stability and continuance, and they have never been able to count on anyone as being there for them, as strong, as permanent. Others have had a trusted and secure relationship suddenly end, perhaps without reason or explanation, that left them feeling abandoned and later wary of new relationships. This feeling is not uncommon in individuals who have had a parent die during their childhood or a parent suddenly leave because of divorce or a trusted boyfriend or girlfriend suddenly end the relationship during adolescence or young adulthood.

Hence, men who are divorcing and who are coming for therapy may have both predisposing and precipitating psychosocial stressors that color their ability to trust the therapist. Now their trust in others, especially in their wife (and perhaps their friends), has been shattered by the separation experience superimposed on a background of vulnerability to loss and mistrust. By interpreting the connectedness of all of these dynamics, the therapist will be able to help the divorcing man gain insight into his difficulties with trust.

Another dynamic that may arise in the transference relationship is manipulation. Examples of this type of behavior might include the following: the patient bids the therapist to exert pressure on his reluctant wife to come in for marital or reconciliation therapy; the patient wants the therapist to communicate to his wife the details of his depressed mood including perhaps his suicidal feelings and intent (I am excluding homicidal thoughts here—in that case, the therapist would have a duty to warn the woman about her estranged husband's intent); the patient attempts to enlist the therapist as an ally against his wife on issues ranging from defamation of her character and morals to custody contests. Acceding to or rebelling against these demands is not the issue here for the therapist, but identifying and working with the loss of control, sense of powerlessness, hurt pride, and desperateness of some divorcing men certainly are.

Patients who are borderline and patients who are pre-psychotic may develop intense transference jealousy, envy, and rage toward the therapist. This may be complicated by alcohol and drug abuse and may be characterized by frequent references to the therapist's marital status, children, or the state of the marriage itself. Assumptions and ideas about the therapist may be aired that are unfounded and perhaps quite distorted. Careful assessment of these statements and of the feeling state behind them aids in diagnosing and revising drug treatment and psychotherapy.

Mr. L was a 42-year-old lawyer and father of three children who came to see me in quite a depressed state shortly after he and his wife separated. He was an acknowledged alcoholic, formerly with Alcoholics Anonymous, who had slipped back into drinking during the past 6 months. His wife, also a lawyer, precipitated the separation because she could no longer tolerate his drinking, his angry outbursts, and his verbal and physical abuse. They had been seeing another psychiatrist for marital therapy for about 3 months; once the decision to separate was made, they were not permitted to continue with the psychiatrist individually because "that was not his policy."

My diagnostic assessment of Mr. L was major depression complicated by alcohol abuse. He was quite symptomatic with suicidal ideation but no plan. He agreed to an antidepressant and immediately returned to A.A. I saw him weekly, but there were one or two phone calls between visits. Initially he was friendly to me but rapidly became overfamiliar. Before first consulting me, he had made some inquiries about my background and learned that we had attended the same university at different times and had been members of the same fraternity. He noted the picture of my wife and children in my office, and that stimulated a barrage of questions. He knew people who knew me including many other physicians in our city.

As their separation continued, and it became clearer to Mr. L that he and his wife would not be reconciling, he became angrier and angrier. He was angry at her, angry at the other psychiatrist for "not helping—and then bailing out," and then angry at me. He insulted me one minute and apologized the next. He was sarcastic about my "having it all" and his "having nothing." On one visit, his walked over to my desk and turned the picture of my wife and children face down. "I can't stand to look at them," he stated (the pictures were not in fact in his line of vision). He accused me of being smug, of lacking sympathy, and taunted me: "Your day will come. Someday you'll be sitting in some shrink's office yourself with nothing to show for all your years of hard work."

Mr. L slowly began to feel better. His angry and attacking outbursts diminished in both frequency and intensity. He began to talk about his feelings of emptiness and loneliness and his hurt pride. My being per-

severing in not giving up on him helped a lot, although at times it was very difficult. I also told him when I felt his verbal abuse was inappropriate. In the long run he appreciated this but not at the time of his emotional ranting and raving. Our work together ended when he joined the Unitarian Church in his neighborhood, and as a consequence of this he made new friends and felt a lot better about himself.

What about the divorcing man who develops a competitive type of transference reaction with his therapist? Although this kind of transference can develop with therapists of either gender, it is more common when men treat men. Competition is so much a part of the socialization experience of boys and men in Western society that I feel that we must accept it as a given in the male personality structure. A competitive transference (and possible countertransference) then is most apt to occur with young, bright, achievement-oriented, and highly intellectualized patients working with male therapists about their own age. Review of their backgrounds often reveals a long history of competition with other men scholastically, athletically, and in the workplace. There may also be a prior history of "losing in love," that is, losing a girlfriend in adolescence or a woman friend in adult life to another man long before the marriage and divorce. The power disparity inherent in the therapeutic relationship is so formidable to these men that their characteristic defenses come into full force. It is essential that the therapist understand how much a "loser" this type of divorcing man feels inside and how much he may have to challenge and defeat the therapist in order to bolster his own sense of self-worth. Inside he feels vulnerable and powerless.

I return now to the issue of intimacy in the treatment of men who are divorcing. My comments about intimacy earlier in Chapter 12 were introductory and generic. I want to focus here on intimacy in the transference relationship when the divorcing man works both with women and with men therapists. Most definitions of intimacy include the concepts of closeness, affection, liking and/or loving, disclosure of feeling, and connection. Although the wish for intimacy is a fundamental need of the human organism (to be held, touched, comforted, and nourished), there are also fears of intimacy (fear of merger, exposure, attack, and abandonment). A certain amount of fear of intimacy is fundamental to good therapy.

When the divorcing man is in treatment with a woman therapist, there may be an ambivalent tone to the intimacy that he feels for her. Once again, depending on his object relations with female figures throughout the course of his life, the man may have many intimate feelings for his therapist, but these same feelings will frighten him. The specific dynamics of his marriage, especially its form and sex-role manifestations, and the circumstances of his separation (that is, who initiated it?) are critical factors in affecting the transference. Commonly, the divorcing man projects many of his feelings about his estranged wife, and often women in general, onto the female therapist. His feelings of intimacy for the therapist often represent a longing for what he did not experience with his wife, or what he misses, or what he hopes for in future relationships. Women therapists must be trained to anticipate this kind of transference when they treat this very vulnerable type of male patient, and further, they must become comfortable helping the man to recognize and verbalize these feelings of fondness, affection, closeness, and so forth.

When the divorcing man develops an erotic transference for his female therapist, this may be more complicated and intimidating for the therapist, especially the younger and less experienced therapist. Often the erotic feelings that the man has are merely an extension of his feelings of intimacy for the therapist. Sometimes they are merely a stereotypically "male" way of feeling and articulating a sense of liking and wanting to be close to his therapist. When either of these dynamics is in operation, these men will feel a lot better just talking about these feelings, because they will be defused and desexualized. They will then feel less anxious and less preoccupied with eroticism. However, the woman therapist has to feel comfortable enough herself to "allow" this and not be made anxious about it or inhibit the man or abandon him as a patient.

The intense and highly eroticized transferences that some divorcing men develop with women therapists are another story. Many of these men are not just simply going through a divorce; their entire world or psychological integrity is disintegrating. Some of them have pre-existing major psychiatric disorders; hence, their erotic transference on women therapists may be of psychotic proportions including delusions of love and possession. Others may have severe underlying personality problems if not diagnosable personality disorders—they make unrealistic demands on the therapist, they actively flirt and try to seduce her, they attempt to "turn the tables" by questioning her about her personal life, or they conduct themselves with an air of entitlement in their work with the therapist. Because these male patients are so difficult and potentially dangerous, the woman therapist must be very careful not to underdiagnose and inadvertently reinforce the man's pathology. It is also wise to get a second opinion from another therapist as quickly as possible in order to prevent the situation from worsening. Even when male patients like this must be terminated, it is important to have advice on how to do it in the best way in order to try to prevent a retaliatory and life-threatening response on the part of the patient.

What about intimacy matters in the transference when divorcing male patients are in treatment with a male therapist? Many male patients will never feel as intimate with another man as they will with their therapist. This helps to explain the resistance of some men to therapy at the outset as well as the separation and abandonment anxiety they may manifest when in therapy. With regard to the latter, I think that there is a tendency for male therapists to underestimate how difficult being in therapy and ending their therapy may be for some male patients. These men may have a much more intimate connection with their therapist than the therapist might understand.

I make this kind of a statement not just from what I've heard directly from my male patients, nor from a purely hypothetical or theoretical perspective, but from what I have heard from the wives of many of my male patients over my years of clinical practice. The following are examples of statements that women have made to me after their husbands have been in treatment with me for a while: "My husband really likes you and trusts you, and I don't tell you this to flatter you—he has never opened up to anyone like this, ever, in his life"; "I know that Bill is very fond of you—he looks forward to his visit every week—and he always feels a lot better after he sees you—he even told me that he likes your taste in ties"; "My husband was really upset after the visit you had with him a couple of weeks ago—apparently you told him that there didn't seem to be much more to work on and maybe he could stop coming—he felt really let down—I don't think you realize, Dr. Myers, how important you've become to my husband, as a confidant—and how much he still needs to see you—there's still so much stuff there, about his father's death, and his relationship with Pat, our son—I hope you keep seeing him."

I am aware that there are other dynamics that these examples illustrate, but there is a chord that resonates throughout: male patients do develop strong and intimate feelings for their male therapists, but they don't directly or easily verbalize them. Person (1985), writing about the male patient–male analyst dyad, has found the erotic transference to be muted when men treat men; yearnings for attachment and dependent gratification do occur but may be experienced as homosexual. And given the anxiety in our society about male homosexuality, it is no wonder that so many men, even men in therapy, have difficulty talking about fondness and caring for another man if they sense that it might be misunderstood as homosexual. When the male therapist himself has problems with intimacy, his own fear of intimacy may obstruct his ability to gauge his patient's fear, to interpret that to him, and to help him work it through.

Divorcing men who are "coming out" as gay men may have even more difficulty with their feelings of intimacy in the therapeutic relationship with another man; they may fear that any expression of open affection for their therapist will be misconstrued as erotic transference. Likewise, male therapists, regardless of their sexual orientation, must be alert to their gay male patients' wish for and fear of intimacy with them. They must overcome any anxiety they feel about this so they don't become emotionally avoidant themselves or, conversely, act out and become sexual with their patients. As we learn more about male-sibling incest, sexual abuse of boys, and sexual assault of adolescent and adult men (Myers, 1989), we must become increasingly sensitive to intimacy issues with our adult male patients. A certain number of men who consult therapists for the first time when they are going through a divorce also have a history of having been sexually abused or sexually assaulted at some time in the past. We hope that as male therapists we can be corrective for these men, but we can also terrify and harm them if we are misunderstood or are professionally naive in our diagnostic and therapeutic work with them.

Another transference feature in the therapeutic work with divorcing men is identification. Again, although identification occurs with the woman therapist as well, identification in the transference is a more common same-gender manifestation as opposed to cross-gender. I will therefore restrict my comments here to the divorcing male patient–male therapist dyad. I am using the word identification loosely here to refer to the process whereby the male patient takes in, imitates, and adopts some of the characteristics of the male therapist. The positive aspects of identification occur when the patient sees his therapist as someone he can respect and someone he may partly wish to pattern his life after. From him, he may learn healthier ways of confronting and coping with stress. By the use of self-disclosure, when carefully timed and brief, the therapist can also help the patient change gender-stereotyped behavior (Olarte, 1985). The identification can become the vehicle or means through which the patient comes to realize his own potential and capacity for growth. Some of this is enacted through the transference, and the rest through the real relationship with the therapist.

But there can be a down side to identification when there is a conscious or unconscious male gender alignment that is blind to certain themes and issues. There may be a collective denial of examining feelings; there may be collusive agreement on stereotypic and distorted ideas about women; there may be reinforcement of male sexism; and emotional closeness may be avoided. Male therapists can enhance their work with their divorcing male patients by asking themselves the question, "How would this patient's therapy be different with a woman therapist?"

Solomon (1982, p. 268) has described two specific transference responses to the male therapist, both of which are germane to the situation in which a divorcing man is in treatment with another man. The first of these, parentification of the therapist, mirrors the patient's relationship with his own father or other male authority figures (an employer or a teacher, for instance). Discussing this type of transference with the man may open the door to examination of his relationship with the important men in his life, past and present. The other transference response, infantilization of the therapist, may induce the man to examine his relationship with younger men in his life, in particular his sons and possibly grandsons depending on his age, as he is progressing through his divorce. The therapist may capitalize on these specific transferences to help the divorcing man talk about these key figures in his life, something many men are not able to do easily.

Let me conclude this section on transference, especially the latter emphasis on what happens when men treat men, by quoting from Jean Baker Miller, who has written: "Men, in general, seem constantly to be seeking to be valued in the eyes of other men and to be simultaneously on a keen alert to the danger that the slightest weakness may put them at the mercy of other men" (Miller, 1972). Her words nicely summarize many of the dynamics in the male–male treatment dyad.

Countertransference

Countertransference has been defined as "the psychiatrist's partly unconscious or conscious emotional reaction to his patient" (American Psychiatric Association, 1975, p. 38). Let me now begin to address many of the myriad variables for the therapist that come into play when he/she treats divorcing men. What are the unconscious conflicts and affects that can influence the course of the psychotherapy? One of the most common and most weighty countertransference reactions when one treats divorcing people, not just divorcing

men, is a primal fear of one's own marriage and family life disintegrating. As I mentioned earlier under transference, many emotional
responses can occur in therapists of both genders, but this particular fear, of family dissolution, is most common in same-sex psychotherapy—when women therapists treat divorcing women and men
therapists treat divorcing men.

There are at least four situations in which the male therapist's
anxiety might be heightened when he is treating divorcing men: (1)
when one is in training and is not experienced in doing divorce
work (that is, it is harder to separate patients' dynamics from one's
personal dynamics); (2) when separations are wife-initiated and appear to occur "out of the blue" with no overt premorbid history of
marital strain or unhappiness; (3) when the man's age, personality,
profession, and family situation are very similar to one's own; (4)
when both the patient and the therapist are struggling with life-
stage issues—especially midlife.

Here is an example of a man whose anxiety about his marriage
ending precipitated a personal crisis and brought him to see a psychiatrist.

*Mr. W was a 36-year-old social worker, married, with two children who
were 8 and 6 years old. He came to see me for two reasons: an overall
heightened level of anxiety and tension for the previous 18 months and
discrete episodes of panic for the previous 3 months. His family doctor
had prescribed a tranquilizer that helped a bit, but Mr. W was more
interested in getting at the source of his anxiety. Mr. W had also developed persistent and repetitive thoughts the previous few weeks that his
wife no longer loved him and that she would surely leave him. Apparently, her attempts to reassure him did nothing to alleviate these obsessive thoughts and relieve his self-doubt.*

*Mr. W was a highly respected marital and divorce therapist in his
community, and he did this work on a full-time basis. When I inquired
about his feelings regarding his work, he told me that he had recently
been seeing "a flood of couples" whose separations were all being initiated by the wives. "I don't know what to make of it—it's like an ep-
idemic—I mean these men are far from perfect but they aren't that
horrible—I really feel sorry for some of these guys—they don't know
which end is up."*

*Mr. W's personal and family history was revealing. He had suffered
from school phobia as a child, and this was related to the very chaotic
and tenuous state of his parents' marriage when he was in elementary
school. They separated when he was in grade 10, when his father took
up with another woman "who I never liked—I was happy when they*

broke up." Although Mr. W was quite popular and active in groups and sports as a teen-ager, he admitted that he was shy and awkward with girls. His one and only girlfriend whom he met in college became his wife when they graduated.

Mr. W described himself as very happy in his first marriage. His wife was a social worker as well, and they shared a similar commitment to working with the economically and ethnically disadvantaged. They had traveled a lot and had worked together in many different parts of the world. While living in Bangkok, his wife became involved with another man, and after several weeks of seeing him and being in crisis, she announced that she wanted to separate. They did this, and after a few weeks, when his wife did not show any sign of wishing to reconcile, Mr. W left that posting to return to North America. He told me that this was the worst period of his life. About 2 years later, he met his present wife. There had been no known marital difficulties, and my interview with his wife confirmed this. Mrs. W also told me that she was thrilled that her husband had come to see me, for several reasons. She felt that he had a lot of unfinished business about his parents' marriage and divorce; that he overidentified with his mother as an "innocent victim"; that he was not "together" yet about his first marriage ending; and that he overworked and identified too strongly with many of his clients who were going through divorces.

Although Mr. W had highly specific predisposing and precipitatory determinants for his breaking out into symptoms, during midlife all men are vulnerable and prone to periods of anxiety and uneasiness. We male therapists, no matter how seasoned, how experienced in marital and divorce therapy, and how knowledgeable about ourselves and our wives, cannot help but feel personally frightened as a consequence of therapeutic work with certain men in the midst of divorce. We see parts of ourselves in our male patients who leave their wives, and we see parts of ourselves in the men who are left by their wives; we witness and share much of the terror and agony and, some time later in treatment, some of the joy and the happy times. For psychiatrists, there are parallels in other branches of medicine: cardiologists fear a coronary, neurologists fear a stroke, and oncologists a sudden weight loss suggestive of cancer.

Not all therapists who are married and who do marital and divorce work are happy in their own marriages. Indeed, given the high divorce rate in our society, it is not uncommon for people who are marital therapists to be divorced themselves. Many of these same individuals began their careers in marital and divorce therapy while their marriages were happy and well functioning; over the years, for various reasons, their marriages have ended. Some may have remarried. When I have treated men who are marital therapists, I have noted two significant factors: their embarrassment and shame for requiring marital and/or divorce therapy and the extreme difficulty that many of these men have had in finding a therapist who is not intimidated by them and who is willing to treat them. They find themselves, because of their training and expertise in marital therapy, shunned and rejected by the very people who are in the community to help!

Before reaching out for professional assistance himself, the unhappily married male therapist may be inclined to feel countertransference envy toward his divorcing men patients who are beginning to do well. He will resent their ability to come to terms with an unworkable marriage, to make a decision to separate, to enlist professional help, and to forge ahead with autonomy and self-interest. The subjective sense of feeling envious of a patient is always important and warrants honest introspection. Divorcing men who leave their marriages of 25 years for women 10 to 15 years younger may spark this type of reaction. This usually says much more about the therapist's problems with aging than the patient!

In Chapter 7, I talked at length about abandoned husbands, those men who feel utterly helpless and completely rejected by their wives. Specific countertransference feelings may arise in therapists treating men struggling with abandonment (Myers, 1986b). Sex-role rigidity may surface in the therapist. Male therapists may overidentify and collude with the man's sense of outrage, indignation, and acts of retribution. Insight building as a goal in therapy may become minimal or lost altogether. Worse yet, adversarial coparenting between the patient and his former wife may be aggravated by the therapist's loss of objectivity and neutrality. Female therapists may overnurture and overgratify dependency needs in these same men and not push enough self-sufficiency and independence. And both male and female therapists may have difficulty with very regressed divorcing men who are highly emotional, passive, and clinging. Their unconscious sex bias that all men should be moderately strong and in control of their feelings causes these therapists to label this as "negative behavior" ("he's acting like such a wimp!") rather than "symptomatic behavior."

Men who are wrestling with a feeling of abandonment in the early stages of their separations can be highly erratic and frightened as well as frightening for therapists who try to help them. I once saw a newly separated woman, in crisis, who had received a phone call from her husband's therapist, a man, the day before. This therapist berated the woman, a complete stranger to him, first of all for leaving her husband "just after he joined A.A." and secondly for refusing to let her husband see her. When the woman told the therapist that she was a battered wife who had left her husband many times before, and he never changed, and that she was still very afraid of him, the therapist, as quoted by the woman, said: "I know all of that; your husband told me all about it. Don't you think he deserves a second chance now that he is not drinking? He's pretty desperate. How are you going to feel if he kills himself?" I supported this woman in her intention to write a letter of complaint to the local professional association to which the therapist belonged. When the therapist denied making the statements, there was no further investigation. The woman, however, did feel a lot better just writing the letter because for her the letter was an assertive and empowering act. It helped to dispel any self-doubts that she had as to the legitimacy of her feelings and her actions in leaving her husband, and it affirmed in her mind that her husband's therapist was indeed out of order.

Another type of countertransference problem is denying or minimizing the divorcing man's emotional and behavioral distress. Trainees and less experienced fully trained therapists are more prone to this kind of countertransference reaction. This seems especially so when they treat younger male patients with and without children. In some cases, this is clearly attributable to the student not having much clinical experience and is not atypical in any teaching setting. In other cases, it is the result of denial and an inability to comprehend the magnitude of pain that can occur in a young man when his marriage breaks up. When describing his patient, one junior resident, a man, stated: "I can't understand why he's so depressed. He's mired in self-pity. Hell, he's young, he's good-looking, he's got a good job—there're all kinds of women out there if he'd only get off his butt and meet some of them!"

Those trainees who themselves have been married and divorced (or who have had committed relationships end) seem to have a greater empathic understanding. One medical student, while discussing his patient, suddenly became tearful, then embarrassed and apologetic. My attending to and focusing on this enabled him to go on: "I asked the patient about suicidal thoughts. He said 'no' ... but that every day he just wants to die. Boy, could I identify with him! How for weeks after my girlfriend and I broke up, how I just wanted to die. And how lonely I felt with those feelings—I thought I was going crazy. I didn't tell anyone. I cover up well. Just like this guy. Whew!"

Many trainees in the helping professions are themselves adult "children of divorce." They have experienced first hand much of what their patients are describing and may therefore have a heightened sensitivity to marital and separation dynamics. However, some may have unresolved issues around their parents' divorce, which, if unrecognized, will interfere with their ability to treat. Supervisors of these trainees must be particularly observant of this kind of countertransference phenomenon and assist the person with his/her idiosyncratic reaction. If the problem is quite severe or persistent, the trainee may require individual therapy in order to be able to work with divorcing men in a compassionate and effective manner.

The emergence of countertransference feelings in treating divorcing men underscores how difficult the work can be, at times, for almost all therapists. Because marriage (or any committed relationship) is something so universal that it is a part of almost everyone's life at some point, therapists cannot help but be affected, via identification, by their patients' concerns. And although not all therapists have themselves been divorced, or have had their personal or family lives touched by divorce, most people have experienced some type of relationship loss at some point in their lives. Many have also had their core relationship threatened at some point by a third party, have been attracted to or involved with a third party, or themselves have been that third party vis-à-vis another couple.

Having said this, let me turn now to the treatment of divorcing men wherein there is a third-party involvement of either the man himself or his wife. This is a common and complicating factor in many divorces. In fact, it is not unusual for the partner who has another involvement to express ambivalence and regret. This is usually enhanced by the spouse's outrage and hurt, by the extended families' upset, and by society's disapproval. It is not easy either for therapists who are attempting to remain as neutral and effective as possible in the face of very painful and intense emotions in the people they are trying to help. And for some therapists, the issue is very close to home, if not too close to home.

A few years ago I was working as a cotherapist with a woman resident in psychiatry whom I was supervising in marital therapy. One of the couples we were treating together was a couple who was attempting a reconciliation after the man's love affair with another woman failed. As this man's wife vented her rage, her hurt, her humiliation, and her mistrust while they went over old ground and unsettled marital issues, Dr. A excused herself and did not return for the remainder of the session. Later, in our supervisory time together, Dr. A explained that she and her husband experienced something very similar in their marriage the previous year. Working with this couple was opening up old wounds for her.

I want to say a few words about role blurring and role discomfort as a countertransference reaction in therapists who treat divorcing men. What I mean by this is that the therapist has some difficulty accepting the role of therapist and what that role entails. Again, this is more of a problem for trainees and younger therapists, where a lack of experience, professional confidence, and maturity may generate feelings of anxiety when treating certain male patients. Examples include medical students or graduate students treating college undergraduate students, residents treating medical students, therapists treating other therapists including therapists of their own discipline, men treating men with sexual dysfunctions, men treating severely regressed men with clinging and dependent behavior, and men treating men who are struggling with conflicts identical to their own. This discomfort and blurring of role may seriously handicap the therapist's ability to assess the patient accurately and to plan treatment. What commonly happens is underdiagnosing and shortchanging the patient with inadequate treatment, for in these situations the therapist is too quick to normalize and to reassure. There is premature closure on many subjects, especially the more difficult ones, as the therapist–patient relationship approaches that of a male friendship rather than a therapeutic and professional one.

Intellectualizing can be both a countertransference and a transference problem when therapists treat divorcing men. This defense is quickly erected by individuals in response to threat, so it is not surprising that this becomes a way of coping for many men who are going through a divorce, especially men who have obsessional and compulsive natures. When it comes to psychodynamic psychotherapy of those divorcing men whose immediate crises have passed, however, therapists must be cautious not to reinforce their patients' use of defensive intellectualization by being highly intellectualized themselves.

I think that there are gender differences here that prompt me to ask a series of questions. Are men therapists more apt to slip into intellectualizing with their men patients than with their women patients? Do men intellectualize more when they treat men than women therapists do when they treat women? Are male therapists more prone to get caught up in the jargon of psychotherapy language or to be so busy cognitively mapping out terrain and planning strategy that they are not being a "participant–observer" while doing psychotherapy? Finally, does the fundamental nature of the male–male dyad foster intellectualization as a normative standard for both the patient and the therapist?

It is well known and generally accepted that the more potentially threatening the patient is to the therapist's professional comfort, the greater is the risk of countertransference or distortion. The most difficult patients for many male therapists are men patients who are very bright or brighter than the therapist, men patients who are socioeconomically and culturally superior to the therapist, and other men in the helping professions, including other therapists.

I can illustrate this with a simple and somewhat amusing situation that happened while I was treating Dr. X.

Dr. X, a 33-year-old psychiatrist, was very bright, very articulate, and very well-read in psychoanalysis. He was also extremely obsessional and intellectualized a great deal of the time. During one particular visit he was using a lot of psychiatric terminology sprinkled with verbatim quotes from the writings of Freud and Jung. This talk also contained subtle references to and veiled insults regarding my intelligence, my training, and my effectiveness as a psychotherapist. I made some type of interpretive statement to him about his use of intellectualization and a suggestion that there might be some resistance and hidden feeling behind the defense. However, as I said this, I began to realize how intellectualized I was in my choice of words and my manner toward him! Inside I felt angry, controlled, rigid, and guarded. Interestingly, he picked this up and interpreted this to me: "Are you O.K.? You seem so uptight these days—you used to be a lot warmer toward me." Initially I felt disarmed by his statement and heard it as a further insult and attempt of his to diminish me. As we discussed this, he was then able to talk about his feelings of inferiority as my patient, his feelings of inadequacy as a man, and a feeling that I no longer cared about him.

As a corollary to the use of intellectualization as a countertransference problem, some therapists also have a strong need to be in control at all times and to be overly authoritarian in their therapeutic work with divorcing men. This type of therapeutic approach will clash with the male patient who himself has problems with control and who is fighting to regain the control that he has lost by his marriage ending. This type of therapist may also have a lot of difficulty expressing and demonstrating empathy for his patient, even though he may actually feel empathy for the patient. When the controlled therapist has trouble with strong affect, he/she may not truly listen to the patient and to what he has to say; instead, the therapist responds in a preconceived and patronizing way. The work of therapist and patient takes on a dominant and subordinate flavor rather than an egalitarian or collaborative mode of working together.

Under transference, I mentioned the situation in which the divorcing male patient attempts to parentify or infantilize the therapist. In a similar vein, the therapist may have an unresolved problem in his life with his father or with his son (or the woman therapist may have unresolved issues with her father or a son). These feelings, conflicts, or attitudes may contaminate the therapy (Solomon, 1982). Obviously, therapists must be alert to their own personal dynamics when treating divorcing men, and if they are not able to come to terms with specific issues, they should seek psychotherapy themselves.

Another type of countertransference problem can occur when the therapist is incapable of appreciating the divorcing man in the context of his racial or ethnic affiliation. This is particularly important when the therapist is of another racial or ethnic group, but countertransference also occurs in those therapists who have the same social and ethnic origins as their patient but have unresolved and inner conflicts of their own. In my supervisory work with medical students of diverse ethnic and racial backgrounds and with psychiatry residents, many of whom are FMGs (foreign medical graduates), I have noted this repeatedly in the trainee. Many of these therapists-in-training, depending on how long they or their families have lived in North America, or depending on their socioeconomic "class" within their racial and ethnic group, are embarrassed or ashamed to be "identified" with the actions and behaviors of their clinically ill divorcing male patients. It is not difficult to empathize with these trainees and their countertransference reactions because of the extremely high degree of racial prejudice and ethnic bigotry that characterizes North American society. They do not want to be linked with the values or customs of their patients, values that they themselves, in the process of acculturation and assimilation into the host country, are trying to discard. This is a complicated countertransference dynamic, but when therapists can recognize it in themselves and can talk openly about it, they can still do very effective and sensitive therapy.

Divorcing men from certain racial, ethnic, and socioeconomic groups may talk, appear, and behave in ways that are extremely upsetting for the therapist. That is, the therapist may become frightened or angry or judgmental about the man's speech or conduct, both in therapy and outside of therapy. What is fundamental is that the therapist attempt to understand the normative values and standards of the divorcing man's reference group. Only then can the therapist gauge the patient's actions and attitudes as to how normal or pathological they are, how much to worry about the man (or his wife and children), and whether to intervene or not. Therapists must always keep in mind that their own personal value system about marital roles, about sex roles, about child rearing, about religious matters, and so forth may be, and often are, extremely different from those of the patients that they treat. Having a clear sense of one's own boundaries of knowledge and a sense of one's own limitations of experience in treating divorcing male patients in the cultural mosaic of contemporary society is a challenge to all therapists.

Conclusion

My objective in Chapters 11–13 has been to define the treatment of men who are divorcing and who are coming for help, in its broadest sense. Because divorce is so traumatic, I have emphasized in Chapter 11 the importance of a comprehensive biopsychosocial assessment of the patient. Divorce makes people ill, certainly psychologically, and frequently physically. Treatment always begins with a proper assessment because only then can the right treatment be initiated for each patient. I have outlined the biological, psychological, and social treatments at length because divorcing men vary so much in their requirements. Some need only one form of treatment, others need several; some need only crisis intervention, others long-term treatment; and some need different modalities all at one time, others need different modalities in a particular order or sequence. A discussion on treatment is not complete without an analysis of the common transference and countertransference issues that arise in therapy with divorcing men. Hence, I have outlined my thoughts, and those of others, in this chapter in some detail.

CHAPTER 14

The Future

In Chapter 1 I reminded the reader that divorce is as old as marriage. Even though the divorce rates in North America have been leveling off throughout this decade, divorce is not going to disappear. In the last chapters, I outlined many different treatment approaches and strategies that are often helpful in working with divorced and divorcing men who are in psychological and psychiatric distress. What about prevention? Is there anything that we as professionals can do to avert the sting of divorce?

Let me start with education. I think that there is a lot more that can be done to inform people about marriage and divorce, beginning with our adolescents and young adults. Schools are one place where more emphasis should be placed on teaching students about the responsibilities and rules of marriage and family life. This should encompass more than sexual education courses; I am also referring to learning communication skills, understanding money management, running a household, appreciating the importance of family planning, and learning to understand and to respect each other in marriage as different but equal.

Marriage preparation courses are becoming more popular and more sophisticated. Some are mandatory in certain religions; others are strongly recommended and advised. There does not seem to be the same degree of resistance to these courses as there was as recently as 5 years ago. Many young men whom I speak to admit to being somewhat reluctant at first to attend such courses, but this feeling seems to pass after the first or second session.

Outreach programs to expectant and new fathers, especially teen fathers, are essential but are really only reaching and serving a small fraction of young men in need of guidance and support. We need a lot more government funding in order to expand and refine this type of service. This, in my mind, is an extremely important issue and one that needs urgent attention if these individuals are to learn a greater sense of control over their reproductive potential. Left unchecked, many of these young men go from relationship to relationship with many of their needs remaining frustrated and unmet.

Societal changes are needed. The more that professionals in the health and social sciences, as well as professionals in the religious, legal, and educational fields, can appreciate the frequency of divorce in our society and speak out about it, the better. I long for the day when people who are living through the transitions of the divorcing period no longer have to feel like failures or have their inner feelings of failure reinforced by those around them. They have enough to contend with as they negotiate their way clear.

As therapists, we must continue to promote the use of divorce mediation for the couples that we assess and treat who are embarking on a separation. The elements of discussion and negotiation that are so fundamental in the mediation philosophy and purpose are the same elements that we as therapists want to see preserved by the men and women we treat. The more that we can help our patients to view divorce (when there are children) as family redefinition or the beginning of a new form for the family, the better. We have to help them to realize, and accept, that divorce is not an absolute end but merely an end to what once was. Their coparenting relationship must be protected, fostered, and nurtured.

Increasingly, the term "divorce therapy" is being heard as a new form of therapy or as a branch of marital therapy. I applaud this. Not only can very pragmatic matters like change of residence, financial support, custody, and visitation be addressed in divorce therapy, but more importantly, there is an effort made on the part of the therapist to bring the separating individuals together to talk. Many, if not most, people who are contemplating a separation or who are already separated appreciate assistance because their own attempts to communicate with each other have been thwarted or aborted by their tension and unhappiness. I think that increasingly we are going to see therapists working not only with divorced individuals but also with the new and very significant individuals in their lives. Much more emphasis needs to be placed on the relationship between the parent and stepparent, not just the relationship that they have with the children.

For some time yet, we will need to educate men about their roles and responsibilities as they pass through their divorces and move into new relationships. Payment of child support will need to continue to be legislated and enforced until all divorcing fathers realize and accept that they are still responsible for their children when a marriage ends. Not only is this the only fair solution, but how else are we as men to regain our credibility as mature and responsible men and fathers? Also, those women who have refused to allow their former husbands access to the children because they have defaulted on child support will no longer be able to do so. In this way, it is hoped, the children will be the benefactors of their father's love, care, and attention.

In the Preface, I said that my purpose in writing this book was based on two premises: that men have a lot of difficulty coping with divorce and that many of these men fall between the cracks and receive inadequate help or no help at all. My hope is that men will continue to evolve into people who are more cognizant of their limitations and vulnerabilities and who are more able to reach out for help when they need it. I also hope that those men who are fathers of sons will impart that knowledge and that sensitivity to them, and they in turn to their sons. Finally, I hope that we who define ourselves as therapists of men keep an open mind and an open heart so that we too can evolve and do our work with more understanding, cooperation, and compassion.

REFERENCES

Abarbanel, A. (1979). Shared parenting after separation and divorce: A study of joint custody. *American Journal of Orthopsychiatry, 49,* 320–329.

Adams, D. (1986). *Treating abusers.* Paper presented at the 139th annual meeting of the American Psychiatric Association, Washington, DC, as part of a public symposium: Family Violence.

Adler, A. (1980). *Cooperation between the sexes* (H. L. Ansbacher & R. R. Ansbacher, Eds.). New York: Jason Aronson.

Ahrons, C. R., & Rodgers, R. H. (1987). *Divorced families. A multidisciplinary developmental view.* New York: W. W. Norton.

American Psychiatric Association. (1975). *A psychiatric glossary* (4th rev. ed.). New York: Basic Books.

American Psychiatric Association. (1986). *Task force report 25: Changing family patterns in the United States* (p. 6). Washington, DC: Author.

American Psychiatric Association. (1987). *Diagnostic and statistical manual of mental disorders* (3rd ed., rev.). Washington, DC: American Psychiatric Press.

Bell, A. P., & Weinberg, M. S. (1978). *Homosexualities: A study of diversity among men and women.* New York: Simon & Schuster.

Benedek, T. (1970). Fatherhood and providing. In E. J. Anthony & T. Benedek (Eds.), *Parenthood* (pp. 167–183). Boston: Little, Brown.

Berman, E. M., & Lief, H. I. (1975). Marital therapy from a psychiatric perspective: An overview. *American Journal of Psychiatry, 132,* 583–592.

Bernard, J. (1972). *The future of marriage.* New York: World Publishing.

Bernard, J. (1979). Foreword. In G. Levinger & O. Moles (Eds.), *Divorce and separation: Context, causes, and consequences* (pp. ix–xv). New York: Basic Books.

Bloom, B. L., Asher, S. J., & White, S. W. (1978). Marital disruption as a stressor: A review and analysis. *Psychological Bulletin, 85,* 867–894.

Bloom, B. L., & Hodges, W. F. (1981). The predicament of the newly separated. *Community Mental Health Journal, 17,* 277–293.

Bloom, B. L., White, S. W., & Asher, S. J. (1979). Marital disruption as a stressful life event. In G. Levinger & O. Moles (Eds.), *Divorce and separation: Context, causes, and consequences* (pp. 184–200). New York: Basic Books.

Blumenthal, M. D. (1967). Mental health among the divorced. *Archives of General Psychiatry, 16*, 603–608.

Bohannan, P. (1980). Marriage and divorce. In H. I. Kaplan, A. M. Freedman, & B. J. Sadock (Eds.), *Comprehensive textbook of psychiatry* (Vol. III, 3rd ed., pp. 3258–3268). Baltimore: Williams & Wilkins.

Bowlby, J. (1969). *Attachment and loss. Vol. I: Attachment.* New York: Basic Books.

Bowlby, J. (1975). Attachment theory, separation anxiety, and mourning. In S. Arieti (Ed.), *American handbook of psychiatry* (2nd ed., Vol. 6, pp. 292–309). New York: Basic Books.

Bowlby, J. (1980). *Attachment and loss. Vol. III: Loss* (pp. 38–41). New York: Basic Books.

Briscoe, C. W., Smith, J. B., Robins, E., Marten, S., & Gaskin, F. (1973). Divorce and psychiatric disease. *Archives of General Psychiatry, 29*, 119–125.

Brod, H. (Ed.). (1987). *The making of masculinities: The new men's studies* (p.2). Winchester, MA: Allen & Unwin.

Brown, G. W., & Harris, T. (1978). *The social origins of depression.* London: Tavistock.

Brubaker, T. H. (1983). Introduction. In T. H. Brubaker (Ed.), *Family relationships in later life.* Beverly Hills, CA: Sage.

Calabrese, J. R., Kling, M. A., & Gold, P. W. (1987). Alterations in immunocompetence during stress, bereavement, and depression: Focus on neuroendocrine regulation. *American Journal of Psychiatry, 144*, 1123–1134.

Cantor, D. W. (1982). Divorce: Separation or separation–individuation? *American Journal of Psychoanalysis, 42*, 307–313.

Cath, S. H. (1982). Vicissitudes of grandfatherhood: A miracle of revitalization. In S. H. Cath, A. R. Gurwitt, & J. M. Ross (Eds.), *Father and child* (pp. 329–337). Boston: Little, Brown.

Cath, S. (1986). Fathering from infancy to old age: A selective overview of recent psychoanalytic contributions. In R. M. Friedman & L. Lerner (Eds.), *Toward a new psychology of men: Psychoanalytic and social perspectives* (pp. 65–75). New York: Guilford.

Cherlin, A. J. (1981). *Marriage, divorce, remarriage.* Cambridge, MA: Harvard University Press.

Chodorow, N. J. (1986). Divorce, oedipal asymmetries, and the marital age gap. In R. M. Friedman & L. Lerner (Eds.), *Toward a new psychology of men: Psychoanalytic and social perspectives* (pp. 202–206). New York: Guilford.

Coleman, E. (1982a). Developmental stages of the coming out process. In J. C. Gonsiorek (Ed.), *Homosexuality & psychotherapy* (pp. 31–43). New York: Haworth Press.

Coleman, E. (1982b). Bisexual and gay men in heterosexual marriage: Conflicts and resolutions in therapy. In. J. C. Gonsiorek (Ed.), *Homosexuality & psychotherapy* (pp. 93–103). New York: Haworth Press.

Coogler, O. J. (1978). *Structured mediation in divorce settlement.* Lexington, MA: Lexington Books.

Dank, B. M. (1972). Why homosexuals marry women. *Medical Aspects of Human Sexuality, 6* (9), 14–23.

Despert, J. L. (1953). *Children of divorce.* Garden City, NY: Doubleday.

Diamond, M. J. (1986). Becoming a father: A psychoanalytic perspective on the forgotten parent. In R. M. Friedman & L. Lerner (Eds.), *Toward a new psychology of men: Psychoanalytic and social perspectives* (pp. 41–64). New York: Guilford.

Dickstein, L. J. (1986). Social change and dependency in university men: The white knight complex unresolved. *Journal of College Student Psychotherapy, 1,* 31–41.

Dinnerstein, D. (1976). *The mermaid and the minotaur: Sexual arrangements and human malaise.* New York: Harper Colophon.

Dullea, G. (1987). AIDS and divorce: A new legal arena. *New York Times,* September 21, p. 23.

Dullea, G. (1988). Child sex abuse charged in more divorces. *New York Times,* January 19, p. 18.

Engel, G. L. (1977). The need for a new medical model: A challenge for biomedicine. *Science, 196,* 129–136.

Engel, G. L. (1984). Clinical application of the biopsychosocial model. In D. E. Reiser & D. H. Rosen (Eds.), *Medicine as a human experience* (pp. 43–60). Baltimore: University Park Press.

Erikson, E. H. (1963). *Childhood and society* (2nd ed.). New York: W. W. Norton.

Federico, J. (1979). The marital termination period of the divorce adjustment process. *Journal of Divorce, 3,* 93–106.

Feldman, L. B. (1979). Marital conflict and marital intimacy: An integrative psychodynamic behavioral model. *Family Process, 18,* 69–78.

Fisher, H. E. (1987). The four-year itch. *Natural History, 96* (10), 22–33.

Friedan, B. (1963). *The feminine mystique.* New York: W. W. Norton.

Furstenberg, F. F., & Spanier, G. B. (1984). *Recycling the family: Remarriage after divorce.* Beverly Hills, CA: Sage.

Gardner, R. (1987). *The parental alienation syndrome and the differentiation between fabricated and bonafide allegations.* New Jersey: Creative Therapeutics.

Gilligan, C. (1982). *In a different voice.* Cambridge, MA: Harvard University Press.

Glaser, R. D., & Borduin, C. M. (1986). Models of divorce therapy: An overview. *American Journal of Psychotherapy, 40,* 233–242.

Glick, P. C. (1984). Marriage, divorce, and living arrangements: Prospective changes. *Journal of Family Issues, 5,* 7–26.

Gold, J. H. (1988). Introduction. In J. H. Gold (Ed.), *Divorce as a developmental process* (pp. xi–xv). Washington, DC: American Psychiatric Press.

Goldfried, M. R., & Friedman, J. M. (1982). Clinical behavior therapy and the male sex role. In K. Solomon & N. B. Levy (Eds.), *Men in transition: Theory and therapy* (pp. 309–341). New York: Plenum Press.

Goode, W. J. (1956). *After divorce.* New York: Free Press.

Green, R. (1978). Sexual identity of 37 children raised by homosexual or transsexual parents. *American Journal of Psychiatry, 135,* 692–697.

Greenberg, M., & Morris, N. (1974). Engrossment: The newborn's impact upon the father. *American Journal of Orthopsychiatry, 44,* 520–531.

Greif, J. B. (1979). Fathers, children, and joint custody. *American Journal of Orthopsychiatry, 49,* 311–319.

Grunebaum, H., & Christ, J. (1976). Introduction. Marriage and society. In H. Grunebaum & J. Christ (Eds.), *Contemporary marriage: Structure, dynamics, and therapy* (p. 3). Boston: Little, Brown.

Hafner, J. (1985). *Marriage and mental illness* (pp. 60–68). New York: Guilford.

Hagestad, G. O., & Smyer, M. A. (1982). Dissolving long-term relationships: Patterns of divorcing in middle age. In S. Duck (Ed.), *Personal relationships 4: Dissolving personal relationships* (pp. 155–188). London: Academic Press.

Halle, E. (1982). The "abandoned husband": When wives leave. In K. Solomon & N. B. Levy (Eds.), *Men in transition: Theory and therapy* (pp. 191–197). New York: Plenum Press.

Hatterer, M. S. (1974). The problems of women married to homosexual men. *American Journal of Psychiatry, 131,* 275–278.

Hetherington, E. M., Cox, M., & Cox, R. (1976). Divorced fathers. *The Family Coordinator, 25,* 417–428.

Hierbert, W. J. (1987). 1986 Marriage, divorce rates down. *Family Therapy News, 18* (5), 10.

Holmes, T. H., & Rahe, R. H. (1967). The social readjustment rating scale. *Journal of Psychosomatic Research, 11,* 213–218.

Hopkins, E. (1988). Fathers on trial. *New York Magazine,* January 11, pp. 42–49.

Horney, K. (1967). *Feminine psychology.* New York: W. W. Norton.

Hyatt, R., & Kaslow, F. (1985). The impact of children's divorce on parents: And some contributing factors. *Journal of Divorce, 9,* 79–92.

Isaacs, M. B. (1988). The visitation schedule and child adjustment: A three year study. *Family Process, 27,* 251–256.

Isaacs, M. B., Montalvo, B., & Abelsohn, D. (1986). *The difficult divorce. Therapy for children and families.* New York: Basic Books.

Isaacs, M. B., Leon G. H., & Kline, M. (1987). When is a parent out of the picture? Different custody, different perceptions. *Family Process, 26,* 101–110.

Jacobs, J. W. (1983). Treatment of divorcing fathers: Social and psychotherapeutic considerations. *American Journal of Psychiatry, 140,* 1294–1299.

Jacobson, D. S. (1978). The impact of marital separation/divorce on children: I. Parent–child separation and child adjustment. *Journal of Divorce, 1,* 341–360.

Kiecolt-Glaser, J. K., Fisher, L. D., Ogrocki P., Stout, J. C., Speicher, E. C., & Glaser, R. (1987). Marital quality, marital disruption, and immune function. *Psychosomatic Medicine, 49,* 13–34.

Kiecolt-Glaser, J. K., Kennedy, S., Malkoff, S., Fisher, L., Speicher, C. E., & Glaser, R. (1988). Marital discord and immunity in males. *Psychosomatic Medicine, 50,* 213–229.

Kimmel, M. S. (1986). Men in particular. *Psychology Today*, April, p. 80.

Kinsey, A. C., Pomeroy, W. B., Martin, C. E., & Gebhard, P. E. (1948). *Sexual behavior in the human male*. Philadelphia: W. B. Saunders.

Kirkpatrick, M., Smith, C., & Roy, R. (1981). Lesbian mothers and their children: A comparative survey. *American Journal of Orthopsychiatry*, *51*, 545–551.

Kitson, G. C. (1982). Attachment to the spouse in divorce: A scale and its application. *Journal of Marriage and the Family*, *44*, 379–393.

Kitson, G., & Sussman, M. (1982). Marital complaints, demographic characteristics, and symptoms of mental distress in divorce. *Journal of Marriage and the Family*, *44*, 87–111.

Kolata, G. (1988). The children of divorce: Joint custody is found to offer little benefit. *New York Times*, March 31, p. B13.

Kressel, K. (1980). Patterns of coping in divorce and some implications for clinical practice. *Family Relations*, *29*, 234–240.

Kressel, K. (1985). *The process of divorce*. New York: Basic Books.

Kressel, K., & Deutsch, M. (1977). Divorce therapy: An in-depth survey of therapists' views. *Family Process*, *16*, 413–443.

Lamb, M. (1979). Paternal influences and the father's role: A personal perspective. *The American Psychologist*, *34*, 938–943.

Lamb, M. E., Pleck, J. H., Charnov, E. L., & Levine, J. A. (1987). A biosocial perspective on paternal behavior and involvement. In J. B. Lancaster, J. Altmann, A. S. Rossi, & L. R. Sherrod (Eds.), *Parenting across the life span: Biosocial dimensions* (pp. 111–142). New York: Aldine de Gruyter.

Laws, J. L. (1975). A feminist view of marital adjustment. In A. S. Gurman & D. G. Rice (Eds.), *Couples in conflict* (pp. 73–123). New York: Jason Aronson.

Lee, J. A. (1977). Going public: A study in the sociology of homosexual liberation. *Journal of Homosexuality*, *3*, 49–78.

Lerner, H. E. (1974). Early origins of envy and the devaluation of women: Implications for sex-role stereotypes. *The Bulletin of the Menninger Clinic*, *38*, 538–553.

Lesser, E. K., & Comet, J. J. (1987). Help and hindrance: Parents of divorcing children. *Journal of Marital and Family Therapy*, *13*, 197–202.

Levinson, D. J. (1978). *The seasons of a man's life*. New York: Alfred A. Knopf.

Lloyd, S. A., & Zick, C. D. (1986). Divorce at mid and later life: Does the empirical evidence support the theory? *Journal of Divorce*, *9*, 89–102.

Masters, W. H., & Johnson, V. E. (1979). *Homosexuality in perspective*. Boston: Little, Brown.

May, E. T. (1980). *Great expectations: Marriage and divorce in post-Victorian America*. Chicago: University of Chicago Press.

Mayer, E. (1985). *Love and tradition: Marriage between Jews and Christians*. New York: Plenum Press.

Merikangas, K. R. (1984). Divorce and assortative mating among depressed patients. *American Journal of Psychiatry*, *141*, 74–76.

Miller, J. B. (1972). Sexual inequality: Men's dilemma (A note on the Oedipus complex, paranoia, and other psychological concepts). *American Journal of Psychoanalysis, 32*, 147–157.

Myers, M. F. (1982). Counseling the parents of young homosexual male patients. In J. C. Gonsiorek (Ed.)., *Homosexuality & psychotherapy* (pp. 131–143). New York: Haworth Press.

Myers, M. F. (1984). The abandoned husband. *Medical Aspects of Human Sexuality, 18*, 159–171.

Myers, M. F. (1986a). Types of marital therapy in psychiatric practice. In L. Frelick & E. Waring (Eds.), *Marital therapy in psychiatric practice* (pp. 80–103). New York: Brunner/Mazel.

Myers, M. F. (1986b). Angry, abandoned husbands: Assessment and treatment. In R. A. Lewis & M. B. Sussman (Eds.), *Men's changing roles in the family* (pp. 31–42). New York: Haworth Press.

Myers, M. F. (1987). *When men treat men.* Paper presented at the 140th annual meeting of the American Psychiatric Association, Chicago, IL.

Myers, M. F. (1988a). Assessing and treating divorcing men. In J. H. Gold (Ed.), *Divorce as a developmental process* (pp. 51–77). Washington, DC: American Psychiatric Press.

Myers, M. F. (1988b). *Doctors' marriages: A look at the problems and their solutions.* New York: Plenum Press.

Myers, M. F. (1989). Men who have been sexually assaulted as adults and sexually abused as boys. *Archives of Sexual Behavior, 18* (3).

Norton, A. J., & Moorman J. E. (1987). Current trends in marriage and divorce among American women. *Journal of Marriage and the Family, 49*, 3–14.

Olarte, S. W. (1985). Changing gender stereotyped behavior: Role of the therapist's personal disclosure. *Journal of the American Academy of Psychoanalysis, 13*, 259–267.

Parkes, C. M. (1972). *Bereavement: Studies of grief in adult life.* New York: International Universities Press.

Parsons, T. (1954). The family symbol. An appraisal in the light of psychoanalytic and sociological theory. In L. Bryson, L. Kinkelstein, R. MacIver, & R. McKeon (Eds.), *Symbols and values.* New York: Harper & Row.

Person, E. S. (1985). The erotic transference in women and in men: Differences and consequences. *Journal of the American Academy of Psychoanalysis, 13*, 159–180.

Pettit, E. J., & Bloom, B. L. (1984). Whose decision was it? The effects of initiator status on adjustment to marital disruption. *Journal of Marriage and the Family, 46*, 587–595.

Pleck, J. H. (1976). The male sex role: Definitions, problems, and sources of change. *Journal of Social Issues, 32*, 155–163.

Pleck, J. H. (1980). *Male sex role identity: Fact or fiction?* Working paper No. 60. Wellesley College Center for Research on Women, Wellesley, MA.

Pleck, J. H. (1981). *The myth of masculinity.* Cambridge: MIT Press.

Pleck, J. H. (1984). *Working wives and family well-being.* Beverly Hills, CA: Sage.

Pleck, J. H. (1987). The theory of male sex-role identity: Its rise and fall, 1936 to the present. In H. Brod (Ed.), *The making of masculinities* (pp. 21–38). Boston: Allen & Unwin.

Pleck, J. H., & Sawyer, J. (1974). *Men and masculinity*. Englewood Cliffs, NJ: Prentice-Hall.

Riessman, C. K., & Gerstel, N. (1985). Marital dissolution and health: Do males or females have greater risk? *Social Science in Medicine, 20,* 627–635.

Robinson, B. E., & Barret, R. L. (1986). *The developing father: Emerging roles in contemporary society.* New York: Guilford.

Ross, J. M. (1982). In search of fathering: A review. In S. H. Cath, A. R. Gurwitt, & J. M. Ross (Eds.), *Father and child* (pp. 21–32). Boston: Little, Brown.

Ross, J. M. (1983). Father to the child: Psychoanalytic reflections. *Psychoanalytic Review, 70,* 301–320.

Rossi, A. S. (1987). Parenthood in transition: From lineage to child to self-orientation. In J. B. Lancaster, J. Altmann, A. S. Rossi, & L. R. Sherrod (Eds.), *Parenting across the life span: Biosocial dimensions* (pp. 31–81). New York: Aldine de Gruyter.

Scanzoni, J. (1979). A historical perspective on husband–wife bargaining power and marital dissolution. In G. Levinger & O. Moles (Eds.), *Divorce and separation: Context, causes, and consequences* (pp. 20–36). New York: Basic Books.

Sifford, D. (1982). *Father and son.* Philadelphia: Westminister Press.

Singer, L. J. (1975). Divorce and the single life: Divorce as development. *Journal of Sex and Marital Therapy, 1,* 254–262.

Solomon, K. (1982). Individual psychotherapy and changing masculine roles: Dimensions of gender-role psychotherapy. In K. Solomon & N. B. Levy (Eds.), *Men in transition: Theory and therapy* (pp. 247–273). New York. Plenum Press.

Somers, A. R. (1979). Marital status, health, and use of health services. *Journal of the American Medical Association, 241,* 1818–1822.

Spanier, G. B., & Casto, R. F. (1979). Adjustment to separation and divorce: A qualitative analysis. In G. Levinger & O. Moles (Eds.), *Divorce and separation: Context, causes, and consequences* (pp. 211–227). New York: Basic Books.

Spanier, G. B., & Thompson, L. (1983). Relief and distress after marital separation. *Journal of Divorce, 7,* 31–49.

Stein, T. S. (1982). Men's groups. In K. Solomon & N. B. Levy (Eds.), *Men in transition: Theory and therapy* (pp. 275–307). New York: Plenum Press.

Steinman, S. (1981). The experience of children in a joint-custody arrangement: A report of a study. *American Journal of Orthopsychiatry, 51,* 403–414.

Stone, A. A. (1984). The Tarasoff case and some of its progeny: Suing psychotherapists to safeguard society. In *Law, society, and morality* (pp. 161–190). Washington, DC: American Psychiatric Press.

Tepp, A. V. (1983). Divorced fathers: Predictors of continued paternal involvement. *American Journal of Psychiatry, 140,* 1465–1469.

Time. (1987). Snip, suction, stretch and truss. September 14, p. 70.

Toufexis, A. (1987). Season of autumn–summer love. *Time*, November 30, pp. 60–61.

Uhlenberg, P., & Myers, M. A. P. (1981). Divorce and the elderly. *The Gerontologist*, *21*, 276–282.

U.S. Bureau of the Census. (1980). *Marital status and living arrangements: March 1979. Current population reports*, Series P-20, No. 349. Washington, DC: U.S. Government Printing Office.

Vaillant, G. E. (1977). *Adaptation to life*. Boston: Little, Brown.

Verbrugge, L. M. (1979). Marital status and health. *Journal of Marriage and the Family*, *41*, 267–285.

Wafelbakker, F. (1975). Marriages of homosexuals. *British Journal of Sexual Medicine*, *2* (4), 18–21.

Wallerstein, J. S. (1986). Women after divorce: Preliminary report from a ten-year follow-up. *American Journal of Orthopsychiatry*, *56*, 65–77.

Wallerstein, J. S., & Kelly, J. B. (1980). Effects of divorce on the visiting father–child relationship. *American Journal of Psychiatry*, *137*, 1534–1539.

Weiss, R. S. (1975). *Marital separation*. New York: Basic Books.

Weiss, R. S. (1976). The emotional impact of marital separation. *Journal of Social Issues*, *32*, 135–145.

Weitzman, L. (1986). *The divorce revolution: The unexpected social and economic consequences for women and children in America*. New York: Free Press.

Woodruff, R. A., Guze, S. B., & Clayton, P. J. (1972). Divorce among psychiatric outpatients. *British Journal of Psychiatry*, *121*, 289–292.

Yogman, M. W. (1982). Observations on the father–infant relationship. In S. H. Cath, A. R. Gurwitt, & J. M. Ross (Eds.), *Father and child* (pp. 101–122). Boston: Little, Brown.

Zube, M. (1982). Changing behavior and outlook of aging men and women: Implications for marriage in the middle and later years. *Family Relations*, *31*, 147–156.

INDEX